The Complete
Legal Guide for
Your Small Business

Small Business Management Series
Rick Stephan Hayes, Editor

The Complete Legal Guide for Your Small Business

PAUL ADAMS

A Ronald Press Publication

JOHN WILEY & SONS
New York · Chichester · Brisbane · Toronto · Singapore

Library of Congress Cataloging in Publication Data:

Adams, Paul, 1936-
  The complete legal guide for your small business.

  (Small business management series, ISSN 0271-6054)
  "A Ronald Press publication."
  Bibliography: p.
  Includes index.
  1. Small business—Law and legislation—United
States—Forms.   2. Contracts—United States—Forms.
I. Title. II. Series.

KF1659.A65A3   346.73'0652   81-11445
ISBN 0-471-09436-6   347.306652   AACR2

Printed in the United States of America

10 9 8 7 6 5 4 3 2 1

To my mother and father, with love

Preface

This book results from the confluence of two careers. Since the early 1960s I practiced law, specializing in patents, trademarks, unfair competition, and related antitrust matters. Since 1973 I have been the president and general manager of a small electronic equipment manufacturer.

It was only natural when I turned to business that I would prepare the necessary legal agreements for the company. However, what was surprising was the change in perspective that accompanied the change in occupation. I became aware that the business manager is in a unique position to draft an agreement. The business manager has an intimate, firsthand familiarity and overview of the problem to be solved. Moreover, there is no need to relate the facts to a draftsman and thus no possibility of misinterpretation during communication.

It also became apparent that agreements required for the business were for ordinary, commercial transactions that did not involve highly difficult questions of law. An understanding of some basic principles of contract law and modest skill with the English language would suffice for many problems presented.

This book attempts to impart these capabilities, thereby enabling a non-lawyer to draft some of the agreements encountered in a small business. The agreements described are particularly suited to a small manufacturing company, especially one with a proprietary product line and a stake in continuous product development. Chapters 4 and 9, "Consulting" and "Licensing," are therefore concerned with proprietary rights—creation, protection, and exploitation.

Chapters 6 and 7 cover the most fundamental business transaction—purchase and sale. In most texts the legal rules relating to sales transactions are set forth without reference to the documents used in day-to-day activities. By contrast, this book suggests how to draft a purchase order.

Since the reader obviously intends use of the purchase order as a buyer, the form paragraphs are clearly and unmistakably favorable to the buyer. Conversely, the Acknowledgment form is biased toward the seller.

It is suggested that the small business will usually employ independent sales representatives for the selling and distribution functions. Form agreements are provided in Chapter 5 for the two most frequently encountered independent sales representatives—manufacturers' reps and distributors.

It has been my observation that in a small business the critical element of success is the people employed. Considerable attention must be devoted to hiring, motivating, and retaining key employees. Because there are special benefits and considerations given to these employees, an employment contract as found in Chapter 8 will be of great utility.

There are portions of all legal contracts that are in common: the beginning, boilerplate, and the closing. These matters are covered in Chapters 2 and 3 by providing forms and an explanation of the functions of the specific paragraphs.

Rarely, if ever, will any specimen agreement provided in this book be usable without modification for particular circumstances. Throughout the text I have suggested alternative approaches but have not provided a specific form paragraph. However, I hope that the reader will develop the confidence to create new paragraphs implementing alternate suggestions that are more appropriate to the situation at hand.

The principal purpose of this text is to provide guidance for drafting agreements; however, this text will be useful in other applications. The headings in each chapter comprise a handy checklist of the main points to be negotiated. A review of the appropriate chapter, prior to the first negotiation meeting, will indicate what matters *must* be discussed and what matters are likely to arise that the negotiator should be prepared to discuss.

Another use of the text is for the analysis of a draft agreement submitted by another party. In most situations I generally prefer to submit the first draft. This can be advantageous in subtle ways. However, when the other party begins drafting, this book can be used to compare a form paragraph with a submitted paragraph and to recognize pitfalls in the latter, if any. The form paragraph may suggest alternative or additional provisions that may be argued convincingly as more appropriate.

Nor is this book solely for use by a small business manager. Although larger businesses more readily engage legal counsel, the manager is usually the prime negotiator; he or she certainly should be the final decision maker in any business transaction. Yet to fully participate in the negotiations you must have some grasp of at least the basic legal issues involved.

For the legal transactions covered in this book, the straightforward contract forms that are provided demonstrate fundamentals. This is not to suggest that this book will equip you to fully understand the many complex and often abstruse legal questions that arise in a complicated transaction. But a comprehension of the fundamentals will at least assist in sifting wheat from chaff.

Finally, a very serious caveat is that this book deals with basic, simple transactions. It would be both imprudent and misleading if I were to suggest that this book is a substitute for legal counsel. The law is a field of expertise that is mastered only through arduous learning, supplemented by practical experience. It is the intent of this book to make you aware of common problems and to suggest possible solutions. This book does not purport to be exhaustive. A specific solution always requires recognition of *all* the problems, some of which are anything but common. Minor variations in a fact situation can make material differences in selecting the proper legal solution. The services of an attorney are well advised.

I wish to give special thanks to my former secretary, Mrs. Marylou Walker, for typing the initial drafts of the text and to Mrs. Evelyn J. Mayfield for typing the final draft.

PAUL ADAMS

Los Angeles, California
September 1981

Contents

Forms

Chapter One
Introduction

This book is not a treatise on contract law. There are numerous books, some of which are listed in the Bibliography, that explain the subject of contracts in general and business contracts in particular. The differences between those books listed in the Bibliography and the present book are threefold: (a) the business agreements in this book are primarily for small, start-up, or closely held businesses, usually with one or two individuals playing a dominant role in operations; (b) this book studies only written agreements; and (c) this book focuses on the process of creating the contract, that is, drafting.

In a typical text on contract law, the subject is divided into three areas: formation, performance, and remedies. Under the topic of performance, the principal concern is actually nonperformance (breach of contract). Within the remedies division, matters of damage and termination of the contract are the primary areas of coverage. This book does not treat performance and remedies as separate matters of discussion. However, when one is drafting any contract one should keep these areas of contract law constantly in mind. Relative to performance and breach of contract the draftsman must ask: Is the promised performance sufficiently definite that failure to perform (breach) can be clearly ascertained? With regard to a remedy, this question should be asked: If the contract has been breached, what are the rights of the nondefaulting party to terminate and recover damages?

In one sense, this book is about contract formation. It does not, however, relate to contract formation from the same point of view as general texts on contract law. The most significant question in general contract formation involves the rules relating to offer and acceptance that are the prerequisites for the mutual assent necessary for a valid contract. But the knotty problems of offer and acceptance are generally found in informal contracts. Informal contracts result from oral and offhand statements from a series of seemingly separate discussions and actions that in the aggregate the law regards as a contract. Identifying the line between discussion and formation is one of the chief matters of concern in the area of general contract law. By contrast, this book assumes an orderly, businesslike, and definite sequence of intended actions and communication. This is not to say that at some point prior to executing a written agreement the parties may not have already formed a valid contract in accordance with general rules of contract law. But a written contract is an attempt to avoid haphazard contract formation. The process of discussion and drafting is an endeavor to embody the statements, writings, and oral communications between the parties that initially may be conflicting or inconsistent into a well-expressed writing which clearly defines the mutual assent.

In the division referred to as formation, general or business contract treatises spend considerable time discussing "consideration." *Consideration* is defined as benefit or detriment that the law regards as a necessary commitment by one of the parties to create an obligation on the other. In a typical written business contract there will be little argument over whether there was adequate consideration. Similarly, problem areas such as the capacity of parties (minors, incompetents, etc.), Statute of Frauds (applicable to oral contracts), illegality, and the failure of mutual assent (fraud, mistake, misrepresentation, duress, etc.) are not areas that normally occur in small business written contracts.

Thus it will be apparent that the scope of this book, at least in comparison to texts dealing with general contract law or even solely with business contract law, is quite specific. There is no attempt to educate or inform in the abstract; instead, the principles of law are used to support and explain form paragraphs used in drafting. The intent is to provide assistance in handling relatively simple, ordinary, commercial transactions and preventing such transactions from becoming, in fact or in appearance, complicated ones. Of course, the book also aids in understanding contracts submitted by others; it is not addressed only to draftsmanship. Furthermore, the section headings in the book and in the form agreements provide a handy negotiation checklist that may be useful before drafting.

One final comment is necessary. Does this book obviate the need for a lawyer? It does not. It should be used as a supplement to provide a legal understanding of a relationship without the cost of legal counseling or the later costs of litigation. When transactions become highly complex there is simply no substitute for direct legal counsel with the skill and expertise in drafting that all lawyers should possess. The corollary of the complexity and need for a lawyer is the value of the subject matter of the contract. The business manager who runs a small manufacturing company with $1 million in annual revenue and who enters into a supply contract with a value of $1 million, without seeking legal counsel, is a fool. Common sense suggests that when a transaction is large in relation to the size of the business and to its success and survival there must not only be an abundance of business judgment applied but also the skill of experts. The line between high-value, complex arrangements and the ordinary transactions that are dealt with in this book is a matter for each business manager to personally draw. If during negotiation the contract becomes increasingly complex, legal assistance should be sought.

PURPOSE

The reason for taking the time and expending the effort to prepare a written contract is to provide a clear definition of the future association of the parties. The purpose of any contract is to regulate or govern one party's conduct relative to another. Despite complete earnestness and sincerity, it is not unusual for two parties to have differing ideas of what has been agreed on in the course of negotiation. Often one or both parties may be surprised, usually unpleasantly, on reviewing the first draft of a written agreement that was intended to simply "confirm" the understanding the parties had reached orally. This may be the result of a difference in usage of a particular term or a difference in what was to come within the scope of the agreement and what was to be excluded. Politicians are not the only ones who talk without listening.

Perhaps the most important objective of a written agreement is to avoid the alternative—an oral contract. There are both legal and practical reasons for avoiding an oral agreement. The legal reason is embodied in the venerable Statute of Frauds that has been adopted in various forms and shapes by every state. This statute states that certain types of oral contracts are unenforceable. In the business world there are three types of oral contracts that courts will not enforce: (a) any agreement that cannot be performed within one year from the date of making; (b) any agreement to answer for debts of another (guarantee, indemnity, etc.); and (c) an agreement for sale of goods having a value in excess of $500 (some states have different values, although nearly all states have adopted the Uniform Commercial Code (UCC) that governs sales transactions and establishes a $500 limit). Clearly in these situations the oral contract is useless.

As a practical matter, oral agreements fail because the human memory is too fallible as a record of events. Except for the most simple transaction to be performed in the immediate future the parties will later disagree on that which was agreed on. In the give-and-take of oral negotiation it is extremely difficult for even the most astute observer to accurately recite what the precise formulation was of each point in an agreement. Good negotiators, like a skilled leader at a business meeting, will attempt to recapitulate and state for the benefit of the persons present what has been discussed and agreed on. But even under good direction the ability to recall a synopsis of each point will vary considerably between the persons present. This failure will give rise to an honest dispute between the parties.

The value of a written agreement is to provide clarity and precision on each point that the parties agree on, thus fully expressing the intentions mutually shared by the parties. The written agreement will then serve as a guide or charter for the future conduct of the parties in the relationship. When a new situation occurs during the performance of the agreement it is the written agreement that may be used as a source of guidance for conduct appropriate to this new event. Ideally, the agreement specifically covers this contingency; at the least, it may provide some light on the parties' intentions with respect to an analogous situation.

Beyond serving as the rule book for the parties to use the written agreement will serve as the official rules that a judge or arbitrator will use to decide whether the parties are fairly playing the game. Any trial lawyer will be quick to point out that the written agreement is the most reliable and convincing evidence one can offer in a contract dispute.

With all those favorable things said a word of caution should be offered. No contract, oral or written, regardless of its length or the skill of the draftsman is a substitute for goodwill and trust. A contract cannot protect a party who enters into an arrangement with a devious, scheming, and deceitful person. The inevitable ambiguities and defects of the English language can be exploited by the unprincipled. One should always be wary in dealing with a person employing sharp business practices; there may be false security in a written agreement. The aggravation, time, and money required to prove that one is right may easily convert a fair arrangement into a costly debacle.

Perhaps the final word on the advantage of a written agreement comes from the movie magnate Samuel Goldwyn who stated: "A verbal contract isn't worth the paper it's written on."

OVERVIEW

The content of a contract must cover two broad segments of the future. The first segment involves what *will* or *should* happen between the parties.

The second encompasses what *may* happen that will affect the future relationship.

The portion of the contract that describes what the parties expect to happen must define the duties and obligations of each of the parties. Each of the parties knows at the outset that certain specific and well defined acts of the other party will be necessary to achieve the result; thus the performance of these acts should be expressly and explicitly stated in the contract. The coverage should therefore be comprehensive, detailed, and not left to inference. Not only should the principal performance be clearly defined but also the contract should go further and define what constitutes a breach of performance. And if the obligation or duty is of sufficient importance the draftsman should consider identifying the remedies the aggrieved partly will have in the event of a breach.

By contrast there is a nearly unlimited range of circumstances that are possible, although not intended. Both parties may prefer that such events never occur, but common experience suggests that the events do arise. Strikes, fire, death of a party, and bankruptcy are a few of the ordinary occurrences that disrupt a business relationship. With only slight imagination a draftsman may conceive of an innumerable list of situations over which the parties have no control. The most simple contract could be extended endlessly if all such contingencies are covered. Furthermore, if for each of such contingencies an attempt is made to set forth what will constitute a breach, a cure, and a remedy, the contract may be worth no more than the paper on which it is written. Superfluous inclusion is a mark of poor draftsmanship. Avoid the tendency to be overly complete. In drafting the portion of the contract describing unexpected possibilities the draftsman must therefore use discretion. In a supply contract with General Motors it is unnecessary to spell out the implications of bankruptcy (although suppliers to Penn Central and Chrysler may have made the same erroneous assumption). On the other hand, a bankruptcy clause may be prudent with a small purchaser. However, as a supplier to General Motors it may be prescient to state that in the event of an auto workers' strike that prevents delivery the auto manufacturer will be required to do the following: (*a*) designate an alternate delivery point, (*b*) pay for finished goods inventory ready to ship, or (*c*) otherwise alleviate the problems that would befall a small company with a large and undeliverable inventory. A labor strike is a real possibility of potentially disastrous consequences. It is a contingency that merits coverage.

Each particular transaction must be independently analyzed with respect to the character of the parties involved, current economic conditions, length of the contract performance, and any unique problems. It is from this review that the likely is differentiated from the merely conceivable. If it is purchasing a small business computer, for example, a company may procure the computer manufacturer's software package or may hire a "software house" to supply the necessary programs. But because they are often small, underfinanced, and a new venture comprising only a small staff, these software houses have a questionable business viability. If after installation the vendor goes out of business, how is the proprietary program to be later modified without any personnel who are familiar with the program? One possible solution for such contingency is to obligate the software vendor to place a copy of the proprietary program for safekeeping with a third party—in effect an escrow arrangement. This approach raises questions about whether the copy must be continually updated, the type of events under which the buyer may have access, and other conditions. In short, the purchase of software raises unique problems after the sale is completed. Some means of protection for the purchaser must be found. Experience suggests that the contingency of loss of support is sufficiently probable that in light of the potential damage the agreement should provide detailed coverage.

Careful planning will exclude some potential events and include others. The resulting agreement will be substantially complete without being ponderous and tiresome. A contract may be frugal with words and still cover the whole.

COMPONENTS

To create a binding, legally enforceable agreement certain essential components must be included in the written document. The agreement must reflect the competency of the parties, the mutual assent that arises through the offer and acceptance process, and the consideration, usually bilateral promises (from each party to the other).

Parties

In general contract law, such matters as age, mental infirmity, and criminal status may vitiate an otherwise valid agreement. But in the area of business or commercial transactions the principal difficulty relating to competency is whether the person executing the agreement has the authority to do so. The rules that permit one person to act on behalf of another to legally bind the other is subsumed under the category of Agency law. The principles of Agency apply in many areas of the business world not the least of which is the employer-employee relationship. In contract formation the question is whether the person executing the agreement can bind the entity for which he or she purports to act.

In medieval England confirmation that a written document was authorized by an appropriate official was established through the presence of a seal. Applying the seal evidenced the fact that the person carrying the seal assented that the document in fact set forth the agreement. That the person had possession of the seal evidenced his authority to act. The seal was eventually replaced by the signature as evidence that the document was genuine. But a signature is not evidence of authority to act for another; there has been no comparable indicia of authority since the seal has fallen into disuse. In a simple written contract, therefore, the authority to execute the agreement must be established by first ascertaining the nature of the entity of the other party. Is it a sole proprietorship, a partnership, or a corporation? There are other more abstruse business forms, but these forms are not likely to be encountered. Also, in international transactions there are unfamiliar forms of business and therefore more difficulty in ascertaining precisely who is the other party and who is authorized to act to bind such party.

Once the type of entity has been established it is still necessary to confirm the authority of the person executing the agreement to act on behalf of such organization. For a sole proprietorship obviously this is an easy task. For a partnership or a corporation there are a few simple rules that must be followed; these rules are set forth in Chapter 2.

Offer and Acceptance

In the usual course of creating a written agreement the process begins with negotiation and ends with formalization. During this sequence of events there may be one or more offers, counteroffers, and finally acceptance. Precisely when an agreement is formed, before or after a written document is executed, is not always easy to establish. Once a properly drafted written agreement has been executed, however, it becomes moot whether at some earlier point prior to execution the parties had reached an oral agreement that was legally enforceable. But if negotiations fail to produce a written agreement, one party may insist that a verbal contract had been consummated. Although this book is concerned only with the creation of written agreements, it is obviously of interest to understand when in the negotiation process a commitment may have been made.

It would be extremely rare for the parties to meet and discuss each detail that normally appears in a written agreement; it would be equally unusual for one party to send another a written agreement without having discussed any of the terms. Normally, the first step of the parties is to meet and discuss what they consider to be the pivotal elements of the relationship. This usually includes price, terms, important duties and obligations, and time. After these discussions the parties may describe their status as being "essentially in agreement" or "in agreement in principle." What is usually meant by such statements is that the parties feel they are 95% along toward a binding agreement. On a moment's reflection each party would probably state that no contract had been formed up to that time. If one party did not have the authority to bind his company clearly no agreement would yet have been formed. But even if there is proper authority it is highly doubtful that the negotiator would feel that the contract formation had been completed.

On the other hand, it is possible that an agreement has been formed even if minor details have not yet been resolved. If the parties should state, "We will let our lawyers put this in writing," an agreement may be completed, and the writing and execution may simply be what the law considers "memorializing" the agreement. That, however, is the more unusual case. Generally, both parties intend that the preparation, review, and execution of a written agreement is the last step in the negotiating process. The agreement is not formed until signed.

There is one other point regarding offer and acceptance that is often ignored to a party's consternation. A prepared written agreement is usually mailed to the other party with a cover letter requesting that the agreement be executed and one copy returned. The agreement enclosed will either be executed by the sender or it will request that the recipient execute the agreement first and then return it for execution and consummation. In the former instance, what has been forwarded to the recipient is an offer. Care must be exercised in making such offer.

Unless the cover letter expressly states that the agreement must be executed and returned within a certain period of time it is an "open-ended" time offer. If no time is stated for it to remain open, the law holds that the offer is open for a "reasonable" period of time based on usage or custom in the trade, the nature of the subject matter, and other circumstances. The method of transmission may also be indicative of the time in which the offer is to remain open. A telegram or Telex offer calls for a more prompt response than a mail-delivered agreement. In either event the problem is that after the letter agreement is forwarded the sender may be in limbo awaiting a response. This can be avoided by stating clearly that the offer is to remain open until, for example, the close of business on a particular day. Obviously, this may be phrased as a number of days from the date of the letter or some similar reference point from which a definite period can be ascertained. Moreover, it may be desirable for even greater certainty to state that the written acceptance must be "received" at the sender's business before the time period expires. Otherwise, depositing of the executed agreement by the recipient into the mail so that the envelope is postmarked before the expiration of the offer will be legally sufficient. Yet this may add several more business days of uncertainty for the sender.

In the event a specific time limit is not placed on the offer when the agreement is sent the matter is best handled after a suitable period of impatience, by a telegram or other written communication stating that the offer will remain open only for a specified period. It is perfectly permissible for a party to revoke an offer completely at any time until it has been accepted by the recipient. Consequently, it is entirely within the prerogative of the sender to qualify or otherwise limit the period for acceptance.

If the document was not executed when sent the written agreement is a draft, a simple invitation to negotiate. When the recipient executes and returns it to the sender, the agreement becomes an offer from the recipient. This offer is accepted when executed by the original sender. This may appear confusing, since the originator is easily assumed to be the offeror. But to do so would be to ignore the significance of the nonexecution. Both parties must sign before a contract is formed.

Another problem that arises with respect to offer and acceptance occurs when one party adds, changes, or deletes one or more terms of the agreement. When the parties are together at final execution and agree on a change there is a simple and proper method for incorporating such change into the written text. The selected phrase or word is deleted by striking; an addition is interlineated. Then the parties place their initials and the date in the margin closely adjacent to the addition, change, or deletion. But suppose an executed written agreement is received in the mail and the recipient desires to make a change? It is common sense for the recipient to call the sender, discuss the change, and attempt to resolve any differences. However, if this cannot be done the change may be incorporated and the agreement executed and returned. The legal effect of the change depends on the nature and seriousness of the modification. Correcting an obvious typographical error will almost certainly be an acceptance. But a change to the price or other material terms will constitute a counteroffer. No contract is formed. When the original sender later initials the change and returns it, there is an acceptance of the counteroffer. A contract is made.

The process of order and acceptance described above is typical of general business transactions. If the transaction involves the sale of goods the UCC will apply. The UCC has codified many of the rules given in the preceding discussion and implemented some deviations from these rules that must be specifically considered. Comments on these exceptions are found in Chapters 6 and 7 dealing with sales agreements.

Consideration

There is no simple explanation of the legal concept of consideration. A clear understanding proceeds from a historical rather than rational perspective. It stems from ancient tradition, the prevalence of illiteracy in early England, and the desire to witness an objective event to give substance to a promise that was oral and ephemeral. Consideration was historically an object that was delivered at the time the agreement was made. Or it was evidence that a promise had been made.

Eventually, it was recognized that a promise standing alone if properly proved would suffice to bind the promisor (the person making the promise) to carry out the performance. Thus an act or a promise can be valid consideration. Suppose that two people meet and one delivers money and the other delivers an automobile. There is a sales contract; the consideration received by one person is an automobile; the other receives money consideration. Now suppose one person delivers the automobile and the other makes a promise to pay (e.g., a promissory note). In this contract the consideration received by one person is the automobile; the other person's consideration is the promise to pay money. Finally, suppose when the parties meet that neither the money nor automobile is available, so the parties prepare and sign an agreement in which one promises to pay money and the other promises to deliver the automobile at a later time. Each party's consideration is only a promise. Yet a valid and enforceable contract has been created.

To put it still another way, consideration is something given "in exchange for" something else. If this example and definition fail to clarify the concept of consideration, there is still hope. For, as noted previously, consideration is rarely a problem in ordinary business transactions. Unless one person intends a gift, something is expected in return. The exchange of one something for another is the very heartbeat of business.

If token consideration exists a court will rarely question the adequacy of such consideration. It is presumed that both parties are capable of bargaining for what they want. A court will not second-guess a decision by a businessperson about whether the consideration received was fair. One limitation on this broad statement stems from the doctrine of unconscionability that also relates to contract elements other than consideration. It is possible that a great disparity between the consideration exchanged may result in a court holding that a contract is unconscionable. The contract would be entirely unenforceable. However, the unconscionability doctrine usually arises in consumer litigation rather than a dispute between businesses. It is fair to say that any consideration, however inadequate it may appear in retrospect, will suffice in an agreement between businesses. For agreements in this book, therefore, consideration is of no practical concern.

SIMPLE MODERN ENGLISH

Lawyers, like all professionals, have developed their own vocabulary. It may be argued that the use of specialized words facilitates the communication of abstract ideas. On the other hand, those who are more skeptical may find in the special verbiage an attempt to exclude nonlawyers, thus justifying the lawyers' existence. Regardless of one's persuasion the law even more so than other professions has the added difficulty of a long history through which archaic expressions have survived. Latin words and phrases that were used extensively during the genesis of the common law still persist. Indeed, sprinkling a few selected Latin phrases through a written document or opinion is believed by some lawyers to be a mark of erudition. Instead, such usage is usually a mark of pomposity.

The continued vitality of archaic expressions in the law is probably attributable to the aura of formality or ritual that is conveyed through the use of such expressions. Of late, there has been extensive discussion in the legal profession and some legislation at both the state and national level which mandates that plain and simple English be used in consumer contracts. This notion is probably an extension of Truth-in-Lending and similar legislation that attempt to establish a balance between the ultimate consumer, usually unrepresented by lawyers, and large corporations. More and more it is recognized that words and phrases that a layman would not understand create an unwarranted disadvantage in consumer transactions. There is no purpose in using a complex, legal expression if a simpler explanation exists, unless one party is attempting to exploit the ignorance of the other. If plain English is to become the rule in business-consumer contracts, then surely it also has a place in contracts between businesses.

Many business managers who draft their own contracts attempt to use a similar agreement previously prepared by a lawyer for another occasion. Unless there is a clear understanding of the expressions employed nothing could be more unwise. It is apparently the feeling that by using another agreement replete with "legalese" the copier will somehow invest the writing with legal force. But as just pointed out it is only necessary to include the basic components of a contract to make it legally enforceable. There is no requirement for magic words. Still worse, other motivations may exist for using an old contract—to give the appearance that the contract was prepared by a lawyer. An attempt may be made to deceive the other party into believing that the draftsman is represented by legal counsel and therefore the document is "proper."

The irony is that the document may be legal but not proper. It may also be an attempt to confound the other party with language that is difficult to understand and for this reason not likely to be challenged. Unfortunately, it probably confounds not only the other party but also the draftsman. Throughout this book there is an attempt to use plain and simple English. Of course, there are terms of art that cannot be avoided. For example, the phrase "specific performance" is a succinct and appropriate label for the legal concept that in certain types of contracts money damages would be an inadequate remedy and a court should force the other party to perform the specific acts promised. When such expressions are believed to be appropriate but not within the vocabulary of a layman, I attempt to explain briefly the legal concept. Thus the reader has at least a rudimentary understanding when the term is later used.

Many terms lawyers use can be properly avoided. Some are archaic and stilted such as "aforesaid," "heretofore," "whomsoever," and "witnesseth." In nearly every instance there are equivalent terms or words that can be used to express the same thought with simpler vocabulary. Perhaps the height of inscrutability occurs in contracts that refer to the parties as "party of the first part," and the like. Not only are the parties' proper names better suited for identification but the agreement is much easier to read. Fortunately, this quaint phraseology is nearly extinct. There are, however, places for such time-honored expressions as "and/or" (although in many cases it can be avoided) and "respectively" (a helpful word for matching two series of enumerated terms).

The modern draftsman will never use "deem" when "consider" will do. It is not necessary to "commence" or "cease" when "begin" or "stop" is adequate. A corporation can be identified as "a California corporation" rather than "a corporation organized and existing under the laws of the State of California." It is sufficient to say that a party "may" rather than "is empowered."

Nor is it necessary to be redundant. Nothing is gained by "each and every" as compared to "each." Nothing is gained by making a payment "due and owing" rather than "due." An agreement that remains "in full force" is just as good as one that remains "in full force and effect." And when it is "agreed," it is obviously "understood and agreed." Doublets are unnecessary.

One last matter concerning vocabulary and contemporary social issues is the use of "man" rather than a neutral term as a suffix. "Draftsman" is used in this book because the available alternative, "drafter" and "draftsperson," are considered awkward. "Business manager" has been used in this text (I hope with only an occasional lapse) in preference to "businessperson." Similar care should be used in drafting a legal agreement. A neutral word can usually be chosen that will save later embarrassment. In an employment contract, for example, "employee" is a suitable word. The same contract, initially drafted for a male employee, can be used later for a female employee without requiring a search for an inappropriate pronoun. In a letter-type employment contract, "employee" would be stiff and formal. But the same effect can be obtained by using the second-person singular pronoun "you." The extent of effort taken to avoid sex-denoting words is finally a matter of discretion and individual judgment. But at least *some* effort is justified.

In summary, it is extremely desirable to be precise and explicit in a written agreement, but it is not necessary to adopt a new vocabulary, particularly one that is understood only vaguely. There is no excuse for using a Latin word or phrase in a business agreement. The object should be to express thoughts in clear, concise English that facilitates understanding. It is not necessary to use legalese to attain precision.

Chapter Two
The Beginning and the End

THE FORMAT

The format of a written agreement can be either "formal"—a complete, separate document—or a "letter agreement"—correspondence from one party to another, signed by the recipient, that includes the necessary components of a legal contract. The choice is strictly a matter of preference. In either case all the promises, terms, and conditions that will govern the relationship between the parties should be set forth in detailed, clear, and unequivocal language. The legal effect is completely unrelated to the format.

The choice of format often will be dictated by the atmosphere of the negotiations. Although it is generally agreed that the letter agreement has an air of informality, some investment agreements involving the most complex terms and with the most serious financial consequences for both parties frequently are found in letter form. Tradition is certainly a factor. It would be extremely unusual to find a lease for an industrial building in a letter format. However, employment and consultant agreements are often in letter format.

Since most of the agreements in this book can be used with either format, this chapter provides a suitable beginning and end for either.

THE BEGINNING

Letter Agreement

In a letter agreement, following the salutation, the opening sentence should refer to the negotiations preceding the letter to provide some background and introduction. If the basic details of the arrangement have been worked out and agreed on the first sentence may recite that the letter will "confirm" the understanding. However, if an important aspect of the relationship—for example, the final price in a sales agreement or the length of the term in an employment contract—has not been resolved, the opening paragraph may make reference to the prior negotiations and point out that complete terms are now included.

As an example, an introductory paragraph to a consulting agreement may read as follows:

2.1   As we recently discussed, we would like you to perform consulting services for us from time to time. This letter will set forth all the terms and conditions for such an arrangement that, if accepted by you, will constitute a legally enforceable agreement between us.

An example of an introductory paragraph for an employment contract letter may read:

2.2   It was a pleasure meeting with you personally after our several telephone conversations regarding employment. This letter contains all the details of our offer of employment that if accepted by you will form a legal agreement between us. Please read the letter carefully and contact me if you have any questions about the terms and conditions.

Notice that in the letter agreement, rather than referring to "consultant" or "employee" and "company," conversational pronouns are used, such as "you," "we," "us," and so on. This is perhaps one of the reasons the letter agreement normally appears to be more informal, since it is more similar to ordinary business correspondence. Presentation in this more familiar context may make the reader more comfortable. In this book, all forms use formal terms to refer to the parties and therefore must be modified to conform to the letter agreement style.

Formal Agreement

Parties.   As in the letter agreement, there are both introductory and background paragraphs normally used in a formal agreement. Unlike the letter contract in which the recipient's name and address precede the body of the letter, and the letterhead of the sender identifies the company and its location, the formal agreement must commence by identifying the parties and their addresses. Such identification should include the full name and complete address of each party. For ease in later reference to the parties it is common to choose a shorthand expression for each party. Some contract draftsmen like to choose functional terms such as "Purchaser" and "Seller," "Distributor" and "Manufacturer," or similar descriptions of the parties' status in the relationship. Other draftsmen prefer to use a portion of the proper name of the parties, for example, "Acme," "XYZ," a company nickname, or an acronym.

In part the choice of the best shorthand identification of the parties may depend on whether the company will be entering into multiple agreements. If the company is establishing a network of dealers or distributors it will be much easier to use the term "Dealer" or "Distributor" throughout the agreement. Reference to the distributor by its proper name would require that each agreement be individually typed with the proper name changed at every occurrence. This approach invites clerical error.

In addition to identifying the parties, it is important to identify and describe the form of the legal entity that is entering into the agreement. The form will be used to determine the type of authority required for legal execution of the agreement. Inquiring about the form of the entity will also prevent contracting with the wrong party. The latter problem often arises when the party uses a fictitious or assumed name rather than a legal name. It is important that the true legal owner be identified and bound by the agreement. If only the fictitious name is used in the agreement the party bound is unknown. It may be presumed that the fictitious-named entity is a partnership but in fact is a sole proprietorship or a partnership composed of different individuals from those presumed. When encountering a party using a fictitious name, the agreement should include the legal name, for example, ". . . John Brown, sole proprietor, doing business as Acme Foundry . . ."

A partnership may be either general or limited. A general partnership is the most ordinary and comprises two or more persons engaged in a joint undertaking. All partners are liable not only for the assets of the partnership but also for their entire personal assets. Each partner in the usual partnership has complete authority to bind the partnership in a legal agreement. A joint venture is a general partnership differing only in that it is usually formed to undertake a project with a definite goal and thus has a defined life. In a legal agreement the general partnership should be defined as: ". . . ABC Company, a general partnership composed of Samuel Adams, John Brown and Tom Clark . . ." A limited partnership, often used in real estate and tax shelter investments, is created under state laws and normally provides limited liability for one or more partners (although there must be one partner with unlimited liability). This protection requires that limited partners refrain from exercising any management authority in the partnership. A limited partnership may be described as follows: ". . . ABC Company, a limited partnership, including John Brown, a general partner . . ." The signature line should be prepared for the signature of only John Brown.

If the entity is a corporation, the description is very straightforward: ". . . XYZ, Inc., a California corporation . . ."

Date. The introductory paragraph will also provide the date of the agreement, just as the letter agreement will normally commence with the date on which the letter is sent. It should be remembered that the date of the agreement may be important if certain events, not the least of which is the term of the agreement itself, are measured from the "date of the agreement." The agreement normally comes into being when the parties execute the contract. When the agreement is being executed by two parties not at the same location at the time of execution, one party obviously will sign earlier. Until the second party signs there is no contract. Therefore, it is reasonable to leave the date blank until the last of the two or three parties to sign the agreement supplies the date on execution.

The parties may specifically intend that the written agreement predate the actual date of execution to reflect an oral agreement that exists. Suppose that in a manufacturer-distributor agreement there is a provision requiring the distributor to purchase a minimum number of units during the first year of the agreement to maintain the exclusive right of representation. The parties doing the negotiation have arrived at all the details to be embodied in a written agreement. While one party is drafting the agreement, or if one of the parties is unavailable to execute the agreement for a short period of time, the distributor may proceed to purchase units. Perhaps to "fill the pipeline" the distributor may enter a very substantial order that amounts to a high percentage of the first year's minimum commitment. In the event that toward the end of the first year the distributor is having difficulty meeting the purchase requirement of the first year, the question of whether the first-year commitment has been met may depend on the date of the agreement. The manufacturer may be unhappy and looking for a reason to terminate the agreement. The distributor may feel that although the first-year results were less than expected the investment in market development justifies at least a second year of exclusivity. Were the goods bought before the written contract was "executed" but after it was "agreed upon" to be counted against the minimum volume commitment?

A suitable way to handle the predating of an agreement is to state that the agreement is "effective" or "made as of" the date stated. Or it may be stated that the agreement is ". . . dated, for reference purposes only, as

of the _____ day of _____, 19_____ . . ." Usually, the date of the
agreement will be of only passing significance. But when there are potential problems because the parties have already begun to operate under an
oral arrangement or the operation is to begin at a later date, some attention must be given to the date chosen for the introductory paragraph.

Recitals.   After the introductory paragraph in a formal contract there is
usually set off on a separate line, as if to give deference to a magic symbol that creates a legal contract, the word "WITNESSETH." For those
people who invite their friends to dinner by saying "Come, let us break
bread together," the word will of course be comfortable. But an alternative choice for those who find this anachronism unbearable is to introduce the following paragraphs by stating "RECITALS." To adopt contemporary language usage the same effect may be obtained by stating
"BACKGROUND."

Exactly what is being done in this part of the formal contract? Simply
enough, there is to follow after the introductory paragraph a short statement of the background facts to provide a preface to the agreement body.
This will enable persons unfamiliar with the agreement to see the promises and covenants of the parties in some factual context. In most cases
this is a mere formality, but often it can be helpful to see what the parties
believed were the facts that led to their entering into the relationship
defined by the agreement. In fact this is probably one of the most beneficial purposes of these background paragraphs—to state the purpose of
the agreement and the reason why the parties have come together.

From a point of view of legal interpretation recitals are not considered
a portion of the substantive parts of the agreement. However, courts have
indicated that recitals may be resorted to if doing such will aid in the
construction or interpretation of ambiguous provisions. It may also be
argued in a later dispute that if the facts recited were untrue the agreement was entered into because of a misrepresentation of the facts. The
difficulty with this argument is that the agreement does not show on its
face which party made the factual misrepresentation. If the representation is material, it is preferable to include a paragraph in the agreement
specifically identifying not only the facts but also which party is making
the representation. For example, in a consulting agreement it may be important to the company that the consultant is not then engaged by a competitive firm. The agreement may recite: "Consultant represents that for
a period of six months prior to the date of this agreement he has not performed, and is not presently performing, consulting services for any company manufacturing widgets." Remember, representations relate to facts,
past or present events, and is not a promise relating to future events. If it

is later proved that the explicit representation was false there is a clear case of intentional misrepresentation which will establish a breach of contract at the very least. By contrast, even a statement similar to that just given appearing in the recitals will have much less force.

One very useful purpose of the background paragraph is to define terms that may be used later. In a consulting agreement the business in which the company is engaged may be defined. In a licensing agreement a group of patents may be identified by title, inventor, and date and then summarily defined as "Patent Rights," a term that may be used through-out the agreement. In an equipment lease the principal piece of equipment, together with all the accessories, may be described in detail and then provided with a shorthand expression such as "Equipment," for later use in the agreement.

If it is decided that WITNESSETH is too formal, the draftsman may also want to dispense with the antiquarian "Whereas" that is usually used to begin each of the background paragraphs. Although this informality may shock many a lawyer, it is entirely sensible to begin each background paragraph with "Considering that . . . ," a reasonable replacement for Whereas. Or one might start each of these background paragraphs as one would any descriptive narrative paragraph. In fact many modern drafts-men completely omit the background paragraphs, considering them un-necessary.

Consideration.   Finally, there is the last of the beginning clauses that starts with the equally portentous "NOW, THEREFORE, . . ." phrase. Like WITNESSETH, these two words are not a magical incantation that invests an agreement with legal enforceability. They mean no more than "in light of the above background facts" the parties are going to get down to business.

Following the "NOW, THEREFORE, . . ." introduction there will usually be found a statement to establish that the vital element of con-sideration is present. Consider this, for example, "NOW, THEREFORE, in consideration of One Dollar and other good and valuable considera-tion . . ." The use of this phrase stems from the early English common law concept of consideration, as discussed in Chapter 1. It was necessary as consideration in ancient English law to recite that some tangible ob-ject was in fact transferred from one party to another and that the prom-ise of the other party was in consideration of this delivery. In transferring land, for example, a clod of earth was delivered! The tangible object later became the dollar. However, no one was ever certain that the dollar alone was adequate. Thus it was recited ". . . for One Dollar *and* other good and valuable consideration . . ." (Emphasis added.) Even though courts held that consideration was established when one party made a promise in consideration of the promise of the other party, many draftsmen still felt the need to specifically recite that there was some tangible consideration.

As noted in Chapter 1, however, few written business agreements are ever found unenforceable because of lack of consideration. Nor is it likely that if an agreement were in fact completely lacking in consideration the mere recital would save the agreement. A simple statement that "The parties agree as follows:" could easily replace the whole of this paragraph. This statement will serve as a convenient introduction to the promises, terms, and conditions contained in the body of the agreement.

A suitable introductory paragraph would therefore read:

2.3   This agreement is made this _____ day of _____, 1979, between WIDGET MANUFACTURING COMPANY ("WIDGET"), a California corporation, 1111 Industrial Street, Los Angeles, California 90000, and Stanley Good, dba GOOD LITTLE DISTRIBUTORS INC. ("DISTRIBUTOR"), a sole proprietorship, located at 7711 Easy Street, Las Vegas, Nevada 77000. The parties agree as follows:

A more traditional beginning, complete with recitals, would read:

2.4   This agreement is made as of the _____ day of _____, 19____, between Robert Inventor ("INVENTOR"), an individual, residing at 10202 Main Street, Chicago, Illinois 60600, and Ace Manufacturing Inc. ("ACE"), an Illinois corporation, 4000 Burnham Road, Chicago, Illinois 60006.

Background

INVENTOR has invented a new, improved mechanical pencil and is the owner of the entire right, title, and interest in and to U.S. Patent No. 5,600,001, entitled, "Mechanical Pencil," issued January 20, 1989 (referred to as the "Patent").

ACE is engaged in the manufacture and sale of engineering drafting supplies, including mechanical pencils.

INVENTOR desires to license ACE to manufacture and sell the mechanical pencils covered by the Patent, and ACE desires to obtain the license and to pay royalties for the use of the Patent.

NOW, THEREFORE, in consideration of the foregoing and the mutual promises, terms, and conditions of this agreement, the parties agree as follows.

THE END

Letter Agreement

The most important point to be made in concluding the letter agreement is this: make it perfectly clear that if the letter agreement is accepted a binding contract results. In addition to expressing the ramifications of acceptance there is the mechanical necessity of providing each party with a copy of the agreement. This is usually done by submitting an original and a duplicate copy of the letter and requesting that one copy be returned.

As noted in Chapter 1, if an offer has no specified time limit the law will imply a reasonable period of time in which the offer remains open. It is therefore desirable to include a sentence in the letter agreement which specifically states that the offer will expire as of a certain date. This will force the recipient to give the offer the prompt attention desired.

The customary manner for providing for the written acceptance by the recipient of the letter agreement is to include a sentence, usually typed below the signature of the sending party, stating that the agreement is accepted as of a particular date, followed by a signature line.

The concluding paragraphs of the letter would read:

2.5 If these terms and conditions are agreeable, please indicate your acceptance by signing the duplicate copy of this letter in the space provided and returning it to me.

This offer expires as of the close of business on _____, 19___.

Sincerely,

XYZ Corporation
President

Accepted this ___ day of _____, 19___.

_____
(Signature of Recipient)

Formal Agreement

In nearly every formal agreement prepared by a lawyer the final paragraph begins: "IN WITNESS WHEREOF, this agreement has been executed . . ." Here again, one is faced with the formalism of early English common law. In days of old when most English agreements were prepared in Latin the concluding paragraph stated: "In Cujus Rei Testimonium." This phrase translates as "In Testimony Whereof" and is equivalent to "In Witness Whereof." All this simply meant that the parties were executing the writing as witnesses to the agreement having been set down in writing to their satisfaction. It is hardly conceivable that omission of the paragraph, followed immediately by appropriate places for signatures of the parties executing the agreement, would in any way affect the agreement's legal validity. On the other hand the concluding paragraph is certainly innocuous and probably ignored by anyone reading or construing the agreement.

There is no objection to using the anachronistic "In Witness Whereof . . . ," but a suitable substitute would be as follows:

2.6 The parties have executed this agreement as of the date first shown above.

ACE MANUFACTURING, INC.
By _____
(Title)
ROBERT INVENTOR

As earlier mentioned, the situation often arises when the agreement should be dated "as of" a particular day preceding or subsequent to the actual date of execution. To be accurate, the concluding paragraph should then read:

2.7 The parties have executed this agreement on _____, 19___, but this agreement is effective as of the day and year first above written.

The date inserted in the blank would be the date on which both parties, or the last to sign, executed the contract.

Authority to Execute

If a written merger agreement between General Motors and IBM, complete with all the formal language normally supplied by a Wall Street legal firm, was executed by a filing clerk for IBM and a building maintenance man in a General Motors field office, the agreement would be completely ignored by the world. Except when dealing with a single individual acting on his or her own behalf the other party must be concerned with whether the executing individual has the appropriate authority to bind the legal entity for which he or she signs. For a corporation, many persons have the authority to bind the company. No one would doubt that a purchase order executed by a junior buyer known to be employed by a particular company would normally bind the company issuing the purchase order. Exceptions will come readily to mind such as long-term contracts or purchase orders involving a dollar amount that is extraordinary compared to prior transactions or the size of the firm. But as a normal matter no company would deny that it was bound by a purchase order on a company form sent by an employee whose regular responsibility is to purchase goods or services.

In determining authority, which involves the myriad rules of agency law, validity is determined from the factual context surrounding the agreement. Because these rules are never entirely unambiguous the party seeking a commitment from a corporation should always obtain the signature of an officer. The basis for this advice is that the usual corporate bylaws generally give all the officers of a corporation the power to bind the corporation. An officer's signature in nearly all commercial transactions should give adequate assurance that the company is bound.

But there are situations for which even an officer's signature would be inadequate to establish proper authority. Any merger agreement, for example, is an act of such importance relative to the conduct of business of the corporation that all lawyers would insist on a certified copy of an appropriate resolution of the board of directors. This may even be true for other corporate acts of a less fundamental nature, such as selling a subsidiary, a division, or line of business or entering into a joint venture.

In many formal agreements there is provision for a corporate officer's signature and another space provided for a "Witness" or "Secretary." The purpose is to obtain the name of a person who saw the agreement executed and can testify to that fact if execution is later denied. In California, execution by the corporate secretary as a witness to signing by the corporate president, chairman of the board, or vice-president is conclusive evidence of proper corporate authority.

Some institutions, usually banks, have simply refused to come forward into the twentieth century and require a corporate seal on certain agreements. This is purposeless, since most state corporation laws include a statute which effectively holds that a seal is of no consequence in terms of binding a corporation. Addition of the seal is not evidence of proper corporate authority.

In concluding a formal agreement to be executed by corporate officers, the final paragraph and signature provisions would be as follows:

2.8   The parties, by their properly authorized officers, have executed
       this agreement as of the date first shown above.

                                              ABC CORPORATION

                                    By _____
                                              Jim Smith, President

                                              XYZ CORPORATION

                                    By _____
                                              Sam Brown, Vice-President

   Questions regarding the authority to execute also arise when a partnership is one of the parties to the transaction. As previously noted, there
are two types of partnerships in common use.

   Since in a general partnership any partner can commit the partnership,
it may be sufficient to obtain only the signature of one of the general
partners. The general authority of a partner may be restricted in the
partnership agreement by a limitation on the authority of one or more
partners so that between themselves not all partners have the power to
bind each other. However, this will not affect the power of a partner to
bind the partnership as to third parties. If it is known that the negotiating
partner does not in fact have the power to bind the partnership (an unusual occurrence), it will result in a nonenforceable contract. It is recommended that each of the partners execute the agreement, particularly
if there are only two or three partners in the partnership.

   To conclude an agreement in which one of the parties is a partnership,
the signature format may be as follows:

2.9   ABC Company
       A General Partnership

       By _____
              Tom Clark, Partner

       By _____
              John Brown, Partner

       By _____
              Samuel Adams, Partner

These rules for corporation and partnership authority will suffice in most commercial transactions.

The matter of determining proper authority may be more difficult when making an arrangement with a foreign company. It would be advisable in such circumstances to request a power of attorney. Or a representation should be set forth in the agreement specifying that the executing person has the power to act. At the very least a letter on the company's stationery should be demanded stating that the person acting in the transaction has the authority to bind the entity.

It can be extremely frustrating to execute an agreement only to later find that the company disavows the act of the representative. If facts can be presented that the representative and the company created an impression of a commitment being proper and authorized, a court may rule favorably. Steps should be taken when negotiating and preparing the agreement to resolve the problem of proper authority.

Chapter Three
Near the End

In all legal agreements there are some standard terms and provisions commonly referred to as "boilerplate." Some of these paragraphs are identical from one agreement to the next without regard to the nature or subject of the contract; in other cases, the paragraphs vary slightly, depending on the context.

As a matter of general arrangement the boilerplate usually follows the principal paragraphs of the agreement. Consequently, the boilerplate is usually positioned near the end of the agreement. This chapter provides typical paragraphs that may be used without modification. There are also other relatively standardized paragraphs that require some modification to fit the particular situation. Suggestions are made about each form paragraph with respect to the type of agreement in which it should be used and the more common modifications required to tailor the paragraph to a specific transaction. The paragraphs first discussed are of almost universal applicability.

NOTICES

During the term of every agreement there will be occasion for one party to communicate with the other with reference to the contract. The agreement should therefore state the manner in which such communication must be given, the time at which the communication becomes effective, and the place to which the communication must be sent.

Any notice or communication between the parties should be in writing. If it is specified in this paragraph that the notice must be in writing, it will be unnecessary each time the word *notice* is used throughout the agreement to state that it is "written" notice that is meant.

There are several means of transmitting written notice. The most widespread is the U.S. mail. But a notice may also be personally hand delivered or may be in the form of a telegram. In most cases the notice concerns a matter on which action must be started or stopped within a defined period of time. Only in a highly unusual situation will the notice be required to be given by rapid means of communication such as a telegram, mailgram, or Telex. When using electronic communication, it is important for the party sending the notice to retain a copy as proof that notice was sent. In all cases the very requirement that the notice be in writing precludes telephonic notice. Emphasis is on certainty and proof that the notice has been given rather than time. If time is important, then it is suggested that at the point in the agreement at which such special notice is required the type of notice be spelled out in detail. In the later Notices paragraph, an exception may be made for the special notice by commencing with the statement: "Except where otherwise stated . . ."

One particular problem with the U.S. mail is possible failure of delivery of the notice. If a letter providing notice is mailed the law presumes that the letter was properly delivered unless the agreement provides otherwise. A denial that notice was received will generally not prevail over testimony that a letter was mailed. However, this contest of memory can be avoided by the sender by choosing a type of delivery for which proof is obtainable. If the notice is personally delivered a signed receipt should be obtained stating that the party received the document as of a particular day. A copy of the signed acknowledgment of delivery should, of course, be retained. If delivery is by mail the letter may be sent either by certified or registered mail with a return receipt requested. This requires that the notice be personally taken to a post office station but is well worth the trouble. When the letter is delivered the recipient will sign a postcard which is returned to the sender and thus constitute proof that the notice was received. This type of proof of delivery is nearly irrefutable.

The second problem surrounding the notice is the effective date. In many instances the date of giving notice will begin the running of a period during which the party to whom the notice is given must begin or end certain conduct. Should this period begin to run on the date on which the notice is delivered, mailed, or dated? The Notices paragraph clarifies this matter by stating what is the effective date. Generally, if the notice is personally served the effective date will be the date of service. If it is mailed then it is usual to provide that the effective date will be several days after the date of mailing. If the notice is sent by registered or certified mail with a return receipt requested, it is possible to use the date of receipt as the effective date, but this is not advisable, since the party may fail to date the return postcard or may place the incorrect date on the card. If only regular mail is used it should never be specified that the effective date is the date of receipt, since such date cannot be easily proved by the sender.

Finally, the Notices paragraph should include the addresses of the parties to whom the notices are to be sent unless they are identical to the addresses given in the introductory paragraph of the agreement. When the agreement involves a large corporation and the address is of a building at which a large number of personnel are employed, it may be desirable to specify a particular person by name and title so that there is no controversy over whether the notice was ever transmitted from the mailroom to the appropriate and responsible person. Although the latter argument may be to no avail as a legal matter, it is one more irritating point of friction that can be avoided by clear and explicit instructions. The entire paragraph will therefore read as follows:

3.1   *Notices.* Any notice provided for in this agreement shall be given in writing. Notices shall be effective on the date of service if served personally on the party to whom notice is to be given, or on the second day after mailing if mailed by first-class mail, postage prepaid. Notices shall be properly addressed to the parties at their respective addresses set forth above or to such other address as either party may later specify by notice to the other.

ENTIRE AGREEMENT

As previously noted, one of the chief purposes of entering into a written agreement is to provide a definitive and complete record of all the understandings between the parties. While negotiating the agreement there will be numerous conversations, exchanges of correspondence, and communications in which various suggestions or proposals are made. In many instances a proposition may not be rejected out-of-hand during a personal or telephone conversation; the party to whom the proposition is made may state that he wants to consider it. At a later meeting the subject may not arise, with one party perhaps thinking that it is of no great significance. Such silence may be interpreted by the other party as agreement. An incipient dispute exists.

It is absolutely mandatory in any written agreement to provide that all prior agreements or understandings between the parties have been superseded. A statement must be included that the agreement is complete and entire and that there are no "side agreements." Yet when this desirable provision is included both parties must be content and satisfied that the agreement is in fact complete. When one party states, "Don't worry about it; it isn't included in this contract, but I give you my personal assurance that we'll do it," the Entire Agreement paragraph belies such statement. A company may disavow the pie-in-the-sky statements of its salesman by pointing to the Entire Agreement paragraph. When properly used the paragraph is greatly beneficial to both sides, since it clarifies that the written agreement, and only the written agreement, defines the relationship between the parties.

The second purpose of this paragraph is to keep the written agreement the only continuing expression of the understanding between the parties. Sometime after the contract is executed it is possible for the parties to discuss a modification of a particular provision. At a still later time one of the parties may contend that as a result of such conversation there was an oral amendment to the agreement over which a dispute has now arisen. To prevent such contention this paragraph must state that only amendments in writing are effective.

Finally, there is a difficulty that arises from benign neglect. If an agreement calls for payment on a particular day of the month, and over a course of time payments arrive a few days late, then a week late, and then two weeks late, many business managers will ignore the first several late payments as being a trivial delay of no real harm. This tardiness may not even be called to the attention of the defaulting party. The very nature of the procedure of giving notice, suggested above as desirable, may be counterproductive in cases of these minor breaches, since written notice may simply be too burdensome and time consuming compared to the slight injury of delay. After many months and several informal oral warnings, when the delay becomes unbearable, the notice may be sent. To the surprise of the sender, the defaulting party may then contend that because the earlier late payments were accepted the nondefaulting party has waived the right to enforce the timely payment provision. The inaction of the party becomes its own undoing.

To cover these matters, a boilerplate paragraph should read:

3.2 *Entire Agreement.* This agreement constitutes the entire agreement between the parties relating to the subject matter contained in it and supersedes all prior and contemporaneous representations, agreements, or understandings between the parties. No amendment or supplement of this agreement shall be binding unless executed in writing by the parties. No waiver of any one provision of this agreement shall constitute a waiver of any other provision, nor shall any one waiver constitute a continuing waiver. No waiver shall be binding unless executed in writing by the party against whom the waiver is asserted.

GOVERNING LAW

The necessity for this provision arises whenever the two parties are in different states and certainly when they are in different countries. Parties subject to the laws of different governments have a problem concerning which law governs the relationship. The determination of which law governs can be crucial in a later dispute. For example, a party in one state may be considered an adult at 18 years of age, whereas in another state the adult age is 21. A company that contracts with a 19-year-old will find that the teenager may be bound if the law of one state applies but not if the other law controls. More subtle, but still vexing problems arise when even though there is no difference in statutory law, there may be court decisions that have construed identical statutes in divergent ways in the two jurisdictions.

As consistently stressed it is the purpose of the written agreement to provide certainty. Therefore if the law of one jurisdiction or another is chosen the possibility of a surprise result by a court about which law is applicable may be avoided. If nothing is said, there are numerous rules under the rubric of Conflict of Laws that courts apply to decide which law governs a contract. The choices are many: the law of the state in which the agreement is executed; the law of the place of performance; the law that the court presumes the parties intended; or the law of the place in which the litigation is brought. Further complicating the whole matter are decisions which state that the law of different places apply to the same contract, depending on the issue in controversy. That is, if the dispute involves a matter of interpretation, the law of the place of execution applies. If the dispute involves a breach, then the law of the state in which the performance was to be rendered will apply.

As a general matter an attorney who drafts an agreement will specify that the law of the jurisdiction in which he or she practices will control. This is the body of law with which the attorney is most familiar. A similar line of reasoning should lead the small business manager to select the law of the home state. In the event that the arrangement develops into a legal dispute, a lawyer from the home state will be hired by the manager. It will be advantageous if the legal questions that arise are to be construed and interpreted under the law of the home state; the lawyer will not only be more comfortable but more knowledgeable.

In most instances, courts will attempt to apply the law that the parties intended to apply; if expressly stated in the agreement, such intent will almost surely be followed. Simply from a point of view of certainty it is desirable to include a paragraph specifying the applicable law, such as:

3.3 *Governing Law.* This agreement shall be construed and interpreted in accordance with, and governed by, the laws of the State
of California.

HEADINGS NOT CONTROLLING

Aside from the use of clear and unambiguous language one of the most
helpful aids in a written agreement is the organization. Like any written
communication of substantial length a proper structure will assist the
parties in finding provisions of interest. A heading or short descriptive
title for each section should be used to assist in locating and retrieving
information. Furthermore, the arrangement of paragraphs—that is, the
order or succession—infers the relative importance of the paragraphs.

Notwithstanding the benefits of appropriate organization and the use of
headings to identify particular paragraphs, there is a latent problem that
may arise. In attempting to succinctly state the content of a paragraph,
the shorthand expression in the heading may affect the interpretation of
the paragraph as a whole. Or it may be contended that the heading was
misleading. In the above Entire Agreement paragraph, the matter of
waiver is included as reasonably related to the subject matter. But it
could be contended in a dispute involving waiver that the heading de-
ceived the defaulting party into believing that a waiver was not covered
in the agreement. The argument may be specious and eventually rejected,
but it is still troublesome. The probability that a heading will adversely affect the intended construction of a paragraph appears to be relatively
small. It is recommended, therefore, that only in a lengthy and complex
agreement should the following paragraph be used:

3.4 *Headings Not Controlling.* The subject headings of the paragraphs
of this agreement are included for purposes of convenience only and
shall not affect interpretation of the paragraphs.

ASSIGNABILITY

The section of the agreement that controls assignment, as well as the remaining paragraphs to be discussed in this chapter, are not entirely boilerplate. Treating such paragraphs as simply boilerplate may give rise to
unintended results and future difficulties.

The purpose of expressly establishing the rules controlling assignment
of an agreement must be clearly understood. A contract creates rights and
obligations of each party with respect to the other.

Both rights and obligations may be assigned, separately or together, depending on the agreement. Suppose in an agreement between A and B, A assigns its rights (but not its obligations) to a third party, C, perhaps as a gift or for some compensation. In general, the other party, B, who bears the obligation that gave rise to the rights of A will be unconcerned with A's being either generous or making another bargain. But B will not take lightly the assignment of the obligations of A. In other words, B may find acceptable that A is giving away the benefits of the contract but will object if A tries to avoid the obligation.

Assume that a business sells a piece of equipment on installment sale after a thorough credit investigation of the purchaser from which a measure of confidence has been drawn that the payments will be forthcoming. If the purchaser could later assign the obligation to pay to a less creditworthy party, it would be a shock to the seller. Of course, the problem does not arise in so blatant a context. Suppose, however, that the purchaser decides to resell the equipment to a third party such that the third party now enjoys the rights of ownership. Is this third-party owner obligated to continue making payments? Clearly, whether or not the third party agrees in writing to continue making the payments the obligation could not be avoided while the rights are being enjoyed. But what if such third party is financially irresponsible? It is obviously desirable for the seller to foresee such occurrence and to preclude any such assignment or to obtain assurance that if assigned the original party will remain obligated. Control is imposed by way of requiring consent in the contract to any assignment. The consent may be given only if the original party agrees to remain obligated.

An aggravated example would involve a personal service contract. If a company contracts with a software programmer and agrees to pay a substantial fee for each hour worked, can the programmer then assign this personal service contract to a man of lesser talents?

There is, therefore, a range of assignment clauses that may be used, beginning with a flat prohibition against either party assigning the agreement and ending with no prohibition at all. The latter, it is suggested, will rarely arise. In some agreements it may appear that there are no continuing obligations on one party and therefore no need to prevent assignment. For example, in the sale of relatively simple goods the purchaser may contract to make installment payments. Does it matter whether the seller assigns the contract to a financial institution, since the purchaser need only redirect its payments from one recipient to another? Usually, it does. For even after the equipment is delivered, inspected, placed into operation, and is functioning properly, what about a failure in the future?

Can the purchaser refuse to pay the assignee (financial institution) if the seller refuses to repair the equipment or if the seller has gone out of business? What is the effect of the warranty? The matter is not free of difficulty. There are numerous rules and principles that apply in these circumstances. Moreover, the law in this area, particularly with respect to consumers, is changing rapidly. Many of the principles that are being created for consumer contract law may find their way into general business contract law.

The following paragraphs are suggested for use in various contexts based on the circumstances and the draftsman's personal judgment. In order, the paragraphs provide for a flat prohibition against assignment; a prohibition, except with written consent; a prohibition, except for specific types of assignments; and a prohibition, except with consent but only nonarbitrary consent. The draftsman must reflect on exactly what is intended before seizing one of these paragraphs. There are many variations, including the possibility that an assignment may be desirable rather than detrimental.

3.5 **Nonassignment.** This agreement may not be assigned nor the rights and obligations otherwise transferred to a third party by either of the parties hereto; any attempted assignment or transfer shall be void.

3.6 **Assignability.** This agreement may not be assigned or otherwise transferred without the express written consent of the other party and a complete assumption in writing by the assignee of all the obligations of the assignor under this agreement.

3.7 **Assignability.** This agreement may not be assigned by either party, except to a corporation that assumes in writing all the obligations of the assignor under this agreement and is the successor of all, or substantially all, the business of the assignor.

3.8 **Assignability.** Neither this agreement nor any of the rights or obligations created by this agreement may be assigned, in whole or in part, by either of the parties without the written consent of the other party, provided, however, that the other party shall not unreasonably withhold its consent.

SEVERABILITY

The purpose of a severability provision is to prevent illegality of one paragraph or a portion of a paragraph from affecting the enforceability of the entire agreement. It is an attempt to prevent one bad apple from spoiling the entire barrel. Certain types of agreements are prone to running afoul of the law despite the intention of the parties. In business agreements the illegality that often arises is a violation of the antitrust laws or state business regulation statutes. In agreements relating to the distribution of goods there may be illegality in a Fair Trade provision; in a patent license there are various technical, equitable defenses that can render a patent license unenforceable (even though it is not an antitrust violation). In an agreement with a distributor, sales representative, or dealer in which there is a restriction against handling a competitor's goods, a severability provision is advisable.

Before incorporating a severability clause some forethought about the consequences is required. If, for example, a prohibition against the selling of competitive goods in a dealer contract is considered to be absolutely necessary to a proper business relationship, a severability clause could be detrimental. The draftsman must ask the question: "If this provision of the agreement were removed, would it be desirable to go on with the relationship otherwise described in the agreement?" Only if that question is answered in the affirmative should a severability clause be included.

Even if the parties agree that a provision found to be illegal should be excised from the agreement but the rest should be saved by the severability clause, a court may not agree. The court may ignore the severability clause on the grounds that the particular provision held illegal was inseparable and indivisible from the remainder of the agreement. The entire agreement will be struck down. Nevertheless, if the parties manifest their intent of going on with the relationship even without the provision that is judicially struck down, most courts will attempt to comply with the wishes of the parties unless the illegality is particularly noxious. Therefore, when appropriate, the following paragraph may be used:

3.9   *Severability.*   If any provision of this agreement is held by a court of competent jurisdiction to be invalid or unenforceable, the remainder of the agreement shall remain in full force and shall in no way be impaired.

SPECIFIC PERFORMANCE

When a party has failed to perform as promised a suit for breach of contract will result in an award of damages against the defaulting party. But courts also recognize that for the breach of certain promises damages may not be an adequate remedy. Under such circumstances a court using its equity power may compel the party to perform specifically as promised.

The classic example in which specific performance is permitted is in the sale of a parcel of land. In the eyes of the law every piece of land is unique; therefore, a buyer is entitled to a specific performance, that is, conveyance, if the seller defaults. Courts have recognized that other property and services may also be unique for which money damages will not properly compensate the aggrieved party. For example, personal property such as an antique, a rare stamp, or similar one-of-a-kind items may be found unique and deserving of the remedy of specific performance.

The emphasis is on whether the subject property is irreplaceable; in sales agreements the availability of a substitute is often referred to as the ability to "cover," that is, obtain identical goods from another source. If the buyer can cover then money damages are obviously sufficient, since the buyer may procure the article elsewhere. Even if the substitute item from the new source costs more, the court will award additional damages to compensate the buyer for the additional cost as well as the effort and time spent in procuring the new goods.

In personal service contracts a court will not force a party to perform against his will, even if such performance is unique. Instead, courts have fashioned an alternative remedy by precluding the party from rendering services to anyone else. Three justifications are normally given for this reluctance to compel performance: (a) to compel the party to act would involve involuntary servitude; (b) courts are reluctant to personally supervise performance, because they lack the appropriate enforcement machinery; and (c) the quality of services performed by a gifted individual cannot be measured against the capability to perform with excellence. An injunction that prohibits a person from working for others, however, will strongly motivate such person to deliver the services as promised.

In a personal service contract, it may therefore be desirable to couch the prohibitory injunction that a court may issue in what is commonly referred to as a "negative restrictive covenant." This simply means that the party agrees to refrain from performing for others under certain conditions which must be set forth in the agreement with great particularity.

The most common type of negative covenant encountered is the noncompete covenant found in agreements for the sale of a business. The seller, whose personal services may be instrumental in competing against the buyer after the sale, agrees to refrain from such competition for a specific period of time and in a limited geographical territory. If properly drafted a court will enjoin a party from acting contrary to the promise made. The applicability of the negative covenant in agreements for consulting or employment services should be apparent. In some states, however, a statute may prohibit a negative covenant in a personal service contract as explained in Chapter 9.

If in either a sale or personal service agreement the defaulting party is compelled by a court to deliver the property or to refrain from performing services for others and the party fails to comply with the court order, the court will then hold the party in contempt. A fine or even incarceration of the individual may result. The latter is a drastic remedy that is not lightly undertaken by a court.

A clause for specific performance should be included in an agreement only after thoughtful attention to its effect. In many agreements, the clause would be inappropriate. The parties may state in the agreement that the subject matter is unique and that there will be no adequate remedy at law for a breach. But a court will use its own discretion in determining whether this unusual remedy applies. A mere recitation in the contract of the required elements for invoking the remedy of specific performance will not suffice.

A suitable paragraph for incorporation into an agreement when specific performance is appropriate is as follows:

3.10 *Specific Performance.* The parties acknowledge that their obligations under this agreement and the subject matter of this agreement are unique and it would therefore be extremely difficult to measure resulting damages in the event one party defaults in its performance. Accordingly, in addition to any other remedies available to the nondefaulting party, such party may demand specific performance, and the defaulting party expressly waives the defense that the loss can be adequately compensated by money damages.

ARBITRATION

For the small business, arbitration may be an ideal method for settling a contract dispute. The principal advantage normally stated for arbitration is that it minimizes time and expense. In some industries, for example, building construction, arbitration has become a well-accepted way of life. Similarly, in foreign transactions the parties may be reluctant to submit to the jurisdiction of a court in an unfamiliar setting. Arbitration by an international commercial body, however, may be acceptable to both parties.

In domestic contract disputes the American Arbitration Association (AAA) is often used for settling disputes. An arbitration hearing may be scheduled in any major city under the auspices of the AAA that has established rules, fees, and an available panel of arbitrators. An arbitration provision in an agreement may specifically provide that such arbitration shall be submitted to the AAA.

The advantages of time and expense can be substantial but must be considered in detail. In an arbitration proceeding there is no "discovery procedure" (the pretrial collection of information through depositions, interrogatories, and similar devices) that can substantially reduce attorneys' fees. Similarly, there is no mechanism for "pretrial motions" (the preliminary sparring between attorneys for an advantageous position at trial) that are both time consuming and expensive. Arbitration may also be simpler and less time consuming than a court trial, because arbitrators are generally chosen who are experts in the applicable field. There is no necessity at the hearing for familiarizing the decision-making body with background facts. Nor is there any provision for a jury trial in an arbitration; therefore, the fees and time-consuming mechanism attendant to the jury process are eliminated. At the hearing an arbitration may proceed with greater speed because there is less delaying disruptions than in a court. Furthermore, a judge may have less time to spend on the hearing than arbitrators whose schedules are more flexible.

Many business managers also like arbitration because it is less technical; that is, the rules of evidence normally used in court which are sometimes complex and confusing are not employed. This provides a better understanding of what is taking place at the hearing and the ability to personally measure the chance of success. The greater appreciation may lead to the acceptance of a compromise if that course of action appears advisable.

Although arbitration expenses are usually less because of the shorter time consumed, arbitration does require administrative fees paid to the AAA, whereas the compensation of a judge is borne by the taxpayers. The AAA has a fee schedule that, for a claim of $25,000, would amount to $600. Finally, it may be desirable to have a reporter at an arbitration hearing; the parties must bear this expense, whereas in a court proceeding the taxpayers are charged. On balance, it is almost certain that the overall expenses for arbitration will be less than for court litigation despite the higher arbitration hearing fees.

One other matter with respect to time is the interminable delay that results in court litigation when the losing party takes an appeal. This may result in litigation, which has already taken several years to complete the court trial, to be extended for another year or more. By contrast, an award in arbitration, except under unusual and limited circumstances, is final.

If the decision has been made to incorporate an arbitration proceeding into the agreement there are several choices for drafting the arbitration clause. First, the matter may be succinctly stated by agreeing to submit the matter to the AAA. This submission incorporates all the procedures, fees, methods, and mechanisms that are set forth in the rules of the AAA. Occasionally, a second choice may be preferred by setting forth in detail the arbitration provisions and submitting the matter to a non-AAA arbitration hearing. In certain industries, a third choice may be available if the industry has informally developed an arbitration mechanism used for intra-industry disputes.

As a general matter it seems preferable to choose the AAA as the arbitration authority. The most common reluctance to submitting the matter to AAA rules is the loss of control over the method of selecting arbitrators. When the parties designate the AAA and submit to its jurisdiction the rules provide the manner in which the arbitrators are selected and a pool from which the arbitrators are chosen. However, if this is the only objection it should be noted that AAA Rule 14 permits the parties to use a different method for choosing the arbitrators but still have all other rules of the AAA control.

Here are two paragraphs for incorporating arbitration into an agreement, the first of which is a total submission to the AAA, and the second provides for a specific method of choosing arbitrators but otherwise submits to AAA rules.

3.11   *Arbitration.*   Any controversy or claim arising out of or relating to this contract, or the breach thereof, shall be settled by arbitration in accordance with the Rules of the American Arbitration Association and judgment upon the award rendered by the arbitrator(s) may be entered in any court having jurisdiction thereof.

This clause is recommended by the AAA. A modified clause is as follows:

3.12   *Arbitration.*   Any controversy or claim arising out of or relating to this contract, or the breach thereof, is subject to arbitration. A party desiring arbitration shall give notice (containing a general description of the controversy) to the other party and designating, by name and address, an arbitrator. The other party shall designate an arbitrator within five (5) days from the date of such notice by giving notice including the name and address of a second arbitrator. The selected arbitrators shall choose a third arbitrator from a list of arbitrators submitted by the American Arbitration Association (AAA). Other than this selection of arbitrators, such controversy or claim shall be settled in accordance with the Rules of the AAA. Judgment on the award rendered by the arbitrator(s) may be entered in any court having jurisdiction thereof.

A provision for arbitration, even in the absence of a specific performance clause, will be specifically enforced by a court. For example, if one party commences arbitration and the other party refuses to participate, then under the Rules of the American Arbitration Association (AAA) an award may be rendered to the participating party. This award will be enforced. Furthermore, if a dispute arises and one party ignores the provision for arbitration in the agreement and begins litigation the other party (defendant) may appear in court and prevent the lawsuit from continuing. If, however, the defendant participates in the court proceeding (also ignoring the arbitration provision), then a court will hold that the parties have waived arbitration and the litigation may continue and will be determinative of the dispute.

It may also be desirable to include a location designation in either type of arbitration clause. If there are several potential places where the arbitration could be held, it may be advantageous to designate a particular city in which the hearing must take place. The location clause will also be enforced by a court. The designation may state: "The arbitration shall be held in the city of _____."

FORCE MAJEURE

Legalese at its finest, *force majeure* is more simply a French phrase meaning superior or irresistible force. Most lawyers would hold that it means Acts of God; but to be persnickety, a better phrase for Acts of God would be *force majesture*—quintessential legalese.

What happens when events beyond the control of the parties prevent one party from performing? Is such performance excused? A well-constructed legal agreement should cover contingencies that are both foreseeable and likely. Accordingly, a provision should be added to nearly any contract to specifically excuse a party from performing when events make such performance impossible or extremely difficult. It is particularly useful in a contract covering a relationship that will continue over a prolonged period of time.

Many events give rise to unavoidable breach. Subsumed under the term "Acts of God" are such catastrophies as fire, earthquake, storms, flood, or other natural disasters. Other events that should be accounted for include war, riot, labor strikes, and acts of government. The types of events that will vitiate the obligation of performance may include some which are intrinsic to the particular relationship. For example, a contract for data processing services may require printed output reports to be made available to the customer. The contract will normally provide for a specific turnaround or elapsed time in which the reports must be delivered. If a general, area-wide power failure occurs that prevents processing the parties may want to designate such power failure as an unavoidable breach.

Other items that may be included in this type of provision include hijacking or other criminal acts which prevent performance. As an example of impossibility of performance due to an "act of government," suppose that a chemical manufacturer had agreed several years ago to supply all requirements for DDT or saccharin in a long-term contract. The producer now finds that the Federal Drug Administration or Environmental Protection Agency prevents its performance. In an era in which government interference in business relations is rife, action taken by the government is not merely likely but expected.

Perhaps this is a good point to observe a canon of interpretation of which every contract draftsman must be aware. If there is a recitation of words or phrases in sequence and there is no general or catch-all phrase at the end of such recitation, all other specific events are excluded regardless of whether they are similar. For this reason, it is normally advisable to dispense with the recitation of the specific and use only the most generic term. But when the generic term may be construed by a court too narrowly, it may be preferable to recite a few specific events, such as "power failure." Otherwise, by interpretation of the standard phrases— "events beyond the control of the parties" or "Acts of God"—an intended excuse for performance may be ignored. After reciting the specific excuses a general phrase must follow. Even then the concluding general phrase will not be given its broadest construction. Another canon of interpretation states that a concluding generic phrase will be limited to the class or kind of matters that are specifically recited.

One last precaution regarding this provision is the necessity to add a remedy for the nondefaulting party. During a long-term supply contract a labor strike at the producer's only manufacturing facility may continue for months or years. The nondefaulting purchaser may desire to make other arrangements even though the defaulting party's nonperformance is excusable. After any significant delay the contract should provide that the nondefaulting party has a right to cancel the agreement. This will enable the nondefaulting party to make other arrangements.

The resulting paragraph will read as follows:

3.13   *Events Beyond Control of Parties.*   Neither of the parties shall be
            responsible for delays caused by Acts of God, government laws or
            regulations, war, epidemic, strikes or lockouts, riots, power failure,

or other causes beyond its control, provided, however, that either party shall have the right to terminate this agreement on thirty (30) days notice if the delay does not abate after a period of six (6) months.

MOST-FAVORED NATION

This term is also legalese. It stems from usage in treaties between national governments in which less powerful countries were concerned about discrimination in multilateral treaties. A "most-favored clause" is used commercially to prevent one party (usually a party in a dominant position) dealing with multiple parties in identical relationships from treating a favored party beneficially. In dealing with a major company a small business must be concerned that a medium-sized competitor may obtain an unfair competitive advantage through some favorable leverage it holds. The small business can protect itself with this provision. It is commonly found in patent license agreements and in sales contracts. In a patent license agreement, for example, the holder of a major dominant patent may grant licenses throughout an industry to many producers. If these licensees compete in the product marketplace, a licensee with a lesser royalty rate or other favorable terms may have a significant competitive advantage.

Normally, the provision provides for an automatic "pass on" of price decreases or other benefits. The draftsman must decide whether price is the crucial item and whether the most-favored-nation provision should relate only to price. If not, then language must be chosen that includes other terms of the agreement, although this may lead to a morass of confusion. What if a new paragraph is more beneficial in some respects but not in others? Can a party demand the benefit of the new more favorable terms while refusing to accept the more onerous terms? This may depend on how the option is phrased; that is, must the party accept "all or none," or may it choose only those terms that in its opinion are more favorable? Problems cannot be entirely resolved even with the most precise drafting.

Another difficulty, at least in the opinion of some lawyers, is that the clause is too easily avoided. A manufacturer having numerous contracts in existence, each containing a most-favored-nation clause, may conjure special circumstances to rationalize more beneficial terms for a newcomer. Through this chicanery, the manufacturer may avoid any effect on the old agreements. The result may be a complete evisceration of the assumed benefits.

There are, however, certain agreements in which adoption of the most-favored-nation clause may provide some benefit and is justified. A typical clause may read as follows:

3.14 *Most Favorable Terms.* If the [vendor or licensor or manufacturer] shall, during the term of this contract, enter into or modify an agreement with more favorable terms or benefits, then [purchaser or licensee or representative] shall automatically become entitled to such more favorable terms.

COUNTERPARTS

This is a provision that attempts to facilitate the execution of the agreement. When it is expected that more than two parties will be executing an agreement at different locations it may be cumbersome and time consuming to obtain the executions sequentially on a single document. If three or four parties are involved that are all geographically separated, it may take several weeks to obtain all signatures. To avoid this delay a paragraph may be included in the agreement stating that there will be multiple copies distributed, one to each party. These will be concurrently signed but will be considered one complete agreement on the execution of the last to sign. The provision reads:

3.15 *Counterparts.* This agreement may be executed in two or more counterparts, each of which shall constitute an original agreement as against a party who had signed it but which in the aggregate shall constitute one and the same instrument.

OTHER PROVISIONS

This chapter begins with standard boilerplate paragraphs and drifts slowly into provisions that are common but not universal. In no sense is it suggested that the paragraphs of this chapter are exhaustive. Particularly in international transactions, there are several boilerplate paragraphs relating to currency, regulations, export-import procedures, and customs that have become more or less standard. Other paragraphs that could be included here would involve liquidated damages which provide that in the event of a breach when damages would be difficult to ascertain a stipulated or "liquidated" amount would be owed. In agreements in which the parties are in different jurisdictions, it may be advisable to include in addition to the Governing Law paragraph a statement that any lawsuit must be brought in a particular forum, that is, the court of a particular state or country. A paragraph may be included providing that in the event of litigation the prevailing party may recover attorneys' fees and costs from the other party. The list of semiboilerplate paragraphs could continue without limit.

The scope of the standard paragraphs included in this chapter must be considered relative to the scope of the book as a whole. The intent is to provide both forms and methodology that are useful for the small business. As transactions become more complex and agreements become more complicated, it will be desirable to include other provisions to encompass a broader range of contingencies. However, the list provided earlier will be found adequate in most transactions discussed in the remainder of this text.

Chapter Four
Consulting

Although he or she wears many hats, the small business owner has only one head—one area of expertise. This specialized knowledge may be the result of educational training or prior experience. It is almost certain to limit the scope of a general manager's detailed involvement. Not only are a general manager's capabilities circumscribed but also in any small organization there are usually only a few other personnel with in-depth skills in complementary areas. Inevitably, therefore, a need will develop for outside consulting services.

The general manager will not be directly engaged in the day-to-day relationship with a consultant. However, he or she will almost certainly be closely involved in selecting, negotiating, and agreeing to the consultant contract. Because of this deep participation in the procurement of such services, the general manager is in an advantageous position to draft the consulting agreement so that it clearly reflects the true intentions and discussions of the parties.

A first consideration is whether a written contract is needed. This may depend on the source of the services. In some instances, the search for a suitable consultant may lead to telephone book yellow pages, consultant directories, or referrals from professional or trade organizations. Results may also be obtained by newspaper advertisement for "temporary assignments" with a detailed description of the services required. When a relationship develops from these sources it will be more formal. Despite the reputation, references, and professionalism the consultant brings to the interview, some type of written contract will give assurance to both parties. By contrast, personal and business sources of consulting services either directly or through referrals may suggest a more informal relationship that may not require a written agreement.

Perhaps a more objective standard for determining the necessity of a written agreement is to examine whether there are critical factors in the performance of either party. One salient consideration that is usually present is the time available for completion of the service. Generally, the outside consulting services are only a portion of a project involving one or more areas of expertise of persons within the company or even other outside consultants. The performance time may simply be too important to be left to an oral understanding. A second area of potential misunderstanding is the consultant compensation. Since this may vary from a simple dollar-per-hour or dollar-per-day arrangement to a complex profit-or sales-based–incentive arrangement, the form of compensation may require more than a simple verbal statement. Certainly, if the contemplated expenditure for the consulting services is large relative to the budget of the entire project it may be desirable to set forth the relationship in writing.

One additional area that in itself may make a written contract mandatory is whether the services will require the disclosure of confidential information to the consultant. It is extremely likely that this will occur. Whether the specialized area of the services is engineering, marketing, sales promotion, or any one of several services, divulging confidential information regarding the small business will almost always be required. If this information in the hands of the consultant raises even the possibility that its disclosure may destroy a competitive advantage, a written agreement is absolutely required.

Several additional reasons may arise for choosing to record the agreement in writing. For example, the arrangement may be intended to produce a report that may be required by third parties such as safety authorities, potential customers, or possible investors for the expansion of the small business. It may be necessary to specify in detail what must be contained in the report, and a written description would be highly desirable. Another reason is that the scope of the work to be performed may require a substantial amount of time. In such instance it is often found desirable to break up the total project into several phases or tasks with a detailed description of each phase. The compensation may be similarly broken up, with given amounts matched to the completion of the services in a particular phase. This type of detail is simply not possible in an oral arrangement.

As indicated in Chapter 2, the agreement may be drafted in a formal contract format or as a letter agreement.

PERFORMANCE OF SERVICES

The initial clause in the body of the agreement sets forth a description of the services to be rendered by the consultant. The extent of this description is proportional to the size of the consulting project.

This paragraph categorizes the types of services performed—technical, marketing, sales, manufacturing, facilities, and so on. It also broadly defines the company's business to provide a background for the description of duties to be performed and for the scope of the proprietary rights clause. It contemplates selective requests by the company for services to be performed. It does not specify when such request will be made, whether the consultant will have time available, or establish any requirement for advanced notice, and so forth. Greater control over access to services is possible by designating a minimum number of hours of availability.

If the time available for completion of the services is critical, the company will be well advised to consider paying a monthly retainer fee. The fee is given in consideration of the consultant's commitment to be available for a minimum amount of time. Without such retainer, the consultant may object to a minimum time obligation. The retainer provision must be drafted with caution. Two approaches are possible. The fee may be strictly for the option on services and will not be applied against charges for services actually performed. Alternatively, the fee may cover a given number of hours of service; the number of hours should be expressly set forth in the agreement. If the specified hours are not used, there is no reduction in fee. But if the number is exceeded, the additional hours are charged for at the established rate. A more elaborate arrangement would carry over unused hours in each month as a credit against later charges. Other possibilities will come to mind.

It may also be desirable to engage the consultant only by requests in writing, to obviate any misunderstanding. Written requests, however, may be too cumbersome in practice. As discussed next, "runaway" costs can be controlled adequately by demanding (and enforcing the demand) that the consultant bill monthly or even weekly.

A paragraph incorporating a description of services and a time commitment may read:

4.1 *Services.* Consultant will advise and assist with respect to [technical, marketing, . . .] problems relating to [describe business, e.g., metal casting]. Consultant will meet and consult with employees of Company at agreed-on times and places and perform services as requested. Consultant agrees to be available a minimum of _____ [hours, days] per week during the term of this agreement.

If the services are for a specific, defined project and the result of the services can be quantified, a "fixed price" arrangement may be used. A good test for whether this is possible, and a suitable starting point for the contract drafting job, is to define the results expected and the interim tasks. This may take the form of a Statement of Work attached to the agreement. The Statement of Work may be elaborate (review of milestones, presentations, approval process, etc.) or straightforward. An example of the latter follows this chapter. The services description paragraph for a turn-key agreement is as follows:

4.2 *Services.* Consultant will perform the services set forth on the Statement of Work attached hereto that describes each task to be performed in the order of such performance.

When the services are defined in detail, the description, during negotiation, should be carefully considered and discussed by the parties. As the specification becomes more detailed, a greater clarity of understanding in the written agreement is possible. But more drafting work is required. The Statement of Work approach to the description of services is particularly useful when it is desirable to terminate the contract short of completion of the entire project. Termination may be required because of dissatisfaction on the part of either party or an abort of the entire project. The Statement of Work may also provide the basis for scheduling progress payments when the parties believe this to be more convenient or necessary than only initial and final payments.

COMPENSATION

Per Diem

There are several different methods of compensation limited only by the imagination of the parties. The obvious and most common type of compensation is on a per-period basis, that is, X dollars per hour, Y dollars per day, Z dollars per week. The length of the period should be chosen in relation to the nature of the work to be done. Office work, such as research, design or report preparation, is conveniently undertaken on a per-hour basis. This unit of time permits considerable flexibility for the consultant, allowing him to interleave services for various clients and still maintain accountability for time spent. On the other hand, services performed outside the office such as a site visit, consultation with company personnel at the company facility, or interviews with prospective customers or experts, can best be undertaken on a per-diem basis. There is little likelihood that portions of the day spent in transit or otherwise nonproductive for the company can be spent for some other client. It may be desirable to structure the engagement on a half-day basis that may be satisfactory to both parties and provide adequate accountability for both office and outside services.

4.3 *Compensation.* As full compensation for the services to be performed by Consultant, Company shall pay Consultant as follows: _____ dollars ($_____) per day for each day worked.

Fixed Price

Another common way to provide for compensation is to determine a fixed price. This may require some advance or "up-front" payment against a predetermined price for the entire job with the remainder payable on completion. The consultant's obligation to perform for a fixed price is obviously based on the hours to complete the work that is specifically defined in the contract. Both parties will be well served by frank and extended discussion.

A practice that should be avoided is the "not-to-exceed" price. It is pure nonsense. It is usually a last-ditch effort by the consultant to save a fixed price offer that is too high. It usually arises as follows:

Consultant: We think we can do the entire job for only $27,000.

General Manager: My God! (Or simply a look of terror.)

Consultant: Well, we might be able to do it for less. It was difficult to estimate the amount of time we would have to spend, and we did not want to compromise the quality of our work by underestimating the time. I think we will be able to do it in less. Let's call that a "not-to-exceed" price, and we will try our best to come well within the figure.

The not-to-exceed limitation is then incorporated into the written agreement. But it is simply a monument to the failure of the parties to continue the negotiation over price until they are both satisfied. It will, therefore, mean that when the consultant's statement comes in at exactly the not-to-exceed price he will feel that he lived up to his end of the bargain; yet the businessman has been telling himself during the period the services were rendered that the final bill will come in for less. Perhaps if this phrase is understood for what it is (or isn't) it is perfectly acceptable. If the businessman believes, however, that the final bill will be less than the not-to-exceed figure he is deluded and will be disappointed.

The fixed compensation paragraph that will accompany the service paragraph in Form 4.2 may read:

4.4 *Compensation.* As full compensation for the services to be performed by Consultant, Company shall pay Consultant on execution of this agreement, the sum of _____ dollars ($_____); and on completion of the services as set forth in Paragraph _____, the sum of _____ dollars ($_____). "Completion of the services" shall mean the delivery by Consultant to Company of [e.g., engineering drawings (including assembly and parts drawings and bills of material) for the widget defined in Paragraph _____, or a written new product marketing plan for the widget, including a discussion and analysis of the items set forth in Exhibit _____.]

Incentive

Still another type of compensatory arrangement involves either of the first two types of present monetary consideration related to the time spent, plus a commission, royalty, or other incentive. The classic example is the technical consulting contract to design a product in consideration of a monetary sum payable on completion and then a royalty based on sales of the product over a period of time. This arrangement is not treated here in depth but may be handled in one of two ways. The royalty arrangement may be set forth in the consulting agreement itself. Alternatively, a separate free-standing agreement may be prepared and attached to the consulting agreement. In the latter case, the consulting agreement may provide that if the company decides to market the product designed it will enter into a license agreement in the form attached to the consulting contract. The parties must arrive at the important aspects of such license agreement: the royalty rate (or at least a royalty rate range); the period over which royalties will be paid; the disposition of the title to any patent; which party has the right to file for a patent and to control the patent application prosecution, and so forth. If the royalty aspect of the agreement is paramount, meaning that both parties believe that substantial remuneration may result from the product designed, it is best to concentrate on the license aspect of the arrangement. License agreement drafting is covered in Chapter 9.

Cost Reduction

Still other types of nontime-based arrangements result from services that produce cost reductions. This may occur in such areas as freight tariffs or telephone costs. Typically, the consultant will promise to reduce the cost presently incurred by the company in exchange for a fixed payment based on time spent, plus some percentage of the cost reduction. The obvious difficulty in this type of contract is the measurement of cost reduction involving general but certainly not specific accounting practices over which the parties may disagree. It would certainly be advisable to incorporate specific accounting methods into the contract to define the methods of measuring cost reduction. This should be done with the advice and assistance of accounting personnel. Consultants who offer such services often have their own contracts; these contracts should be cautiously approached and reviewed regarding the proper definition of cost reduction.

Travel Expenses

Most per-diem consultant agreements provide for payment of travel expenses incurred by the consultant while performing the services called for by the agreement. It is not recommended that the agreement attempt to anticipate the myriad types of travel expenses that could be incurred. Such detail would be unwarranted in the ordinary situation. A simple statement that such expenses should be "reasonable" and "out-of-pocket" should suffice. The latter phrase is intended to prevent a standard charge for meals and lodging that some consultants prefer to simplify bookkeeping. The out-of-pocket provision will also preclude double billing of expenses for a business trip taken on behalf of two clients.

Company approval should be required in advance to prevent the possibility, however unlikely, that the company may be presented with a bill for a trip to Japan that the company neither authorized nor had reason to expect. On the other hand it is not suggested that such approval be required in writing. For the trip across town written approval would be an unnecessary burden and would be ignored. Yet, if the company pays for such trips without advance written approval, it may be found to have waived the entire provision. This would be disastrous for the surprise trip to Japan. The intermediate position would be to provide that written approval is requested for any trip that exceeds, say, $1000. This sum should cover most domestic trips of reasonable length and prevent any abuse. The following paragraph may be used with the per-diem arrangement (Form 4.1):

4.5   *Travel Expenses.*   Reasonable, out-of-pocket travel expenses (tourist-class transportation, hotel, and meals) incurred by Consultant in connection with any trip made by Consultant at the request, and with prior approval of Company, will be paid by Company.

Incidental Expenses

Whether to include a clause for incidental expenses is left to the discretion of the draftsman. In every consulting assignment there will be incidental expenses such as long-distance telephone calls, photocopies, and the like. Some consultants consider this normal overhead, not chargeable to the client; others may as a matter of policy attempt to pass on to the client all expenses incurred that are identifiable with a particular assignment. The choice for the draftsman is whether to even mention incidental expenses, since this will constitute an invitation. If mentioned, the manner of handling these expenses in the agreement is to use general phraseology. Or a middle-of-the-road position may be taken, calling for approval only if such expenses exceed a certain amount per item or per month. Of course, the incidental expenses provision would be used only with the per-diem compensation paragraph (Form 4.1); it may read:

4.6   *Incidental Expenses.* Reasonable expenses actually incurred by Consultant incidental to the services performed will be paid by Company.

Invoice and Payment

No treatment of compensation is complete without adding the "when" and "how" to the amount. Except for the fixed price arrangement described previously in Form 4.2, a periodic invoice is suitable for controlling the relationship. The typical period chosen is a month, but a lesser time such as a week may be more satisfactory to both parties. It is not recommended that a period longer than a month be used. It is strongly recommended that a single billing at the completion of the services should be avoided.

The procedure for invoice and payment provides security to each party to the agreement. The consultant is continually assured that the company is in a financial position to afford the services. The company is not surprised by a large lump-sum billing over a prolonged period of time that far exceeds its expectations. The arrangement for services is on the request of the company, as set forth in Form 4.1. The company can, therefore, terminate the relationship by simply refraining from requesting services after any bill is received in which the amount is unsatisfactory. In other words, the monthly billing is a continuous cost control that the company can use to see that the project does not get out of hand.

The typical method of payment is to provide that the consultant must submit an invoice every month, or "at least every month," or for some other period as agreed. If expense details are requested this may be included in a description of the invoice. It should definitely include compensation and expenses for travel or incidental expenses. Furthermore, it should provide that the company will have a certain period of time after receipt or from the date of the invoice to make payment.

4.7   *Invoice and Payment.* Consultant shall submit a monthly, itemized invoice specifying the time spent and expenses incurred (including receipts for items in excess of $25) and Company shall make payment within ten (10) days of the date of the invoice.

CONFIDENTIAL RELATIONSHIP

In drafting the confidential relationship between the consultant and the company, there are two principal considerations—offense and defense. Offensively, it is desirable to preclude the consultant from giving away any confidential information received from the company. But it is equally important that the company not receive any confidential information in the consultant's possession that he had obtained from a third party in a nondisclosure relationship. Particularly in technical consulting arrangements in which a well-respected consultant provides services to many companies in the same industry, it may be difficult to handle the conflict of interest possibilities. A good defense against a claim by a prior client of the consultant begins with a proper warning to the consultant and evidence of awareness of potential problems and the intent to avoid them.

For offensive protection of valuable proprietary information, the agreement should provide a broad and all-encompassing definition of the information that is covered. There are essentially two types of information the consultant should be prevented from disclosing. First, there is the information developed by the company, either before or during the consulting relationship, that is given to the consultant to permit him to perform the services. Second, the consultant in the course of his work may create information that should be available exclusively to the company.

With respect to protecting proprietary information transferred or created, it is important to draft a strong but fair prohibition against disclosure or use. The prohibition must be against both use by the consultant, perhaps as a competitor, and disclosure to third parties. It should last indefinitely, subject only to the information having lost its proprietary nature, expressed as "entered the public domain" or "become public knowledge." The point is that once the information is disclosed to the public by someone other than the consultant, the consultant should be relieved of any further obligation to maintain confidence. On the other hand, the language must not permit the possibility that through the consultant's own acts the matter becomes public knowledge.

With respect to the defensive nature of confidential information, the matter is most easily expressed by way of representation and indemnification. The information must be defined and then the consultant must represent and warrant that he is free to disclose such information to the company without violating an obligation to a third party. The paragraph goes on to provide that if the representation is false, the consultant will hold the company harmless from any damage to the company—for example, a lawsuit by an injured third party. Obviously, it is not likely that the consultant will be in a financial position to truly indemnify the company for any meaningful loss or damage as a result of a lawsuit. Nevertheless, the language helps to impress on the consultant the gravity of the matter so that he does not lightly undertake the representation.

4.8   *Confidential Information*

(a)   Consultant agrees not to disclose or divulge to Company, or to induce Company to use, any confidential information or trade secrets (Third-Party Property) that Consultant now possesses or which may be acquired from any third party during the term of this agreement. Consultant represents and warrants that Consultant is free at the present time to disclose to Company, without breach of any obligation to a third party, any and all information, ideas, suggestions, developments or know-how which Consultant will divulge in performing the services under this agreement. Consultant further agrees to indemnify and hold Company harmless from and against all losses, liabilities, damages, expenses, or claims against Company based on a breach of obligation by Consultant to a third party in disclosing any Third-Party Property to Company during performance of the services under this agreement.

(b)   During the course of performing services, Consultant may become aware and receive confidential information, including data, designs, ideas, methods, reports, plans, or other proprietary matters of Company. Consultant agrees to receive and hold in strict confidence for and on behalf of Company all such confidential information acquired from Company and all information that Consultant creates in connection with or as a result of performing services under this agreement, including data, designs, ideas, methods, reports, suggestions, or other confidential information. Consultant agrees not to use, or disclose, any of such information to any person either during or after the termination of this agreement unless such information is, or becomes, through no act or omission of Consultant, public knowledge.

INTELLECTUAL PROPERTY

In all consulting arrangements, it is important to expressly set forth that all intellectual property created by the consultant becomes the property of the company. Indeed, the principal if not the singular objective of some arrangements is the property to be derived from the consultant's services—that is, a "contract to create." Certainly, the most common type of subject matter encompassed in intellectual property rights are U.S. or foreign patents, but copyrights are equally valuable in many relationships. Trade secrets, although not afforded statutory legal protection, may be even more important than the first two.

Briefly, ownership problems regarding copyrights arise when the company engages an advertising agency, creators of technical publications, or copywriters for instruction booklets, manuals, or similar written or visual materials. The entertainment industry has refined and carried the art of contracting for copyrighted works to a dazzling degree of verbosity. No such elaborate precautions are ordinarily required in the types of arrangements described previously; the value of the copyrights would not warrant the effort and cost. Still, an important ancillary objective of the arrangement may be the written or visual material supplied by the consultant. The definition of the intellectual property in the form paragraph should be modified if copyrights are involved by reference to "written and visual materials or other copyrightable subject matter."

As for the property rights in technical ideas, there are two important aspects to be covered in the contract clause: (a) disclosure by the consultant to the company and (b) an assignment of ownership of the property. The key to a properly drawn intellectual property right contract provision is a careful definition of the rights to be disclosed and assigned. There are many words that may be used to describe the products of individual creation or discovery. Technical creations are usually referred to as "inventions" or "innovations." "Improvements" is a broader term, not as directly associated with technical advances but connoting a more minor contribution. "Idea" is a still broader term not limited to technical, or even rational, creative products; however, it suffers from a lack of definiteness. Courts have often held that only the expression of an idea can be protected, not the idea itself. "Suggestion" is also a vague word not limited to technical concepts but implying a relatively insignificant or simple contribution. The "suggestion box" used in many companies usually produces simple, pragmatic ideas; in the industrial world, therefore, a suggestion is associated with a relatively trivial advance. "Discovery" is distinct from creation, since it relates to the act of ascertaining the existence of something, previously existing but unknown. A discovery may be as commercially valuable as a creative product.

It is desirable to cover what may appear to both parties as initially trivial, since the commercial value of an idea is not always immediately apparent. Of course, the description should firmly encompass major technical advances. It is therefore common to use a collection of words to describe property rights in the agreement. Since it will become necessary to thereafter refer to this entire congeries of definitions, it is convenient to gather all of them into a word such as "Developments" or "Rights."

It is similarly important to clarify that the definition of the rights is not dependent on whether the idea is patentable. This has several purposes. First, there are some types of technical advances that do not fall within the ambit of statutory patent protection. A notable example being contested at the present time is software programs for computers. Second, although the advance is within the scope of patent protection, a patent application may be finally rejected. The subject matter of the application may thereafter be used by any third party. However, it is entirely possible that the idea (for example, a process used within a manufacturing plant) is maintained in secrecy during the pendency of the patent application and is known to no one other than the consultant and the company. Under such circumstances, the idea may be a valuable trade secret. But because the company has elected to attempt to cover the process by patent, and such attempt at protection was finally rejected, the consultant may feel that he should be on the same footing as third parties—that is, free to use the idea. Although the preceding clause relating to Confidential Relationships may come into play on the issue, it is desirable to expressly negate that the consultant and third parties are of the same status.

As a practical matter, the definition of the rights to be disclosed and assigned must also be limited with respect to time. Not all ideas of the consultant preexisting on the date of execution of the agreement should be encompassed. Nor after the relationship terminates should the consultant be bound indefinitely. It is desirable, therefore, to state that only such ideas that are made during the term of the agreement are covered. Patent law has divided the process of invention into steps such as conception and reduction to practice. Other types of ideas may be covered by the generic word *created*. It is common practice to describe all the various ways in which an idea may arise during the applicable time period by reciting: "conceived, made, reduced to practice, or created."

In all likelihood, the consultant will be performing services for others simultaneously with the consulting work being done for the company. The extent of the rights that the consultant is bound to disclose and assign should be further limited by referring to those ideas which "result from" or "arise out of" the services being performed by the consultant for the company. This will prevent a conflict of the consultant's obligations. A more contentious point is whether the ideas should be further limited to those that "relate to the business" of the company in addition to resulting from the services performed. Conceivably, if the subject matter of the consulting contract were entirely foreign to the company's present line of business, uncertainty would develop by referring to ideas "which are related to the business of the company." On the other hand, in the more likely occurrence in which the subject matter of the consulting arrangement is directly related to the business of the company, the latter clause would expressly limit the scope of the rights encompassed and thus clarify the relationship. If reference is made to the business of the company, the nature of the business has been defined in Form 4.1 that defines the services to be performed.

Having defined these rights, it is then necessary to state that they should be promptly disclosed to the company, preferably in writing, and that they will thereby become the property of the company. There are numerous mechanical acts that must be performed by the consultant in the process of obtaining a patent. If the company intends to apply for a patent, therefore, the clause should further state that the consultant will be obligated to cooperate with the company to secure the patent rights. It is common industrial practice to state that the performance of these acts will be without any further expense to consultant. However, this phrase may carry a latent dispute. The company generally is willing and intends to pay all expenses incurred in the preparation and prosecution of a patent application just as it would do in procuring any other piece of valuable property. Although the consultant would easily agree with this assumption of the expenses by the company, it may also be felt that "without expense to the consultant" means that there will be compensation for any time expended in assisting the company in acquiring the rights. The generally straightforward process of consultation with a patent attorney, review of a patent application, and executing the formal papers required for filing a patent application may be performed without charge by the consultant. But if in the course of the patent prosecution some considerable difficulty arises, such as a contest of priority of invention (referred to as an "interference"), then tens, hundreds, or even thousands of hours could be expended by the consultant in assisting the company in obtaining the patent. Clearly, neither of the parties could foresee such massive expenditure of the consultant's time. Perhaps reference to "reasonable" assistance and support may be sufficient to require the parties to bargain in good faith on a point on which the contract is not explicit.

As discussed with reference to defensive aspects of a confidential relationship, there is the need to assure that the consultant is free to transfer the property rights described earlier. Because of prior contractual commitments, either as a consultant or an employee, it is possible that the consultant has already given away ownership to the idea before the consulting agreement begins. For example, if a prior engagement contained an intellectual property right definition as suggested previously, the idea "conceived" while the consultant was so engaged will have become the property of the prior employer. It is no longer available for transfer at the time the idea is reduced to practice, even if such reduction occurs during the consulting agreement term. Although this may be an unusual circumstance, an appropriate warning to the consultant to the effect that he represents that he is free to disclose and assign such ideas to the company is worthwhile.

Finally, there is the matter of whether the requirement for disclosure and assignment devolves on employees, agents, or subcontracting parties engaged by the consultant. Obviously, in a one-man consulting firm the problem is minor. When the firm is larger, however, effectiveness of the property rights clause may depend on the form of business organization of the consultant and whether employees of the consultant have been properly bound by an agreement to assign and disclose inventions made. A recommended clause covering these matters may read:

4.9 *Intellectual Property.* All inventions, innovations, discoveries, improvements, ideas, and suggestions (Rights), whether patentable or unpatentable, conceived, made, reduced to practice, or created by Consultant, resulting from or arising out of the services performed by Consultant under this agreement and relating in whole or in part to the business of Company, will be promptly communicated in writing by Consultant to Company and shall become the sole property of Company. On request, and with no expense to Consultant, Consultant will assist Company in every proper way to obtain patents on such Rights. On request of Company, Consultant will execute any and all documents, considered necessary or desirable by Company, to obtain patent protection on the Rights in the United States and foreign countries and to secure title in the Rights in Company. Consultant represents and warrants that Consultant has no obligation to any third party that would be breached by the disclosure and assignment of Rights to Company.

INDEPENDENT CONTRACTOR

The purpose of the next clause is to limit the liability of the company for conduct of the consultant. To effect this limitation, it is important to establish that the relationship created is not one of employment. Although this will be obvious if the consultant firm is large and well established, it is in the one-man firm that the problem often will arise. If a consultant works daily for a company, works exclusively on the company's premises, uses the company's equipment, and is given certain benefits (e.g., holidays or medical insurance), it may be difficult to deny an employment relationship. A court will determine the nature of the relationship based on all the facts relating to the transaction rather than rely on the parties' characterization of it. Yet it is advisable to express in the agreement the intention of the parties.

Why is it important to distinguish between an employee and a consultant relationship? First, there are government-imposed obligations that must be discharged by the company if the relationship is one of employment. The company must withhold state, federal, and local taxes from the employee's paycheck. In many states, workmen's compensation and disability insurance premiums must be paid by an employer for every employee, either to the state or a private state-approved insurance carrier.

Second, in addition to state-imposed obligations, there are principles of law that hold a company bound by acts of an "agent"; however, the company will not be responsible if the person is an "independent contractor." Again, simply using the label will not convince a court that a relationship is what it clearly is not. But establishing certain aspects of the relationship in clear and express language will assist in characterizing the relationship as intended. It should be set forth that the consultant is responsible for all agents or employees hired by the consultant. Not only will these factors be helpful in establishing that the legal relationship is between independent parties but also will foreclose any misunderstanding that could arise at a later time between the parties.

4.10 *Independent Contractor.* Consultant, with respect to the services performed under this agreement, is acting as an independent contractor, and not as an employee. Consultant may be employed by other persons, firms, or corporations during this agreement. Any employees or other personnel engaged by Consultant shall be under the exclusive direction and control of Consultant. Consultant shall assume and discharge for its own account all costs, expenses, and charges necessary or incidental to the performance of services under this agreement. Consultant shall indemnify and save Company harmless from and against any losses, liabilities, damages, expenses, or claims against Consultant unless specifically assumed in advance in writing by Company.

TERM AND TERMINATION

All contracts should contain an express definition of the duration of the term. Contracts, such as one for consulting services, are typically for a relatively short period of time—one or two years. If the parties contemplate that a single project or assignment to be undertaken by the consultant will extend beyond such period, the longer term obviously should be specified. However, it is well for both parties to weigh the fixed compensation rate versus the length of the contract, particularly in these days of high inflation.

If the suggested one- or two-year period for the contract is acceptable, the continuation can be handled in one of two ways. First, the term of the agreement may be automatically renewed at the end of the first term unless one party gives notice to the other party that it wishes to terminate the agreement. The alternative is that the agreement will end unless those parties agree to extend it for an additional term. The latter is merely an "agreement to agree" and would not obligate either party to a continuing term. The only ostensible reason for the inclusion of such a term in the operative portion of the contract is that it is an expression of the parties' intent. If one or the other of the parties is given the unilateral right to extend the contract, then an option is effectively created for the benefit of the party who may unilaterally act. This should be done very cautiously, since one party may find itself obliged to an extended period that it did not contemplate.

It is of considerable importance when using an automatic renewal provision that the clause specify that the agreement will be extended "on the same terms and conditions as set forth in this agreement." Otherwise, there may be a dispute between the parties about the length of the subsequent term, a change in the rate of compensation, or other substantive matters in the original agreement.

It should be apparent that concern with the length of the term of the contract is important only if during the term the parties have the right to terminate solely for specified causes. If either party has the right to cancel the agreement on 30 or 60 days notice "without cause," then the effective length of the contract is not the stated duration but rather the length of the notice period. This is important not only from the viewpoint of what will be the period of engagement of the consultant but also bears on renegotiation of the terms. Suppose the consultant can cancel the agreement by giving 30 days notice. After giving such notice the consultant may approach the company with an offer to continue, providing that the rate of compensation or other provision is modified. To put it another way, a contract without any right of termination, except for specified causes, effectively limits renegotiation until the term expires.

Assuming that there is no right to cancel "without cause," then the agreement should specify the causes that permit the aggrieved party to cancel during the contract period. Typically, the specified causes include (a) termination of business, voluntarily or involuntarily, by one of the parties; (b) breach of one of the terms of the contract; or (c) in personal service contracts, inability of the person to perform the services. In some consulting arrangements, the first specified cause may be ignored. The second cause is of much greater significance, since it permits either party to terminate the agreement immediately (if so provided) in the event of nonperformance by one party. This may be highly desirable from the consultant's point of view. Failure to make payments for services in accordance with the provisions of the agreement would permit the consultant to immediately terminate the agreement. This would foreclose the possibility that the company would stall in making payments while continuing to demand the services of the consultant. Finally, from the company's point of view it is important to terminate the agreement in the event of death, illness, physical or mental disability, or other incapacity of the consultant. A term such as "mental disability" is extremely ambiguous; if the matter is of great importance then the provision can be set forth in terms of the failure to perform services for a period of several months, regardless of the reason, rather than setting forth a specific reason. The matter of balance—detail versus probability of occurrence—is again called for.

After specifying the reasons that permit either party to terminate the agreement the clause should then state the method of termination. Normally, this comprises written notice from the allegedly injured party setting forth an intention to terminate at the end of the notice period. The parties may want to provide one another with a "second chance" with respect to breach of a provision. The agreement may then provide that on curing the default within a certain number of days the contract will again be in force.

It is also advisable to identify any obligations of the parties that extend beyond termination. For example, the consultant is normally obligated to maintain confidential information beyond the full term of the agreement. Such obligation should also continue when the agreement is terminated early for cause. This result should obtain without express language. Caution dictates, however, that the termination clause of the agreement provides for specific obligations (usually identified by reference to specific paragraphs) which will continue beyond the early termination. A suggested paragraph reads:

4.11 *Term and Termination.* This agreement is effective from the date first written above and shall terminate one (1) year from such date. The agreement shall be extended automatically on the same terms and conditions for additional periods of one (1) year unless either party shall terminate the agreement by notice to the other not less than thirty (30) days prior to the expiration of the year or any renewal period.

(a) This agreement may be terminated by Company, by giving thirty (30) days notice to Consultant, in the event of death of Consultant, or an illness or injury that will permanently prevent the performance of services required under this agreement, or if for any reason Consultant fails to perform any services, after request by Company, for a period of two consecutive months.

(b) Either party may terminate this agreement on breach of any of the terms by the other party on giving thirty (30) days notice to the other party.

(c) Termination of this agreement for any reason shall not affect Consultant's obligation under Paragraphs _____ and _____ .

GENERAL

Several of the standard paragraphs should be included in the consulting contract: Entire Agreement (Form 3.2), Governing Law (Form 3.3), Assignability (Form 3.5), and Notices (Form 3.1). If a breach of the Confidential Relationship or Intellectual Property clauses occurs, the paragraph on Specific Performance (Form 3.10) would be advantageous. The clause on Arbitration (Form 3.11) should also be considered.

STATEMENT OF WORK

Scope. The object of the work to be performed by CONSULTANT is the design of a molded plastic external housing for a portable, hand-held data entry terminal. The terminal is intended for use in office and commercial environments by clerical, nonscientific personnel with a minimum of training. The principal subassemblies will include a pushbutton pad, a four-digit LED display, battery recharge jack, and an On-Off switch. The housing shall be constructed of a high-strength plastic material for manufacture by the injection molding process.

Phase/Task	Phase/Task Description	Delivered Item
	A. Design Analysis and Definition	
1	Schedule and gather background information through meetings with project engineer, review of competitive devices, and familiarization with nature of environment	
2	Prepare initial design concept drawings exemplifying possible approaches	
3	Present preliminary concept designs to COMPANY	Concept sketches
4	Select preliminary design concept and obtain approval by COMPANY	
5	Identify alternative preliminary design concept for fallback	
	B. Preliminary Design Model	
1	Prepare cardboard or wood scale model	
2	Present preliminary model to COMPANY	Preliminary design model
3	Obtain COMPANY approval of preliminary model	
	C. Plastic Model Fabrication	
1	Prepare design drawings for plastic model	

Phase/Task	Phase/Task Description	Delivered Item
2	Present design drawings and review with COMPANY project engineer	Plastic model design drawings
3	Select model shop and negotiate price, terms, and delivery for plastic model	
4	Coordinate model preparation	
5	Present model price, terms, and conditions to COMPANY and obtain approval for model fabrication	
6	Present plastic model to COMPANY and assist in assembly problems	Plastic model
7	Obtain approval by COMPANY	
8	Schedule all modifications and changes to model for production version and coordinate and assist in fabrication of revised model, if required	

D. Injection Mold Drawings

1	Prepare final drawings for mold maker	
2	Present final drawings to COMPANY and obtain approval by COMPANY	Final drawings
3	Assist COMPANY in discussions with mold maker regarding tolerances, materials, and suggested changes	

Chapter Five
Marketing

The simplest and most direct method for selling to a customer is to employ a sales force that calls directly on the final user and to ship and bill the goods directly to the user. Most small businesses, however, cannot make the investment in a direct sales force. The product line of the company may not generate enough sales volume to justify the costs of salesmen covering the entire country. If the customer base is large and potential sales volume is high, it would be necessary to field a large number of sales personnel. Start-up costs would be extremely expensive. Conversely, if there are only a limited number of customers (because of the specialized nature of the product) then each sales territory will be large. Few salesmen will be required, but considerable travel will be necessary with a high cost per sales call. Small businesses, therefore, ordinarily choose to work with independent sales firms that represent the company in a defined territory.

The nature and type of independent firms and the function they perform are largely determined by industry pattern. This pattern is established by a dominant company in the industry, usually through trial and error to arrive at the most cost-effective distribution method. The nature of the product also strongly influences the sales channel. And tradition has a part to play simply because customers become accustomed to a particular mode of marketing and distribution. Patterns are changed only with great difficulty and expense, not easily afforded by the small business, and therefore choice may be limited.

To oversimplify, there are essentially two distribution channels involving independent, intermediary sales firms. One of the most familiar forms is the distributor. A *distributor* is a sales representative that purchases goods from a manufacturer and resells them to either another independent firm along the chain (such as a retailer) or to the ultimate consumer. The distributor, sometimes referred to as a "wholesaler," is used in industries that distribute products such as automotive parts, hospital supplies, pharmaceuticals, jewelry, industrial hand tools, electrical supplies, and similar goods. The second channel is the sales agent or representative, often referred to as a *"manufacturer's representative."* A principal distinction between the distributor and rep is that an agent or rep never purchases the manufacturer's goods. The rep calls on customers, solicits orders on behalf of the manufacturer (that may be taken by the rep or forwarded by the customer to the manufacturer), and is paid a commission when a sale is consummated.

A distributor purchases goods and normally carries an inventory; a rep does not. A distributor receives its remuneration by purchasing goods at a discount from the manufacturer and reselling the goods at a higher price. A rep receives remuneration directly from the manufacturer based on a percentage of sales. From the point of view of credit management, the financial condition of a distributor is significant, since the manufacturer must look to the distributor for payment. For the representative, it is the credit standing of the customer to whom the goods are shipped that is of greater importance.

There are numerous variations on these two basic types of nondirect channels. The most commonplace variation is the addition of one or more subsidiary levels in the distribution chain. Most manufacturers of consumer goods employ distributors which in turn may sell to retailers that service the ultimate consumer. A manufacturer may circumvent the distributor by selling directly to retailers selling a single product line, referred to as "dealers." Furthermore, a manufacturer may employ representatives that call on wholesalers which in turn service retail accounts. Either distributors or manufacturers may use jobbers, whose function is that of a sales representative, to call on retailers. Further complicating the matter are those distributors that add value to the product, whereby the distributor becomes similar to an Original Equipment Manufacturer. Although a distributor normally takes possession of the goods in addition to title, the distributor may order the goods for "drop shipment" directly to the customer. The movement of the goods (as contrasted to the billing) resembles a sales representative channel. Because the terms used to identify an independent sales representative vary from industry to industry, the labels should be ignored and the substance carefully examined.

Despite some overlap in the functions performed by the two basic types of firms, the relationship can be characterized as one or the other for purposes of explanation. This chapter sets forth a sample agreement for each type of distribution relationship.

SALES REPRESENTATIVE AGREEMENT

While it is possible to work without a written agreement, it is hardly advisable when working with multiple sales representatives. It is desirable to obtain uniformity in the methods used to transact business with each sales representative. Before beginning to form the sales organization, therefore, a written agreement should be prepared that can be offered to prospective representatives for negotiation. Unless this is done, the sales representative will normally suggest the execution of an agreement similar to one it may have executed with another manufacturer. The manufacturer will work with numerous representatives; it will greatly complicate the administration of the rep organization if each representative has a different agreement.

There are several manufacturers' representative trade organizations that have standard form agreements. In general, these forms are favorable to the rep. Great care should be exercised before executing any standard form.

In developing a standard agreement, it is highly recommended that the terms be prepared with fairness to both parties. An overreaching, one-sided agreement will be difficult to negotiate and will create ill will. The agreement should be of reasonable length and with the utmost clarity so that negotiations and consummation of the contract may be completed without either party resorting to legal counsel. Only when the relationship calls for unique provisions will the agreement involve a complexity that necessitates the services of an attorney. It is also recommended that the agreement be printed. This will generally reduce the length of the physical document and avoid the ponderous look of the multiple-page contract. Moreover, there is a certain psychological reticence to modifying a printed agreement vis-à-vis a typewritten document. Experience suggests that if the contract is printed and fair, it will not be heavily negotiated, thus preserving uniformity and minimizing sales management time in forming the rep organization.

One further observation with respect to form and uniformity is the use of exhibits. Exhibits are appended to the agreement to accommodate those differences between each contract that are inevitable. Blanks in the body of the agreement may be used for short provisions filled in at the time of execution. Exhibits will be found to be more convenient when the terms to be filled in are extensive. Many agreements define a territory as a state or group of contiguous states; this brief description can be supplied by filling in a blank in the body of the agreement. But there are many territories that cannot be defined easily. It may be desirable to divide a state between two representatives by defining certain counties to be covered by one and other counties by another. In a highly populated area, it may become necessary to divide a county or even a city. In those instances, the easiest method for defining the territory is to prepare a map of the area, with the territory outlined in red, and incorporate the map as an exhibit to the agreement.

Other variable terms that may be easily handled by the use of exhibits include definition of the product line (when multiple lines are manufactured and sold), complex commission structures, or a list of excluded accounts ("house accounts").

The usual format for a sales representative agreement is formal. The introductory paragraph, as explained in Chapter 2, will set forth the identification of the parties, including their addresses. The manufacturer's name is usually shortened to a nickname or abbreviation; in the form agreement in this chapter the manufacturer is called "MANUFAC-TURER." The sales representative may be referred to throughout the agreement by a convenient term such as "REP" that is introduced in the beginning paragraph. Attention should be given to the date of the agreement, as suggested in Chapter 2.

No good purpose is seen in the use of recital paragraphs, since the background will usually be factually uneventful.

Definition of the Relationship

Appointment. Initially, there is a simple statement of the nature of the relationship. The manufacturer appoints the representative, and the representative accepts such appointment. The scope of the appointment should be identified immediately: exclusive or nonexclusive. It appears safe to say that most sales rep agreements are exclusive. A specific territory is defined, and all sales made by the manufacturer to customers in the territory earn a commission for the rep. There are some industries, however, in which sales representatives are neither exclusive nor assigned a specific territory. The method for crediting sales to a representative's account will be based on the use of sales orders written by the rep. These orders are submitted to the manufacturer. Alternatively, specifically identified customer accounts are agreed on as the commission base; the rep is credited with a commission on every sale to that account. This latter method must be set forth in considerable detail in the paragraph of the agreement covering commissions.

Duties. Following the appointment and acceptance, it is desirable to set forth in general terms the duties that each of the parties will undertake.

For the representative, this is usually stated as the obligation to use its best efforts to introduce and promote the products of the manufacturer, to obtain orders for the products or services, and to provide sales support. These general terms are used to express the normal sales activities of a representative and are subject to some varying interpretation. Occasionally, when the manufacturer adds a new product to its line, the agent may be nonreceptive, based on its subjective evaluation of the potential success of the product. The obligation to "introduce" the products of the manufacturer is intended to clarify this obligation.

Many manufacturers also expect sales representatives to assist in such activities as trade shows, product seminars, group customer presentations, and similar activities that do not fall strictly within the term "sales calls." Yet this promotion is highly necessary for successful product sales. Similarly, nontechnical after-sales support may be crucial to establishing a sound, continuing customer relationship. Every good marketing person recognizes the need of the goodwill visit to assure that the customer is satisfied and to handle such inevitable occurrences as delivery delays, incomplete shipments, or the inability of the customer to use the product initially. To attempt to recite and detail all the necessary tasks required from initial contact to final customer satisfaction would burden the agreement with unnecessary terms. General language expressing the obligation of the rep is a necessary alternative.

Time and Effort. It is desirable to make clear that the manufacturer expects the rep to devote reasonable time to its products. The greatest problem in dealing with sales representatives is securing adequate representation for the manufacturer's line, as opposed to other product lines, handled by the rep. It would be impractical to set forth a specific percentage of the rep's time that must be devoted to the manufacturer's product; indeed, a good rep would recoil from any attempt to control its activities. It should not be forgotten that most reps initially started as salesmen for organizations and found that controls and restrictions placed on personal sales techniques were too onerous. There is hardly a rep that does not abound in the entrepreneurial spirit. It is the desire to avoid control and to use stylized sales methods that usually leads reps to start their own businesses. In spite of this recognition that the rep needs freedom to control its own activities, it is still desirable to point out that the rep has some obligation, although generally expressed, to pursue business on behalf of the manufacturer. In the final analysis only the success of the product, the remuneration from commissions, and the motivational skills of the manufacturer's sales management will secure adequate representation.

Communication. For the small manufacturer, the day-to-day relationship with a rep will be conducted by telephone, Telex, and correspondence. Reps generally follow sales leads provided by the manufacturer in addition to calling on their own customer base. The manufacturer should attempt to see that sales leads are followed up promptly and thoroughly. It may be necessary for the rep to investigate requests for quotations from customers in its territory and to follow up on quotations made by the manufacturer through personal contact to resolve minor difficulties. The rep may handle price quotations directly in accordance with the instructions of the manufacturer or may correspond with the customer in writing. The manufacturer should be kept advised by having copies of these written communications. In the event the rep receives an order directly from the customer, orally or in writing, the order should be passed on to the manufacturer without delay and in explicit detail. All these are matters that normally occur in effecting sales. A general statement in the agreement serves as a clear understanding between the parties of the rep's obligations. At best, it would be difficult to litigate this obligation because of the difficulties of proof. But even this general language should aid in resolving the controversy in favor of the manufacturer in the event that an inactive rep must be canceled and a dispute arises as to whether there was a breach of the duties of the rep.

Marketing Services. It is not unreasonable for the manufacturer to also expect the sales representative to provide marketing support. A good rep, like a professional salesperson, should report on the activities of competitors and the requirements and needs of customers. The rep should forecast sales for the territory. These are chores that take on the appearance of close control to which some reps will demur if too much detail is included. Motivation is the only successful method for accomplishing these tasks. Yet, again, reciting that these duties are expected of the rep will help in clarifying the expectations of the manufacturer in the continuing relationship. This will promote harmony.

Facilities. Specific requirements regarding facilities are often ignored in a sales representative agreement. Some manufacturers, however, insist that the rep have an office other than the rep's residence. Depending on the product line and the customer base, a manufacturer may even require the rep to have a showroom where customers may visit for a demonstration of the equipment. In such event, it is often also required that the rep purchase a demonstration unit on execution of the agreement as a part of the rep's commitment to the product line. These requirements are much more common in distributor agreements than in rep agreements.

Sales Meetings.   There are varied opinions regarding the value of sales meetings. Many manufacturers adopt a policy of having annual or semi-annual sales meetings; because the meeting represents a substantial investment, the manufacturer will require that each rep firm attend the meeting. This can often be a point of contention in negotiating the agreement. The rep will usually counter with a provision that the manufacturer should pay at least some of the expense if attendance is required. If the reps are merely invited, not required, to attend one or more sales meetings, it is safe to omit any mention of sales meetings from the agreement.

Samples.   There are endless variations on manufacturers' sample policies toward their sales representative primarily based on the value of the product. For inexpensive items, the manufacturer may provide free samples in limited quantities. If this is the manufacturer's policy, it should be expressly stated, since it will favorably impress the representative. If the product is more expensive, the manufacturer may agree to ship the product with a "memo" billing that is a recordkeeping document. The memo provides that the rep must return the unit after a suitable period of time or the manufacturer will send an invoice requiring payment under normal terms. A third manner for handling samples is to sell the samples to the rep at cost or at a substantial discount from retail.

If the manufacturer wants to handle the samples on an individual basis, perhaps supplying a sample in one sales situation or for one customer but not another, then the matter may be omitted from the agreement. Or the agreement may provide that the manufacturer will supply samples "as necessary." Although ambiguous, the statement at least indicates the manufacturer's policy.

Advertising.   With respect to product literature, the manufacturer invariably supplies literature to the sales representative for distribution. In nearly all cases the manufacturer will bear the entire cost. It will do no harm to place an obligation on the manufacturer to supply literature as required by the representative. It is a good statement of intention that the rep will appreciate. With respect to direct mail, neither or both of the parties may have a direct mail program. Some well established and well run reps have a local mailing list that has been developed at considerable expense. The rep may take literature from the manufacturer and perform a local mailing either with or without the manufacturer's sharing of expenses. Conversely, the manufacturer may have a direct mail list and may agree to make mailings in the rep's territory that specifically identify the rep. Whatever the policy of either party, care must be taken not to contractually commit to a policy that may later be changed. It is preferable to state the obligation in general terms to accommodate desired flexibility.

As for media advertising, either party may assume an obligation to advertise but usually without any definite commitment about expenditure. The manufacturer may agree to advertise in national trade publications without any commitment about the number of ads, the selected magazines, or the advertising budget. In general, rep firms do not ordinarily advertise, but occasionally local, inexpensive trade journals may be used by a rep to identify product lines carried. In such event, the rep may seek permission to use the manufacturer's name and may ask for some contribution to the cost of the advertising. The manufacturer should reserve approval.

Some products are particularly amenable to demonstration by audiovisual devices. A manufacturer may develop a sound film, an audiovisual cassette, or a slide presentation for effective demonstration of the product and its application. The rep may be provided with these materials free of charge or at cost. The manufacturer may require the rep to have suitable equipment for the presentation or may sell, lease, or lend the equipment to the rep.

The type of advertising in which a party may engage and the range of policies of manufacturers vary so widely from one industry to another that the agreement must speak, if at all, in broad generalities. If the matter is of serious consequence to the manufacturer's marketing plan and specific details are required in full, it may be advisable to include a separate paragraph relating to advertising.

Training.   No manufacturer should be expected to provide sales training to members of the rep firm. On the other hand, every manufacturer must assume the burden of providing product training. The manufacturer that fails to provide training to the rep does a disservice to both. There are various techniques for providing training: plant visits, accompanied field calls, application notes, new product bulletins, and many others. The particular policy chosen by the manufacturer need not be committed in writing.

Competing Lines.   The matter of competing products should also be addressed. One of the greatest values that a rep can provide to a manufacturer is in handling complementary product lines. A sales call for the express purpose of selling one product may result in the sale of another. A small, new manufacturer may get a free ride on name-brand products carried by the rep that are purchased by its customer for a related need.

It is this synergism that enhances the value of the rep to a limited product-line manufacturer. But it is also the seed of discontent.

Because the rep is handling complementary product lines there is the possibility that an expansion of one manufacturer's line may encroach on another. By definition the businesses of the several manufacturers handled by the rep are closely based. Few reps are likely to take on, after the agreement is established, a directly competing product without terminating the first manufacturer. The conflict of interest is too obvious. A disagreement is more likely to arise when a second manufacturer handled by the rep slowly expands its product line until it becomes indirectly competitive. Reasonable men may differ on whether two products actually compete.

It is recommended that the agreement contain a prohibition against handling competing products. But that will usually not be enough. Because of the possible difference of opinion the manufacturer should insist that it be advised of all products the rep handles and notified in writing when the rep acquires a new product or line. The manufacturer will thereby be made aware of a possible conflict. It is then in a position to exercise its own judgment and terminate the agreement if it strongly feels that the new line is competitive. If a rep has the obligation to notify the manufacturer of a new product line and fails to do so, the breach will be clear and sufficient regardless of whether the product is competing.

From this lengthy list of points that may be covered in the paragraph defining the relationship between the parties, the draftsman can choose the appropriate measures. It is difficult to draft a standard paragraph, because nearly every business situation will differ. Moreover, nearly every business manager has specific ideas about the most important aspect of the relationship between the rep and manufacturer. If very specific and detailed treatment is felt necessary for any one or more of these points, a separate paragraph should be drafted, complete with precise details, covering the subject. This will help to draw attention to the importance of the matter at the time the contract is negotiated as well as during the relationship. The following paragraph covers all these points but employs a very generalized definition of the duties and promises of the parties.

5.1 *Appointment and Duties.* MANUFACTURER appoints REP as exclusive sales representative for ["all of the" or "the XYZ line of"] products (defined in Paragraph _____) of MANUFACTURER within the territory defined in Paragraph _____. REP accepts this appointment.

REP shall use its best efforts to introduce, promote, obtain orders for, provide support for the products covered by this agreement, and devote such time and attention as is necessary and reasonable to effect sales in the territory. REP shall handle promptly all inquiries, quotations, and other matters relating to the business of MANUFACTURER and shall furnish MANUFACTURER with copies of all correspondence, price quotations, and orders relating to the products of MANUFACTURER. REP shall advise MANUFACTURER promptly and fully about customer requirements and competitive activities. REP shall prepare sales forecasts and other information required for successful marketing of the products of MANUFACTURER. REP shall assist MANUFACTURER at all trade shows in which MANUFACTURER participates in the territory. REP shall maintain a business office in the territory.

MANUFACTURER shall furnish to REP catalogs, sales literature, and advertising materials for distribution by REP. MANUFACTURER shall provide samples to REP on memo billing if MANUFACTURER determines that such samples are necessary for a proper promotion of the products. MANUFACTURER shall hold periodic sales meetings and may require REP to attend such meetings, providing MANUFACTURER pays at least fifty percent (50%) of the cost of travel, lodging, and meals of REP at such meeting. MANUFACTURER shall furnish REP with copies of all orders received and accepted, invoices rendered, and inquiries and replies from customers located in the territory. MANUFACTURER shall supply the necessary training on its products and keep REP informed about product features and competitive information.

REP agrees that it will not handle products that compete with the product of MANUFACTURER. REP will give notice of any new product line that is added to the product line presently sold by REP within thirty (30) days after REP assumes such product line; the notice will include the manufacturer's name and descriptive sales literature.

Products

This very brief paragraph describes the goods offered for sale by the manufacturer that the rep is authorized to sell. If the manufacturer has a single line of products, this paragraph could be deleted entirely; the Appointment paragraph would state that the rep is appointed to sell ". . . all the products offered for sale by MANUFACTURER . . ."

If the manufacturer has more than one line of products, a more detailed definition is required and a separate paragraph may be warranted. If each line of products is sold under a different trademark, the products covered by the agreement may be referred to as ". . . products offered for sale by MANUFACTURER under the trademark XYZ." If the delineation between product lines cannot be based on a trademark, the description must be more exhaustive. This may be best handled by attaching an exhibit to the agreement. The exhibit may include all the products to be covered by the agreement, or, alternatively, it may refer to ". . . all products offered for sale by MANUFACTURER, except . . ." Another alternative, rather than a typewritten list of products, is to use a price page that identifies the products to be sold by the rep.

When a specific list of products is set forth in the exhibit, as suggested in the foregoing, some reference must be made to future products that the manufacturer may later offer for sale. Conversely, a generic designation may be used in the body of the agreement such as "fasteners," "pressure regulators," or "computer memory devices." It then will not be necessary to refer to future products that will be subsumed automatically into the agreement when introduced.

In some businesses it may be necessary to exclude services that are offered by the manufacturer that are ancillary to the primary business of manufacturing products. Many small manufacturers welcome the opportunity to create a new product for a customer that is willing to pay for the research and development and engineering work. The manufacturer may enter into a contract (that may be in the form of a purchase order and acceptance) to perform such services; the order may include one or two prototypes. This business may represent a small portion of the sales volume in the rep's territory. Furthermore, follow-up business for production units will generate commissions for the rep. The parties may therefore agree to exclude such services and the prototypes from the definition of *products*.

A typical paragraph may read as follows:

5.2   *Products.*   The "Products" included within the terms of this agreement shall be the [widgets and accessories] normally offered for sale by MANUFACTURER, except those products listed in Exhibit 1. Any contract for research, development, or engineering services, including any developmental products delivered pursuant to such contract are excluded from this agreement.

Territory

Normally, this paragraph will also be succinct. If the agreement encompasses a well-defined territory such as a state, county, or other readily identifiable region, it is easily defined. Previously, it was suggested that in a more difficult case for which a written description will not suffice a map including the territory covered by the agreement may be appended to the agreement as an exhibit.

Although it is desirable to restrict the agent from soliciting orders outside the territory, it should be unnecessary to include an explicit prohibition against such activity. As seen subsequently, the commission base is identified as shipments made into the territory covered by the agreement. With such definition it is unlikely that a rep will pursue customers outside the territory unless the goods are being shipped within the rep's territory.

There are several ways of handling the matter of the exclusion of certain customers from the agreement. One obvious way is to include a separate paragraph that defines specific customers by name or by generic term. A simpler technique is to add a sentence in the territory paragraph.

The territory may be defined as follows:

5.3   *Territory.*   The "Territory" included within the terms of this agreement is described in Exhibit 2 attached to this agreement. Customers excluded from the Territory are [ABC Chain Stores, Mammoth Corporation (including all its divisions and subsidiaries), all agencies of the U.S. government . . . , or any firm engaged exclusively in purchasing Products for export . . .].

Acceptance of Orders

Legally, when an agency relationship is created there is power in the agent to bind the principal. When a rep is appointed to solicit orders, the scope of the rep's power to bind the principal would include acceptance of a purchase order. This possibility creates two dangers. First, the rep may quote prices that the manufacturer may be unwilling to accept. If the prices are those published by the manufacturer no difficulty will usually arise. But situations may occur in which the rep, in its business judgment, may want to discount prices for a large volume order. Conversations between the rep and the manufacturer may lead the rep to believe that the manufacturer is willing to offer a discount from the published price. Under the pressure of a highly competitive situation communications may be too vague. When the order is received, the manufacturer may realize there was a misunderstanding or may even have second thoughts about the discount discussed. Yet, under the circumstances, a court could find that the rep, as the agent of the manufacturer, had the power to bind the manufacturer to the quoted price.

Second, the manufacturer will always want to exercise credit control. The manufacturer should establish credit qualifications that are communicated to the rep. However, exceptions may arise for which the manufacturer may want to limit the extension of credit to a particular customer. If the rep can accept orders on behalf of the manufacturer the manufacturer loses credit control.

To avoid these risks it is desirable to include a paragraph stating that only the manufacturer has the power to accept an order solicited by the rep. A statement may be included that the manufacturer is responsible for any risks associated with credit extended and for the collection of monies from the customer. Furthermore, an orderly procedure for communicating to the rep that an order has been accepted should be included. If the manufacturer uses an Acknowledgment for orders accepted, a copy should be sent to the rep. If shipment is normally from stock shortly after receipt of an order, the manufacturer may elect to provide the rep with a copy of the invoice rather than the Acknowledgment.

It is also desirable to establish that the manufacturer has the right to change or alter prices at its discretion. The manufacturer should attempt to keep the rep advised of current prices by forwarding any price changes and revised price lists. If the rep has quoted prices based on an obsolete price sheet, then as discussed, the manufacturer will have retained for itself the right to reject such order. However, to assure a satisfactory relationship with the rep it is advisable to make it unequivocal in the agreement that the manufacturer has total control over prices and terms of sale.

These matters may be covered in a paragraph as follows:

5.4 *Acceptance of Orders.* All orders shall be subject to acceptance or rejection by MANUFACTURER. The extension of credit and collections shall be the sole responsibility of MANUFACTURER. REP shall quote only the prices and terms established by MANUFACTURER. MANUFACTURER shall have the right from time to time to change prices and terms of sale; MANUFACTURER shall notify REP of any change in prices or terms of sale.

If it is the nature of the business that most sales are made on quotations from the manufacturer, the manufacturer should assume the duty of transmitting a copy of such quotation to the rep when issued. If the manufacturer customarily sends a notice of shipping date or shipping advice (that may be advisable when delivery times are long after receipt of an order), a copy of such document should be transmitted to the rep. The practices in various industries and by different manufacturers regarding the flow of paperwork involved in order processing make it difficult to generalize about the documents that should be transmitted to the rep. The draftsman should consider the practices used by the manufacturer and attempt to balance the competing interests of satisfying the rep's desire to be kept informed and preventing a blizzard of paperwork.

Commissions

For both parties this is the heart of the agreement. The matter of primary interest is, of course, the amount. It is not the purpose of his text to offer advice or assistance on establishing the amount of commission payments. It is safe to say that in nearly all rep agreements the commission is based on a percentage of sales. The average percentage, and the range of percentages, varies widely from industry to industry. In a survey undertaken by the Manufacturer's Agents National Association, it was reported that the commission rate may be as low as 2.5% (food) and as high as 40% (parks and recreation equipment). Yet, within the food industry alone, commission rates ran as high as 20%, and the average commission was 12%. The variation for industrial products ranges from 3 to 20%, but in most industries the average commission ranges between 7 and 10%.

Obviously, this range of commissions is too broad to offer guidance for establishing the proper amount. There is simply no alternative to discussion with reps and other manufacturers on what is the common, established, average commission used in the industry. Even then, the manufacturer must take into account other variables such as uniqueness of the product, reputation of the manufacturer, whether the territory was previously worked by another rep, the desirability of attracting the most qualified reps, and so on. These considerations are used to modify the industry-established rate upward or downward.

Once a percentage has been established the next step is to define the base for computing commissions on each sale. The usual measure is the "net invoice value." This should be stated in the agreement as the total or gross invoice price, minus trade discounts or allowances, freight charges, taxes, COD charges, and insurance. Having spelled out the base for each particular order, it is then necessary to identify those orders that are aggregated to arrive at the total sales base. It is recommended that the term "shipments" should be used to define the sales base. The reason is that shipments are readily identifiable, explicit, and definite. It would be a mistake to state that the commission will be paid on all "sales" made in the territory. Despite the fact that the term "sales" is in common parlance and is readily understood it is not easy to state where a sale takes place. The rep relationship is tied to a territory or place and depends on the activities that occur there. In fact, most sales are made at the manufacturer's plant, where the offer has been received and accepted. When the goods are shipped by common carrier, "title passes" when the carrier departs with the goods, even if an acceptance document is not used. The terminology is highly important here. A good foundation must be laid that readily and yet precisely defines those sales of the manufacturer on which the rep is to receive commissions. The term "shipments" is chosen because the destination of the goods is always ascertainable from shipping documents. It therefore provides the data from which computation of commissions can be made. The difficult problem of handling sales when more than one rep in different territories participates in the activity can be best resolved by tying the commission base to shipments.

The next aspect to be defined is when commissions are payable. Here, too, it is important to understand that there are two events which are distinct but often confused. The obligation or duty of the manufacturer to pay the commission will arise on the occurrence of a specified event. Since the manufacturer will not instantaneously make payment on such occurrence, the obligation exists to be discharged in the future. Commissions are therefore "payable" at one time and "paid" at another.

There are several events that may be used to identify when the obligation to pay of the manufacturer arises: acceptance of the order, shipment, invoicing, or collection. If the commission becomes payable on acceptance of the order, the manufacturer obviously runs the risk that if the shipment is never made (the plant burns down), the debt must still be paid. This is not a likely event that a manufacturer would choose when drafting an agreement. At the other extreme, the manufacturer would prefer that the obligation arise only when payment is received from the customer; this is particularly favored if the manufacturer is not well financed. From the rep's point of view, the sale is completed after shipment, and it should be credited with an earned commission, since the rep's work on that particular transaction has been completed. Furthermore, since the manufacturer controls the credit policy, it may be argued that the slow-paying customer has been approved by the manufacturer which should bear the burden of its own selection. The manufacturer may have sloppy collection practices that should not be borne by the rep. The manufacturer may also accelerate payment by offering a time discount (for example, 1%–10 days), a matter of financial choice at its discretion. From the manufacturer's point of view, it would be desirable to avoid a commission payable liability on its books as long as possible to improve its financial picture.

The middle ground is to create the obligation on shipment or invoicing. The distinction between these two events is usually trivial, since it is simply good business practice to invoice as quickly after shipment as possible. Perhaps invoicing is more commonly used because the date is more readily accessible within the accounting department than the date of shipment. Although it is difficult to generalize, choosing the date of invoice as the event on which the duty to pay the commission arises is probably the most prevalent.

Having defined when the commission payment obligation arises, it is then necessary to define the date on which payment will be made. As a matter of accounting convenience, the date for payment is usually established as a fixed number of days following the month in which the invoice is sent (or payment is collected). If numerous transactions take place during the month, they are accumulated, the commission is calculated, and the commission checks are prepared and forwarded to all the reps. For the small business the effect on cash flow by choosing either "invoicing" or "collection" as the event on which payment must be made should not be ignored. If payment is made on the tenth day of the month following the month in which invoices are sent, and the credit terms are net 30, then commission payments will be made on the majority of sales prior to the receipt of cash. Conversely, if collection is used, then the manufacturer will have the use of the cash for at least 10 days, and as many as 40 days, prior to disbursement of commissions. Of course, the effect on cash flow can be mitigated by extending the date for payment to the rep beyond the tenth day, say, the twentieth day of the following month.

To keep the rep informed of the status of orders and shipments, the manufacturer may promise to send copies of all invoices to the rep at the time the invoice is forwarded to the customer. At the time of payment, the manufacturer should provide some summary or proof of the computation of commissions by listing all the invoices sent during the preceding month from which the commission calculation has been made.

Provision should also be included for "returns." A rep's commission payable account is credited and may be paid shortly after invoicing by the manufacturer. If the customer later returns the goods, then the credit or payment should be deducted from commissions payable during the month in which the return is made. If the customer fails to make payment, a similar reversal and deduction should be made. The manufacturer should reserve the right to determine if an account is uncollectible. When that decision is made the rep's account should be debited and an appropriate deduction taken from the payment in the month following the month in which the account is written off. Informing the rep of these deductions is easily handled if a commission statement is used by the manufacturer with each monthly commission payment.

A difficult matter to handle in any rep agreement is commission splitting. The problem arises because the solicitation of orders may take place in more than one territory. For example, a large customer may have headquarters (where authorization of a major purchase must be approved) in territory A, an engineering department in territory B, and a manufacturing plant to which the goods will be shipped in territory C. The rep in territory B may expend considerable effort in working with the engineering group to obtain approval for purchase of a product. The rep in territory C may be simultaneously working with manufacturing engineers or local purchasing personnel to obtain the order. Finally, the rep in territory A may be working with upper management of the customer involved in engineering, manufacturing, or procurement. When shipment is made to territory C, fairness and equity require that some division of the commission be made with the other reps.

Perhaps the simplest way to solve this problem is to state that under such circumstances the manufacturer will split the commission among the reps and will advise the reps of their proportion of the whole at the time the order is placed. This permits the manufacturer to make a decision based on its knowledge of the respective contributions of the reps involved toward securing the sale. It may, however, leave the rep with a certain insecurity about the fairness of the manufacturer in making this determination. This latter objection may be overcome by a commitment that each rep shall obtain at least a minimum percentage of the total commission. Alternatively, a specific percentage may be set forth for various types of rep contributions. Since there is no way to foresee the various combinations of possibilities that may arise, there is no alternative to leaving a certain amount of discretion in dividing the commission to the manufacturer. In all events, the manufacturer must have the final determination of the split.

A typical paragraph may read as follows:

5.5   *Commission Payments.* MANUFACTURER shall pay to REP as commission for services _____ percent (_____%) of the net invoice value (gross invoice value, minus trade discounts, freight charges, taxes, COD charges, and insurance) of all shipments of Products into the Territory. MANUFACTURER shall pay the commission on or before the tenth (10th) day of each month following the month in which the customer is invoiced.

MANUFACTURER may deduct from the commissions owed the REP any sums previously paid the REP for sales of Products that are returned or which the MANUFACTURER determines in its sole judgment are uncollectible.

At the time MANUFACTURER invoices any shipment made into the Territory, MANUFACTURER will send REP a copy of such invoice. At the time payment of commissions is made to REP, MANUFACTURER will provide a summary of invoices sent during

the preceding month and a computation of the commission payment.

If REP shall participate in the sale of Products shipped to a customer located outside the Territory, MANUFACTURER will allocate the commission among the REPs participating in the sale,
but no participating REP shall receive less than _____ percent
(_____%) of the full commission. MANUFACTURER will allocate the commission at the time the order is received and notify all
participating REPs of their respective allocation, and such determination of the allocation shall be final.

In addition to the standard commission paragraph just provided, several other matters should be considered. If commissions will be paid on
sales to the U.S. government, care must be taken that the government
agency will allow such payments. In a solicitation for bid from a government agency, the document may include rules that permit commission
payments when itemized as a contract expense. Some government agencies, in some circumstances, prohibit or qualify the type of commission
payments that may be made. Unless it is expected that a large proportion
of sales will be made to government agencies, the agreement may remain
silent on this issue. When the situation arises the matter can be discussed
and resolved with the rep.

Another consideration is the use of incentive commissions. When a new
product line is being introduced or the situation suggests that sales will
not be easily secured a cash incentive may be used. The incentive may
be formulated as an additional percentage of sales in excess of an established quota set forth in the agreement. It must be made clear that the
manufacturer has the right to establish this quota and revise it from time
to time.

Another possible variation of the commission structure is a sliding commission schedule for a single order. A sliding commission schedule simply reduces the percentage as the order amount becomes larger: 10% on
the first $10,000; 8% on the next $10,000; 6% on the next $10,000, and 4%
on the remainder. The declining percentage may be appropriate when
the nature of the product and the purchasing methods used in the industry result in blanket purchase orders with releases over an extended period of time. A rep's expenditure of time and overhead expenses will
probably be less on a single, large dollar-volume order than the equivalent dollar amount from 20 separate customer orders. It is therefore ar-
guable that a lesser average commission is justified. It may also be argued
that such policy will prevent the rep from chasing a single large customer
and neglecting a smaller customer. The latter may provide a more stable,

distributed customer base that may be best for the manufacturer in the long run. Most reps, however, would convincingly reply that the time spent on a single large order may equal or exceed that of many small orders. Moreover, a large dollar-volume commitment from a single customer may significantly enhance the manufacturer's reputation and thus deserves a full commission. The sliding schedule must therefore be carefully considered before implementation.

Finally, and akin to the above suggestion, the manufacturer may want to negotiate commissions on large orders or for particular customers. This is not an easy practice to effect legally. To refer to such orders as "special" or "exceptional" as opposed to "normal" is simply too indefinite. Either the specific customer must be identified or a minimum dollar volume must be established, followed by a mechanism for arriving at the applicable commission. The agreement may provide that the manufacturer may offer a reduced commission for the portion of the order in excess of the minimum amount. The rep may then have the opportunity to accept or reject within a defined period. If no agreement on the commission is reached the matter may be submitted to arbitration.

Numerous commission schemes are used in practice. Certain industries have well-established patterns that deviate from the simple commission structure suggested above. As the commission structure becomes more complex the drafting problems increase exponentially. The point may be reached where the services of a lawyer would be well advised.

Term

Broadly speaking, there are two ways of defining the term: (a) a fixed term (one year, five years, etc.); or (b) an indefinite term.

In a fixed term agreement, the period should be measured from the date of the agreement that, as discussed in Chapter 2, may be the date of execution or the effective date. If a fixed term is recited without any further qualification it will expire naturally at the end of the period. Since both parties will desire to have advance notice about whether the other party wants to continue, it is common to provide for renewal periods after notice is given. If the agreement automatically renews the period of the renewal term should be defined clearly. To provide advance warning if the agreement will not be renewed, the party desiring to terminate the agreement should be obligated to deliver notice within a fixed period, 30 or 60 days, prior to the expiration of the then-extant term.

An indefinite term agreement, as implied, provides for a continuing relationship that exists until terminated by one of the parties. This is done by stating that written notice must be given by the party desiring to terminate the agreement to the other party of its intention after a prescribed period of time. This is normally referred to as termination "without cause."

If a fixed term agreement is used, it will be desirable to enumerate certain events that will give a party the right to terminate prior to the end of the term. One of the more common reasons for providing one party with the right to terminate is bankruptcy, insolvency, or similar financial collapse of the other party. The solvent party must specifically be given the right to terminate the agreement on the filing of a petition in bankruptcy or a general assignment for the benefit of creditors. Otherwise, it may become involved in the legal proceedings of the insolvent company. Filing a petition in bankruptcy will not in and of itself terminate the agreement, unless the agreement so provides. Therefore, the manufacturer may be prohibited from appointing a new rep without running the possibility of being sued for breach by the trustee in bankruptcy or other party that takes control of the failing company's business. Bankruptcy proceedings, especially if reorganization is attempted, can last for an uncomfortable period of time.

Another event that should explicitly permit a party to terminate the agreement is a breach by the other party. Merely because one party breaches the terms of the agreement (for example, the manufacturer fails to make commission payments) does not automatically permit the other party to terminate. The injured party may have the right to sue for damages emanating from the breach, but the breach itself may not terminate the agreement unless the agreement so provides.

The fixed term agreement, therefore, has some complications involving termination for cause. The entire matter may be simplified by choosing an indefinite term agreement. So long as the notice period is of reasonable length, a simple notice of termination (without cause) can be used if the other party becomes insolvent or breaches the terms of the agreement. The indefinite term is used in many manufacturer-rep agreements. The right to terminate an indefinite term agreement at any time, following the method prescribed in the agreement, has been establishd as lawful under the UCC.

If the indefinite term agreement is used, what is a fair and equitable termination period? Naturally, when a party gives notice the other party will be less than cooperative and may immediately begin seeking a new business partner. However, a short notice period may be unfair especially to the rep that has provided long years of service. There are several ways of handling this problem. As discussed next, there may be a provision for severance payments based on the number of years during which the relationship existed. An alternative is to increase the required notice period during each successive year of the relationship, for example, 30 days during the first year, 60 during the second, and so forth, to a maximum of, say, 120 days. The rep will normally receive commissions on orders entered or shipments made during the notice period. Consequently, by increasing the length of the notice period earned commissions will be greater in recognition of the years of service.

If a long notice period is used, another problem that may arise for the manufacturer occurs when the rep takes on a competitive product line during the period. Since a rep has a close customer relationship, the manufacturer is at the mercy of the rep during the notice period. The matter may be solved by providing that if the rep starts to represent a competitive product line during the notice period no commissions will be paid thereafter. This should discourage the rep, but even if it does not, it will allow the manufacturer to immediately appoint a new rep without double commission payment obligations.

Since the indefinite term agreement is preferred, the following paragraph is representative:

5.6 *Term and Termination.* This agreement shall begin on the date set forth in the introductory paragraph and shall remain in effect until terminated by either party, without cause, by notice given to the other party, indicating an election to terminate this agreement at a date that shall be at least thirty (30) days after the date of such notice.

Rights after Termination

During the notice period prior to termination, all the terms and conditions of the agreement will be in force—commissions will be paid, the rep will solicit orders, reports will be exchanged, and the rights and duties of both parties will continue. The Rights after Termination clause is specifically directed to the status of orders and shipments immediately after the termination date (the last day of the termination notice period). What specifically should be done with orders that have been booked but not shipped as of the termination date? What should be the status of those orders that follow so closely after the termination that they are the apparent result of the rep's prior activity?

If orders are booked but not shipped prior to the termination date, the manufacturer's obligation to pay commissions (unless based on bookings, which is inadvisable) will arise only after the agreement has ended. It is common to provide that for all booked orders commissions will be paid according to the terms of the agreement when the goods are shipped and invoiced. In some agreements, the time is limited to shipments made within a specified period, such as 90 days. This limitation can be particularly important when blanket purchase orders with scheduled releases over an extended period of time have been entered. The new rep in the territory will normally take on the responsibility of servicing each account and will expect commission payments for such activity even though an order was entered by a prior rep. The manufacturer can be assured of a more orderly transition of reps in the territory by limiting the shipping period during which commissions are paid to the old rep. A compromise between providing for payments on shipments indefinitely versus a fixed period is to provide for a second period in which commissions will be paid at a reduced rate. For example, the agreement may provide that normal commissions will be paid on all orders entered prior to the termination date if shipped within 90 days and that 50% of the commission rate will be paid on shipments during a subsequent 90-day period. The manufacturer may then be able to negotiate with the new rep an agreement which provides that the new rep will also receive 50% commissions on shipments during the second 90-day period for orders placed prior to the termination date by the old rep.

For orders entered immediately after the termination date the agreement may provide for either full, partial, or no commissions. Any commission payment is generous; whether any payment is made may depend on the length of the notice period. In other words, if there is a relatively short notice period, such as 30 days, there may be provision for payment of commission on orders placed following the termination date for a period of 30 days. Conversely, if a notice period of 60 or 90 days is used, it is usual to pay commissions only on orders entered prior to the termination date.

An alternative approach to providing for rights after termination regardless of which party terminates is to vary such rights, depending on the terminating party. Typically, if the rep terminates the agreement, a hard line may be taken, stating that commissions will be paid on orders placed prior to termination only if shipments have been made prior to the termination date. If the manufacturer terminates the agreement, commissions will be paid on booked orders if shipped within a relatively long period, such as 90 days. The fairness of this type of provision that adjusts the period during which commissions will be paid has much to commend it.

Another approach for compensating a rep for past services is to provide "severance payments." Severance payments are in addition to the payments on orders discussed previously. The amount of the payment is normally adjusted to the length of service. It will normally start with a minimum period of time such as two years. For each additional two-year increment an additional payment would be made up to some maximum amount. The amount of payment is usually based on the commissions that have been paid to the rep during the year immediately preceding the termination date. The commissions for the year may be divided into 12 equal increments, each representing "one month severance pay." The agreement may then provide that for service longer than two years but less than four years one month severance pay will be paid; for service greater than four years but less than six, two months severance pay, and so on.

While a severance pay provision is often discussed by reps and advocated by rep organizations, actual occurrence of the provision is believed to be relatively limited. It is not recommended that a manufacturer draft a standard agreement including severance payments. If a rep requests severance payments, the manufacturer should investigate the practice in the industry to determine that such payments are actually required.

There are other matters that must be covered in the clause for Rights after Termination. First, it is desirable that the manufacturer have a "right of setoff" against any commissions due the rep on the date of termination or commissions earned subsequent to termination if the agreement so provides. This will permit the manufacturer to deduct from commissions owed any amounts owed by the rep to the manufacturer, including the return of materials, equipment, and samples that may have been provided free of charge to the rep. To make such provision effective, it is necessary to provide that the manufacturer may temporarily withhold payments from the rep for a limited period of time beyond the normal payment date. During this period the manufacturer may compute any amounts that are to be deducted from commission payments. In the absence of such provision, the manufacturer will in all probability exercise this right of setoff, but there will be no legal authority to do so. Thus the manufacturer will be in breach of an obligation to make commission payments after termination that may precipitate litigation. Proper drafting can avoid potential problems.

Also, the agreement should contain explicit instructions on the return of all materials of the manufacturer in the possession of the rep on the termination date. This should include all sales literature, photographs, price lists, newsletters, and any other written materials supplied by the manufacturer during the term of the agreement. It should expressly encompass sales samples, demonstration equipment, visual aids, or other items the manufacturer has given to the rep for sales support. To avoid any dispute over whether the manufacturer or the rep owns the items, the agreement should state that all documentary and physical materials supplied to the rep during the agreement are the property of the manufacturer and remain its property at all times.

Further, all items of confidential information should be returned by the rep. If the rep has been sent engineering drawings, formulations, or other documents that are treated as trade secrets by the manufacturer, the request for all written materials, discussed previously, will include these materials. However, confidential information should be identified as such at the time it is sent to the rep. The identification warns the rep that the documents are not to be disclosed to others or used by the rep for any purpose other than that which has been authorized by the manufacturer. A good company trade secret policy will attempt to avoid any distribution of such sensitive materials to reps because wide distribution may in itself defeat the claim that the information is proprietary. However, occasions will arise when such disclosure is necessary. If the documents were not properly identified at the time they were transmitted to the rep, it will not be possible to claim at the time of termination that the documents are proprietary and must be returned. Confidential information will have a much greater value than ordinary written materials, and it is important that the identity of confidential material as well as restrictions on its use is clear. A court will enforce the return of proprietary materials more readily than ordinary documents. Summarizing these suggestions, a properly drafted paragraph follows:

5.7 *Rights after Termination.* In the event of termination of this agreement by REP, MANUFACTURER will pay commissions in accordance with Paragraph _____ on all shipments made within thirty (30) days after the date of termination on all orders booked prior to the termination date. In the event of termination by MANUFACTURER, MANUFACTURER will pay commissions in accordance with Paragraph _____ on all orders placed prior to the thirtieth (30th) day following the date of termination on shipments made within ninety (90) days following the date of termination. However, if REP begins to represent a competitor of MANUFACTURER at any time prior to the expiration of the 90-day period, commission payments will not be made on any shipments after the date of termination.

MANUFACTURER may deduct from commissions due REP any credits or adjustments arising out of the terms of this agreement or breach of the terms of this agreement and may withhold commission payments due REP for a period of thirty (30) days after the date on which such payments are due for the purpose of determining such deductions.

All written materials—including but not limited to sales literature, price lists, newsletters, or manuals—all confidential or proprietary information, and all samples, demonstration equipment, or other physical items given to REP during the term of this agreement is and shall remain the property of MANUFACTURER and shall be returned by REP, no later than the date of termination, to MANU-FACTURER at its expense and in accordance with its directions.

Independent Contractor

It is essential in any rep agreement to include a paragraph that expressly sets forth that the rep is an independent contractor and not an employee, partner, or other affiliate of the manufacturer.

The problems here are similar to those considered in Chapter 4 for consulting contracts. If a rep is an individual rather than a firm, the problems relating to the characterization of the relationship as one of employment are similar to those discussed in reference to a consultant. If the rep is a firm, there is the possibility of construing the relationship as a joint venture or other business affiliation that makes the manufacturer responsible for the actions of the rep. It is therefore highly desirable to expressly state that the rep has the sole responsibility for its expenses, liabilities, and other obligations, including those to employees of the rep. Despite the statement, it must be recognized that if the manufacturer exercises too much control over the conduct of the rep business, the language may be ignored in a contested action. Liability could follow.

The manufacturer must also guard against exposure to warranty statements of the rep. There are well-advised precautions that should be taken against implied warranties. However, there is always the possibility that the law in a particular jurisdiction may ignore a disclaimer or find some technical defect in the manufacturer's attempt to limit its warranty. It is therefore advisable to include an express limitation on the right of the rep to make statements regarding warranty that in any manner exceed the warranty offered by the manufacturer.

At the same time, it should also be made clear that the rep has no authority to modify prices, specifications, or other data supplied by the manufacturer for use by the customer in making the purchase decisions.

Express limitations on the power of the rep to modify or extend the manufacturer's warranty or to vary prices has several salutary effects. First, it will foreclose future disagreements between the parties over the extent of the rep's authority. Second, it may be referred to when informing a customer that a rep had exceeded its power to bind the manufacturer to a lower price, for example. Third, in a legal dispute it will aid in establishing that the rep was, in fact, not merely in words, an independent contractor without power to impose obligations on the manufacturer.

A paragraph that covers these several matters is as follows:

5.8 *Independent Contractor.* REP is an independent contractor with respect to all activities of REP and its agents or employees. REP assumes sole responsibility for its activities performed in accordance with this agreement. REP shall be responsible for all expenses, liabilities, or other obligations incurred by REP and its agents or employees and shall be solely responsible for payment of such obligations. REP is not an agent of MANUFACTURER, nor is REP authorized to transact any business, enter into any agreements, or contract with any person, firm, or corporation that would impose an obligation or liability on MANUFACTURER.

REP has no authority to make any representations or warranties concerning the products of MANUFACTURER not specifically authorized in writing by MANUFACTURER and has no authority to modify any product specification or price unless authorized in writing by MANUFACTURER.

General

Several of the paragraphs set forth in Chapter 3 should definitely be included in any rep-manufacturer agreement. These include Governing Law (Form 3.3), Notices (Form 3.1), Entire Agreement (Form 3.2), and Assignability (Form 3.8). With respect to assignment, it is recommended that a flat prohibition against assignment by either party, or at least the rep, should be included. Since many rep agencies are small and loosely formed, a change in partners or principals requires a careful investigation by the manufacturer. If it is found that a new partner or principal is undesirable, a flat prohibition against assignment will prevent the new entity from taking over from the old rep firm. Problems may also arise, for both the rep and manufacturer, if an acquisition takes place and the agreement is assignable. The new party may be making or selling competing products. Such problems are easily resolved by a total prohibition against assignment; an alternative is assignment only with the written approval of the other party.

Rep agreements are also likely to give rise to controversies or disputes that can be handled by arbitration. The amount of money involved in a dispute arising from a rep agreement will usually not be large enough to justify the expense of court litigation; arbitration is a satisfactory compromise. The clause for Arbitration (Form 3.11) is generally recommended.

Two other paragraphs that may be included are Headings Not Controlling (Form 3.4) and Severability (Form 3.9). The latter will call for an analysis of the situation and the desirability of continuing in the event that a critical paragraph of the agreement is stricken by a court.

The closing paragraph of the agreement, including the signature provision, can be drawn from Chapter 2. Attention should be directed to whether the person executing the instrument is properly authorized.

DISTRIBUTOR AGREEMENT

Many aspects of the distributor agreement are identical to the manufacturer-rep agreement. When similar considerations are involved, reference is made to the foregoing discussion.

It bears repeating that one of the critical distinctions between a distributor and a rep is that the manufacturer is relying on the credit standing of the distributor. Thus a more exhaustive financial investigation is required. The distributor is normally a more financially solvent entity than the typical sales representative. Since the distributor possibly stocks products for several different manufacturers, there will exist a considerable inventory investment. The size of most distributor firms suggest that there may be more negotiation of terms in a printed form than in the sales rep agreement. Other differences between a rep and distributor agreement are noted in the following discussion.

In some industries, it is common to identify distributors as a "franchised distributor." Recently, the Federal Trade Commission (FTC) has promulgated new rules relating to disclosure requirements concerning franchises. The rules are applicable to distributorships and should be averted if possible. Compliance with the disclosure requirements will be costly and time consuming. To effect such avoidance, the manufacturer must not use the term "franchise" in the agreement or negotiations, or it will forego several exemptions to the rules that are otherwise available. One exemption turns on minimal control over the distributor's operations; only essential items should be mandatorily controlled, with items of lesser importance, such as various types of assistance, made optional. Unfortunately, there is no objective test that can be applied. Further, the rules will apply when a payment for the franchise right is required as a condition for receiving the distributorship—that is, a "front end" fee. Therefore, no payment must be demanded. If a start-up inventory is required the prices must be comparable to other ongoing distributor prices;

no hidden franchise fee may be contained in the prices for the minimum inventory purchase.

Another exemption may be available (although there is "control" and "payment") if the distributorship is a "fractional franchise." A franchise is fractional if (a) the distributor has already been in business for at least two years and (b) the parties in good faith do not anticipate that the new product line sales will exceed more than 20% of the distributor's total sales (even if actual events prove that the forecast was in error). These facts could be incorporated into the recital paragraphs (that are appropriate for this purpose) or a clause in which the distributor makes representations about these facts. Because they are new it is difficult to predict with any measure of confidence how the rules will apply in concrete situations; however, the guidelines just provided will aid in plotting a course that avoids running afoul of FTC disclosure requirements.

The typical distributor agreement has a formal format of the type suggested in Chapter 2.

Appointment and Duties

Appointment. The appointment and acceptance by the distributor is similar to the provision found in the rep agreement. Simply to show a variation in form, the appointment paragraph directly incorporates a definition of the territory and the products covered rather than set these forth in separate paragraphs. In the following form, the manufacturer affirmatively states that the distributorship is exclusive.

A statement that the distributorship is exclusive is not entirely dispositive of the manufacturer's rights to sell directly. Unless the agreement further defines what is the meaning of the term "exclusive," a court will be forced to consider customs in the industry in which the parties are engaged. In some industries an exclusive appointment would not allow the manufacturer to deal directly with customers in the territory, unless specific reservations are added with respect to identified customers or classes of customers. In industries such as electronics, the manufacturer and distributor accept that certain customers may place large volume orders directly with the manufacturer. The manufacturer will provide "order protection" up to a certain unit volume on a single purchase order but will deal directly with the customer for larger orders. The nature of the product may suggest one or the other construction of the term "exclusive." If the manufacturer is selling farm tractors, an exclusive distributorship will likely be construed to preclude the manufacturer from direct sales to dealers. Only when the unit quantities purchased are large and the unit price is relatively low will there be an insistence by the manufacturer to deal directly with high-volume customers. An exclusive appointment in such circumstances may be interpreted as applicable to other distributors but not to the manufacturer itself.

If the manufacturer decides to sell directly from the factory to certain customers, or through branches, in competition with its distributors, the agreement must make this clear. One cautionary note must be given. Since a recent U.S. Supreme Court decision, it is clear that a manufacturer may impose territorial restrictions on its distributors when a purely vertical arrangement exists. However, when the manufacturer distributes in competition with its distributors—that is, plays a dual role, a "dual distribution" situation arises in which the antitrust rules are not completely settled. Because the manufacturer-distributor and distributor have effectively horizontally divided territories the agreement may be unlawful. The entire matter involves some esoteric antitrust principles that can trap an unwary manufacturer in a subsequent dispute with a distributor over an unrelated matter.

The following form is for an exclusive distributorship but with reservation to permit the manufacturer to sell to certain classes of customers. The paragraph should read as follows:

5.9   *Appointment.*   MANUFACTURER appoints DISTRIBUTOR as the exclusive distributor for the products of MANUFACTURER defined in Exhibit A ("Products") in the territory defined in Exhibit B ("Territory"). DISTRIBUTOR accepts this appointment. MANUFACTURER may sell Products directly, without any compensation to DISTRIBUTOR, to any agency of the United States, any person, firm, or corporation engaged principally in export sales or any factory of XYZ Corporation located in the Territory.

Duties.   Many of the duties in the distributorship agreement vary from the sales rep agreement because of the nature of the distributor's operation. A primary concern of the manufacturer in a distributor arrangement is the facilities that the distributor has available. If the product is large and complex, the manufacturer may demand that the distributor have a display room or some other substantial facility where customers or dealers can visit. For complex products, it may be mandatory that the distributor have an adequate service department and an installation and maintenance staff. Alternatively, the parties may intend for the distributor to establish a network of dealers that will be responsible for service or maintenance. The manufacturer should then obligate the distributor to establish dealers with the necessary facilities. This obligation on the part of the distributor may also extend to the requirement that it maintain replacement parts of a quantity sufficient to satisfy the manufacturer. If a product is simple, the requirement for facilities may be no greater than that in the ordinary sales representative agreement.

As noted in the foregoing, the distribution channel may involve a hierarchy of entities through which the goods move to the end users. Indeed, the primary function of the distributor may be to establish dealers or authorized retail establishments to serve the consumer. The manufacturer should demand to have the distributor-dealer contract in a specific, approved form. At the least, the manufacturer should insist that it be advised and provided with a copy of all agreements entered into between the distributor and dealer. Even if the distribution channel does not involve dealers, the manufacturer may obligate the distributor to appoint salesmen or representatives in a number satisfactory to the manufacturer. This obligation will assure that the product is represented properly in the territory.

Other means to assure that there is a proper level of effort by the distributor is to establish an annual minimum sales volume requirement as a condition to the exclusivity of the territorial appointment. This may be done by establishing a given volume of sales either in dollars or in units. If the agreement has a relatively long term with no right to terminate without cause, a fixed, tangible standard for distributor performance is well advised. At the very least, a "best efforts" clause should be included in the agreement.

Another provision not normally found in a rep agreement is the requirement that the distributor have a financial statement prepared at least annually and furnished to the manufacturer. This will enable the manufacturer to review the continuing financial strength of the distributor.

The manufacturer may also require the distributor to maintain a minimum inventory level based on the manufacturer's assessment of the market potential of the territory. The initial inclusion of such term in the agreement depends on the manufacturer's bargaining leverage and therefore may be beyond the reach of the typical small manufacturer. However, if the manufacturer later receives complaints from customers or dealers that there is an inadequate stock available from the distributor for immediate delivery, the manufacturer may renegotiate the agreement at the end of any fixed term and insist on a minimum inventory level.

Most of the other duties that will be placed on the distributor are not dissimilar from the rep agreement. These will include samples, advertising, sales literature, attendance at trade shows and sales meetings, sales reports, and marketing support services. These terms must be individually tailored, based on the products, industry custom, and the marketing policy of the manufacturer.

Since it would be impossible to provide a form that would cover all products and distribution channels, the following paragraph would be typical for use when a product is relatively expensive and complex, requiring maintenance and service directly by the distributor. No dealers are involved, nor is any sales quota or minimum inventory level required. The paragraph may provide:

5.10   *Duties.*   DISTRIB JTOR shall maintain a place of business in the Territory, including facilities where the Products of MANUFACTURER will be displayed. DISTRIBUTOR shall provide maintenance service on all Products sold in the Territory and will maintain qualified technical personnel and service policies satisfactory to MANUFACTURER. DISTRIBUTOR shall carry a repair and replacement parts inventory satisfactory to MANUFACTURER based upon the approximate number of units sold in the Territory.

DISTRIBUTOR shall appoint sales personnel or representatives to introduce, promote, and obtain orders for the Products of MANUFACTURER and will use its best efforts and devote such time and attention as are necessary to sell and service MANUFACTURER'S Products.

At least annually, DISTRIBUTOR shall prepare or have prepared financial statements by a qualified, independent accountant and shall furnish a copy of such statements to MANUFACTURER.

MANUFACTURER shall have the right to examine the physical inventory and inventory records of DISTRIBUTOR at any reasonable time during business hours to determine the adequacy of Product and spare parts inventory.

The other duties of the distributor with respect to advertising, and the like, may be added following the form paragraph just provided. Sample provisions for these additional duties may be drawn from the corresponding form paragraph in the rep agreement.

Prices, Terms, and Sales Policy

The following matters may be grouped into a single paragraph or may be the subject of separate paragraphs. For ease in explanation, the seven points covered here are provided under a single paragraph with appropriate subparagraphs.

Prices.   It is not actually necessary to establish the price of the product sold to the distributor in the agreement itself. The agreement may simply recite that the manufacturer agrees to sell to the distribuor at prices that it will establish from time to time. Typically, a distributor price list will be prepared by the manufacturer. The agreement may provide that the price list in effect on the date of execution will establish the initial prices at which the manufacturer agrees to sell. Alternatively, the manufacturer may have a retail price list and provide that the distributor shall receive a specified discount from the suggested retail prices. This percentage discount must be specified. If it is the manufacturer's policy to sell Free on Board (FOB) factory, this should be clearly stated. Most important, the manufacturer should retain the right to change prices and other terms of sale, at its discretion, on giving the distributor notice, perhaps 30 to 60 days prior to any prospective price change. It should then be added that orders received prior to the effective date of the price change will be invoiced at the old price.

Payment.   The credit terms of the manufacturer should be explicitly set forth. It has become vogue to charge interest on past due accounts and to the extent that such provision may be enforced realistically it may be added. If credit terms are not extended then the specific manner and time of payment, such as COD, sight draft, or cash in advance, should be specified. The method of payment does not normally appear in domestic distributorship agreements. However, if unusual requirements exist, for example, a domestic letter of credit is demanded, this should be spelled out.

The manufacturer should also protect itself against slow payment by the distributor. Since the manufacturer has the right to accept or reject each individual order from the distributor, as explained subsequently, it could be assumed that an adequate remedy is to reject orders when payments are in arrears. Yet this may not be a satisfactory solution. The manufacturer may want to accept but to delay shipment as leverage to obtain payment. By accepting the order the distributor is bound; withholding shipment can be used to apply pressure. The agreement should expressly give the manufacturer this right.

Risk of Loss.   As in any sales agreement, it is desirable to specify which party will bear the risk of loss after shipment of the goods by the manufacturer. Ordinarily, the seller or purchaser will insure against loss or damage in transit. Determination of which party bears the responsibility, therefore, primarily affects the insurance requirements and thus the premium of each party. As a manufacturer it will be desirable to state that the risk of loss falls on the distributor. Assuming that the distributor is agreeable to such provision, the distributor may insist that the manufacturer will properly prepare and pack the goods for shipment.

Allocation. If the manufacturer periodically cannot maintain an adequate level of production to meet orders, it may become necessary to allocate production capacity until the crisis is past. Although this is typically done by simply filling orders on a first-come–first-serve basis, this may not be the most desirable customer policy. When a large volume order will substantially delay delivery on many smaller orders entered later, the manufacturer may want to allocate. To clarify that the manufacturer reserves the right to allocate, a statement should be included.

Acceptance of Orders. The agreement should also state that all orders received from the distributor are subject to acceptance by the manufacturer. Although this may seem obvious, it will foreclose the possibility that the distributor agreement itself will be construed as having created an obligation on behalf of the manufacturer to accept any order submitted by the distributor. When the financial condition of the distributor becomes impaired, the manufacturer may want to exercise its right to reject one or more orders of the distributor during the period of financial difficulty. If the manufacturer has a minimum dollar-order policy this should also be stated.

Returns. It is important that the manufacturer establish its policy with respect to the return of products. Normally, this is done by stating that the manufacturer is not obligated to receive returned products or to credit the distributor for any returned product unless the manufacturer authorizes such return for credit in writing. The manufacturer may also impose a restocking charge on returned goods.

A paragraph encompassing all these terms is as follows:

5.11   *Prices, Terms, and Sales Policy.* Sales of Products to DISTRIBUTOR shall be at the prices established by MANUFACTURER from time to time; current prices are set forth on the Distributor Price List attached to this agreement and identified as Exhibit C. All prices are FOB MANUFACTURER's plant. MANUFACTURER has the right to change all prices, terms, and conditions of sale and agrees to give DISTRIBUTOR thirty (30) days written notice of any such change.

The risk of loss due to damage or destruction of the Products shall be borne by DISTRIBUTOR after delivery by MANUFACTURER to a carrier for shipment. MANUFACTURER agrees to properly prepare and package all Products for customary methods of shipment.

MANUFACTURER will attempt to promptly fill all accepted orders, but MANUFACTURER has the right to allocate production or inventory according to its sole discretion.

DISTRIBUTOR shall make payment within thirty (30) days from the date of invoice. MANUFACTURER reserves the right to withhold shipment of accepted orders in the event DISTRIBUTOR fails to make timely payment for previous shipments.

All orders received from DISTRIBUTOR are subject to acceptance by MANUFACTURER.

Term

As in the sales representative agreement, the term may be either indefinite or for a fixed period of time. If an indefinite term is used, there must be a provision for termination by written notice within a fixed number of days. This type of Term paragraph is set forth in the sales representative agreement (Form 5.6). As noted in the discussion of a fixed term agreement in the context of the sales representative arrangement, provision must be made for termination for cause during the term. Furthermore, if the agreement will automatically renew for an additional term, a provision must be added for an election to terminate within a defined period prior to the expiration of the original or additional term.

A sample of a fixed term paragraph with the right to cancel for selected events follows:

5.12 *Term and Termination.*   This agreement shall continue for a period of five (5) years from the date of this agreement and shall automatically renew on the same terms and conditions for additional periods of one (1) year each unless one of the parties gives notice to the other of its election to terminate the agreement at least ninety (90) days prior to the end of any period.

This agreement may only be terminated by either party prior to the end of the original or additional periods for the following causes: (*a*) in the event that a party fails to perform any one or more of its obligations set forth in this agreement, notice may be given to such party giving sixty (60) days to remedy the same, and, on failure to remedy, this agreement shall terminate at the expiration of the sixty (60) days; (*b*) in the event that one party discontinues business, becomes insolvent, has a receiver appointed, goes into liquidation, or becomes a party to a bankruptcy or insolvency proceeding, notice may be given that terminates the agreement immediately.

Rights after Termination

If the agreement is terminated, provision should be made for the disposition of orders booked and orders placed shortly thereafter. The agreement should also define the rights of the parties with respect to the distributor's inventory.

Unlike the sales representative agreement, the manufacturer may take a soft position regarding orders. Orders that have been received and accepted must be filled. For orders placed by the distributor shortly after termination, there is no reason for the manufacturer to be restrictive about the period involved. Only if the manufacturer cancels the distributor to establish its own distribution and sales center or desires to immediately appoint another exclusive distributor should the post-termination honoring of orders be limited to a short period. After termination and selection of a new distributor, it will be necessary for the manufacturer to stock the new distribution point with sufficient product to accomplish a smooth transition. A 90-day period should therefore be easily acceptable to both the distributor and the manufacturer.

What should be done with the distributor's inventory? Normally, the manufacturer will repurchase it. The repurchase may be at the price paid by the distributor, including any freight costs incurred. The repurchase may be made optional, but the manufacturer will usually find that it is desirable to recover the goods. The repurchase should be conditioned on the products being returned in mint condition. An alternative approach is to charge the distributor for restocking in the event the distributor cancels the agreement but to repurchase the goods at full price if the manufacturer cancels the agreement.

A sample paragraph defining the rights after termination follows:

5.13 *Rights after Termination.* Upon termination, the terms of this agreement shall apply to any orders for Products from DISTRIBUTOR that have been accepted by MANUFACTURER and to any orders submitted by DISTRIBUTOR for a period of ninety (90) days after termination.

Upon termination, MANUFACTURER agrees to repurchase and DISTRIBUTOR agrees to sell, within one hundred twenty (120) days after termination, all Products in DISTRIBUTOR's inventory, purchased by DISTRIBUTOR within six (6) months before the date of termination, at the price paid by DISTRIBUTOR, including freight, provided that such Products are in new condition.

Prior to shipment by DISTRIBUTOR, MANUFACTURER shall have the right to inspect and examine all Products to be repurchased and to direct the shipment of the Products. DISTRIBUTOR will ship on MANUFACTURER's instruction, and MANUFACTURER shall make payment within ten (10) days after shipment.

Warranty

Every manufacturer is advised to have a warranty statement incorporated in sales literature, catalogs, and invoice and acknowledgment forms. Legal considerations in drafting the warranty, and a sample form, are contained in Chapter 7 (Form 7.7). In the distributor agreement, the warranty extended to the distributor should be identical to that given to the end user. Accordingly, the distributor paragraph on Warranty may simply incorporate the standard warranty into the agreement as an exhibit. If the standard warranty limits the warranty only to the purchaser, then the manufacturer should state expressly in the distributor agreement that the warranty may be passed on to the distributor's customer. There are, however, two additional matters that it may be advisable to include in the distributor agreement.

First, one of the purposes of establishing an express warranty statement is to negate certain warranties that the law implies. One troublesome implied warranty is that of "fitness for a particular purpose." The statement of the distributor may give rise to an implied warranty of the manufacturer. It is therefore recommended that a provision be included in the distributor agreement which cautions the distributor against making such warranty-creating statements. The provision should place on the distributor the sole obligation for any warranty claims based on its statements.

Second, it is reasonable to place additional obligations on the distributor with regard to the procedure and mechanism for warranty claims. The normal warranty provides that the goods must be inspected before the goods are returned for repair, replacement, or a credit. Most manufacturers would like to place other obligations on the buyer: a requirement that the warranty claim be made within a short, defined period; a condition that written authorization for return must be obtained before shipping goods back to the manufacturer; and a requirement that a report indicating the basis of the rejection must accompany the goods. In practice it would be difficult to enforce these warranty provisions, at least on consumers, and maintain good customer relations. But it is not unfair to place these additional burdens on the distributor, who may be expected to handle a large volume of goods and have the staff and facilities for complying with these additional requirements. A more orderly and easily administered warranty policy will result.

A recommended paragraph is as follows:

5.14   *Warranty.*   The standard warranty of MANUFACTURER, a copy of which is attached hereto as Exhibit D, shall apply to all sales to DISTRIBUTOR and resale to its customers. DISTRIBUTOR shall not make any representations, statements, or declarations to any customer of DISTRIBUTOR with respect to warranty that in any manner exceed the standard warranty. DISTRIBUTOR agrees to hold MANUFACTURER harmless from any claims, damages, or liabilities that may arise from use of the Products of MANUFACTURER where such claim, damage, or liability is based on representations, statements, or declarations of DISTRIBUTOR which exceed the standard warranty.

Liability of MANUFACTURER to DISTRIBUTOR under the standard warranty is conditioned on prompt written notice by DISTRIBUTOR to MANUFACTURER of any warranty claim, written authorization for the return of allegedly defective goods, and a written report from DISTRIBUTOR indicating the basis or reason for returning the goods.

Trademarks and Trade Name

In advertising the manufacturer's products, the distributor may want to use the manufacturer's trademarks and trade name. The manufacturer should have at least a basic understanding of the legal concepts that underlie trademarks and trade names for self-protection.

A *trademark* is a word, symbol, or device used on or in connection with the goods to identify such goods as those sold by the manufacturer as distinguished from goods sold by others. Unlike a patent or copyright, a trademark is created through first use rather than through a process of filing and examination by some governmental authority. It is protected under the common law doctrine of unfair competition (that encompasses, among other claims, common law trademark infringement). However, greater rights may be obtained by filing for a federal or state trademark registration that substantially proves and confirms that the trademark belongs solely to the user. If goods are shipped in interstate commerce bearing the trademark, federal trademark protection may be obtained; if the business is local, a state trademark registration may be available. Such statutory protection is recommended, for which the services of an attorney practicing in the specialized area of patents, trademarks, and unfair competition should be engaged. This protection precludes others from using the mark on similar goods or products.

By contrast, a *trade name* is the name of the manufacturer itself; it distinguishes one business from other businesses. It also is created through first use of the name and may be protected under the common law concept of unfair competition. Trade names are not normally protected by statute. If a business is incorporated, the state providing the charter for the corporation will generally have a procedure for examining names of existing corporations in that state. It will refuse to permit the use of a corporate name that is confusingly similar to one already existing. The search does not, however, purport to cover names of partnerships, corporate names approved in other states, fictitious names, or trademarks similar in sound or meaning. In many states, there are also laws that permit doing business under a fictitious name. Such laws usually simply record the name without an examination for confusing similarity and do not establish presumptive rights to use of the name.

The matter becomes confusing, since it is possible that a dominant portion of a trade name may also be used as a trademark. For example, Acme Inc. may sell a line of nuts and bolts under the trademark ACME. If the state authorities had permitted the corporation to be formed under the name Acme Inc., it will prevent any later company from being formed with a similar name. But this would not prevent a competitor from using the word ACME on goods sold in competition with Acme Inc. For this protection, the manufacturer would have to pursue the competitor with an action for trademark infringement under either common law or statutory rights. In carrying the illustration further, Acme Inc. could also begin using the term SUPER-X for a particular product line of nuts and bolts that it sells in commerce. Acme Inc. would then have trademark rights for the terms SUPER-X and ACME, in addition to its right to the tradename Acme Inc.

Suppose that Acme Inc., located in California, establishes a distributor in Florida. If a new business is being formed especially for the purpose of selling the ACME line of nuts and bolts, the distributor may want to select a corporate name such as Acme Inc. of Florida. This would be ill advised. Even though Acme Inc. was the first user of the trade name in California, the use of the name Acme Inc. of Florida may become associated in the minds of purchasers located in that state with the distributor rather than the manufacturer. If the relationship is ever severed, the distributor may procure a line of nuts and bolts from another manufacturer but may insist on continuing the use of "its name." Expensive litigation may result.

Suppose, however, that the manufacturer is eager to have its name widely used and recognized. The manufacturer will want to permit distributors to use both the manufacturer's trade name and trademark. The manufacturer may provide in the agreement that the distributor expressly has such right. But the agreement must further provide that on termination the distributor will discontinue any further use of the manufacturer's trade name (or any part thereof), trademark, or any confusingly similar word, term, or symbol that may be likely to lead to purchaser confusion.

A paragraph expressing and defining these rights is as follows:

5.15 *Trade Name and Trademark.* During the term of this agreement, DISTRIBUTOR may use the trademarks and trade names of MANUFACTURER in connection with the sale of MANUFAC-TURER's products on signs, advertising literature, catalogs, and other promotional materials. In the event of termination of this agreement, DISTRIBUTOR shall immediately discontinue use of such trade names and trademarks and shall not use any trade names or trademarks in connection with its business that, in the sole judgment of MANUFACTURER, is confusingly similar to the trade names and trademarks of MANUFACTURER.

Competing Products

Several factors may impel the manufacturer to prevent the distributor from selling competing products. If the distributor has an exclusive territory, the manufacturer is wholly dependent on complete dedication of the distributor to the manufacturer's line of products. Furthermore, if there is no minimum sales quota, there is no assurance the distributor may not handle a competing product with serious loss of sales to the manufacturer. The manufacturer may therefore choose to protect its interest by prohibiting the distributor from selling competitive products. Such provision is not without potential antitrust problems.

In the jargon of antitrust law, the prohibition against selling competing products is termed "exclusive dealing." Such restrictions are not automatically illegal but are scrutinized under what is termed the "rule of reason." For the manufacturer with a small market share and minimal economic leverage the fear of government attack is minor. But attack by the distributor is a definite possibility and could lead to expensive litigation, even if unsuccessful. For this reason, a provision against handling competing products should always be accompanied by a severability provision in the agreement, subject to the considerations surrounding the use of such provision as previously discussed. An appropriate paragraph is as follows:

5.16   *Competing Products.*   DISTRIBUTOR shall not sell any products that, in the sole judgment of MANUFACTURER, compete with the Products of MANUFACTURER. DISTRIBUTOR will submit a complete list of products and the name of the manufacturer of each product to MANUFACTURER on execution of this agreement, and at least once during each calendar quarter during which this agreement is in effect will submit in writing to MANUFAC-TURER any additional products (including the manufacturer's name) added to DISTRIBUTOR's line.

If desired, an option may be given to the distributor, preferably in the paragraph describing the products covered by the agreement, to decline to accept any new product that the manufacturer introduces. This permits the distributor to avoid handling competing products.

General

There are other clauses that may be required to fit differing circumstances. No form, or general discussion, can possibly include the myriad number of unique conditions that may arise for a particular manufacturer or for specific products. A few matters not covered above are mentioned subsequently.

As noted, the manufacturer may want to retain for itself the right to sell directly to certain national merchandising firms or mail-order houses. These may be specifically excluded from the agreement by carefully identifying the class of customers. An alternative is to pay the distributor a commission on sales made to customers in this proscribed class located in the distributor's territory just as in a sales representation agreement. This may ameliorate the distributor's objection to customer exclusion.

Quite common in distributor agreements is a provision for cooperative advertising. Advertising by the distributor should not be made mandatory. Therefore, the distributor and manufacturer will sign a separate agreement relating to cooperative advertising that may be incorporated by reference into the distributor agreement.

Some manufacturers permit a distributor to return slow-moving goods. This may be done on a one-time basis shortly after the start of the agreement. At the beginning, neither the manufacturer nor the distributor may be able to forecast realistically the product mix that should be carried by the distributor in the specific territory. A manufacturer may give the distributor the right to return items from this initial order after, for example, one year of operation. In other instances, a manufacturer will allow a distributor to periodically return slow-moving items either at full credit or with a restocking charge. The manufacturer should require the distributor to first obtain authorization for the proposed return, indicating the products, number of units, and so forth. From the manufacturer's point of view, this must be done very carefully. One method to prevent the return of old, obsolete products is to limit returns to products purchased within six months from the date of the request for return authorization.

Another potential product definition or exclusion problem occurs when the manufacturer makes identical products for sale under private label. Although this avoids intrabrand competition, the private label seller may still provide stiff competition to the distributor. This problem is not easily resolved, except by total prohibition of this practice. The effects of private labeling should be appraised carefully by the manufacturer as a matter of policy, before introducing it into the agreement.

Finally, there are selected boilerplate paragraphs that should be included. As in the rep agreement, these include Notices (Form 3.1), Governing Law (Form 3.3), Headings Not Controlling (Form 3.4), Entire Agreement (Form 3.2), Assignability (Form 3.8), and Severability (Form 3.9). Other provisions that may be considered would include Arbitration (Form 3.11) and Most-Favorable Terms (Form 3.14). A standard closing is used from Chapter 2.

Chapter Six
Purchasing

This chapter and the next are concerned with the very essence of business—the purchase and sale of goods. The purchase or sales contract is a unique species of contract, since it is usually not a single, negotiated document. Moreover, special rules of law apply—the UCC. In most business law courses, a general approach is used in studying the formation of contracts, regardless of the contract subject matter. These principles of law, however, are only dimly related to specific documents used in forming the purchase contract. It is therefore difficult to apply the theory to everyday business transactions. In contrast, the approach taken in these chapters is to examine the purchase contract from the point of view of the basic documents normally used.

In this chapter, the basic document reviewed is the Purchase Order; a recommended form is given. In Chapter 7, a recommended Sales Order or Acknowledgment (sometimes called an "Acceptance" or "Confirmation") is given, with emphasis on the differences between Purchase Order terms and Sales Order terms.

THE PURCHASE TRANSACTION

The purchase transaction is studied from the buyer's point of view; proper steps are outlined so that the buyer can obtain a contract on terms most favorable to itself. These steps attempt to control the formation of the contract by anticipating the documentary responses of the seller to parry their effect.

Why is control of the terms so important? In many instances, the differences between the terms of the buyer and those of the seller in the Acknowledgment may produce significantly different results. Some terms cover exceptional circumstances that arise only occasionally. But although infrequent, these circumstances can be of serious consequence. For example, a properly prepared Purchase Order will assure that the seller indemnifies against patent infringement. Perhaps only once in a lifetime will a buyer be sued by a patent owner, but the costs of that one defense can be catastrophic. On the other hand, situations that arise more often (a breach of warranty, nonaccepted goods, an attempt to make a change in the Purchase Order) can have, if not serious consequences, at least a disruptive effect on the buyer's everyday business activity. To place the matter in another light, all the care exercised in drafting terms to protect the buyer will be of no avail unless those terms are the final terms controlling the transaction.

Consider a simple transaction in which there has been no prior negotiation between the buyer and seller. The seller has provided a catalog or sales literature through the mail. The material provided will contain a physical description of the product, a technical specification, the seller's identification of the product (model or part number), and perhaps price. Normally, such sales literature does not constitute an offer to sell.

After reviewing the literature, the buyer sends a Purchase Order. The Purchase Order contains a list of terms favorable to the buyer. Assume a basic, simple Purchase Order that fails to contain a clause about which document will control the final purchase contract.

The Purchase Order constitutes an offer. It will incorporate the catalog description regarding the part number and price and will specify the quantity required and the date on which delivery is requested. These are the "nonstandard" terms; that is, they vary from transaction to transaction; the standard terms are contained on the reverse side of the document. Whether the standard terms will prevail depends on what the seller does in response to the Purchase Order. Several hypothetical situations illuminate the effects of varying the basic Purchase Order and show that the documents exchanged and the conduct of the parties affect the final result.

First, suppose that the Purchase Order form of the buyer includes a duplicate copy entitled "Acknowledgment" that instructs the seller to execute the Acknowledgment at a space provided on the copy and return it to the buyer. If the seller signs and returns such Acknowledgment copy, the contract is formed on the buyer's Purchase Order terms at the time the Acknowledgment is mailed. This is straightforward and results in a contract on terms favorable to the buyer.

Second, suppose that there is no Acknowledgment copy with the buyer's Purchase Order form. The seller, however, returns a "clean" Acknowledgment. A *clean* Acknowledgment is one that has no terms or conditions (usually favorable to the seller) and simply provides notice that the Purchase Order has been received and accepted. A contract is formed on the buyer's terms as set forth in the Purchase Order when the seller mails the clean Acknowledgment.

Third, suppose that the buyer uses an Acknowledgment copy with the Purchase Order (requesting that the copy be signed and returned) but the seller ignores this form and instead returns a clean Acknowledgment. This is probably an unusual situation. Whether a contract is formed, and on what terms, depends on the language in the Acknowledgment copy attached to the buyer's Purchase Order. If the Acknowledgment copy states in effect that "this order may be accepted only by signing and returning the attached Acknowledgment," no contract is formed when the seller sends the clean Acknowledgment of its own. If the seller later ships the goods, and they are accepted by the buyer, a contract is made, formed in part by documents and in part by the conduct of the parties. It is probable, although not certain, that the contract is on the buyer's favorable terms.

Fourth, suppose that the buyer uses a Purchase Order form, either with or without the Acknowledgment copy, and the seller uses its own Acknowledgment document. Terms of the Acknowledgment are, of course, favorable to the seller and conflict with those of the Purchase Order. The battle of forms is now joined. Under general contract theory, since the Acknowledgment of the seller was not a "mirror image" of the buyer's Purchase Order (offer), there is no acceptance and no contract would be formed by the exchange of documents. But UCC Section 2-207 changes this long-standing rule of law, with great consternation to commercial lawyers. It replaced the certainty that a contract was not formed with— it depends.

It depends on the language of the seller's Acknowledgment. If the Acknowledgment states that "this acceptance is expressly conditional on assent to the additional or different terms contained herein," no contract is formed so far in the exchange. However, if this conditional Acknowledgment includes a place for execution by the buyer, and if it is executed and returned to the seller, a contract will be formed on the seller's terms. If the buyer does not respond to the conditional Acknowledgment (the usual situation) and shipment follows from the seller, with acceptance of the goods by the buyer, then the conduct of the buyer and seller forms a contract at the time the goods are accepted. But on what terms is the contract based? Under the UCC, the contract contains all the terms in the Purchase Order and Acknowledgment that are in agreement, but none of those which are in conflict, plus all the rules set forth in the UCC. Since some but not all of the rules of the UCC are favorable to the buyer (for example, implied warranties), the buyer may not be in the best of positions, but at least it will not be in the worst.

Fifth, suppose that the seller's Acknowledgment is not conditional on the assent by the buyer to the additional or different terms it contains. What then happens depends on the terms in the Purchase Order. If the

Purchase Order states that "it expressly limits acceptance to the Purchase Order terms," then all the different terms in the seller's Acknowledgment are merely refused proposals. This statement is the most critical clause in the Purchase Order. Without the statement, the additional terms of the seller would have been automatically incorporated in the contract so long as the terms did not "materially alter" the terms of the Purchase Order or the buyer had not notified the seller that it objected to such terms. But with the statement, a contract is formed on the terms of the Purchase Order.

What advice do these hypothetical situations offer? The answer is simply this. The Purchase Order should be drafted so that it expressly limits acceptance to its terms, then (a) if the seller does nothing but ships the goods, a contract is formed on the buyer's favorable terms; (b) if the seller sends a clean Acknowledgment, a contract is formed on buyer's favorable terms; (c) if the seller sends a "dirty" Acknowledgment, all the additional terms of the seller are rejected proposals and the contract is formed on the buyer's favorable terms, *provided* that the buyer does not sign the seller's Acknowledgment form; and (d) if the seller's dirty Acknowledgment is of the "expressly conditional" type, no contract is formed in the document exchange; but if the seller later ships and the goods are accepted, a contract is formed by conduct, and the compatible terms in the documents, plus the UCC rules of law comprise the contract terms.

Thus the "limited acceptance" Purchase Order, plus unequivocal instructions to the purchasing department not to sign a dirty Acknowledgment will always produce the best results. For the small business, if a large seller insists on the execution of the Acknowledgment before shipment there may be no choice. But if the seller so insists, and the purchasing department is properly instructed, the matter will be brought to the attention of top management that can then decide what to do. This is precisely the purpose of the UCC rule: to escalate the war of the forms to the level of negotiation if the matter is of serious consequence to the parties.

Combinations and permutations of the documents and conduct become more complex if the document exchange starts with a quotation from the seller. The quotation, if properly drafted, constitutes the offer; and the Purchase Order, if clean, would constitute the acceptance, forming a contract on the seller's terms. If the Purchase Order is not clean (the usual case), the analysis must be pursued using a methodology such as that in the foregoing. Advice for the quotation form is found in the next chapter (terms favorable to the seller).

With this unfortunately belabored explanation as background, a recommended Purchase Order follows.

PURCHASE ORDER

The following paragraphs are suggested for the company's standard Purchase Order. These terms are printed on the reverse side of the Purchase Order, preferably in as large a type as possible. On the face of the Purchase Order, a sentence must be included that incorporates all these terms and conditions into the offer to purchase. This statement additionally calls the seller's attention to the terms that the buyer intends to govern the transaction. A suitable sentence reads: "This Offer is Subject to the Terms and Conditions on the Face and Reverse Side of this Purchase Order."

The draftsman must again be cautioned that the terms and conditions that are here recommended for the Purchase Order are not exhaustive. The nature of the materials purchased and purchasing customs in the industry may require special terms. Terms and conditions unique to an industry may be found by examining purchase orders of other corporations in the industry.

The recommended Purchase Order in this chapter is specifically drawn for the smaller business. There is no attempt here to include detailed provisions relating to government contracts. Instead, since the small business will normally be in a subcontractor status, a general provision is used to incorporate by reference all the terms of the prime contract for which the goods are being purchased.

Acceptance

As pointed out earlier, the most critical provision in the documents which define a purchase transaction is that which determines which party's terms and conditions control. Following the argument advanced previously, the Acceptance paragraph should prevent additional terms in the seller's Acknowledgment from becoming part of the contract. Unless the seller's acceptance is expressly made conditional on the additional or different terms contained in the acceptance, a contract will be immediately formed with all the additional terms constituting refused proposals. The paragraph should go on to state that in the event the seller ships, such conduct will constitute an acceptance of the Purchase Order terms. It was also noted earlier that in addition to the use of this provision in the Purchase Order the best effect (i.e., the terms most favorable to the buyer) also requires that the purchasing department of the buyer be directed not to execute any Acknowledgment sent by the seller without first calling the matter to the attention of management.

The following paragraph is recommended:

6.1   *Acceptance.*   Acceptance of this order is expressly limited to the terms and conditions of this order, and none of Seller's terms and conditions shall apply in acknowledging this order or the acceptance of this order unless agreed to in writing by an authorized representative of Purchaser. If any part of the goods ordered is shipped by Seller, such conduct will constitute an acceptance of the terms and conditions of this order. Acceptance of any part of the goods delivered by Seller in response to this Purchase Order will not constitute acceptance of Seller's terms and conditions.

Delivery

There are four points that should be made regarding delivery. First, it should be stated that "time is of the essence" to the transaction. These are words of art long used in legal documents to express the idea that time or dates specified in the contract are not simply approximate but are in fact critical. Presumably, the buyer will have carefully considered the requested delivery date in the Purchase Order and is anxious to receive the goods at the specified time. Should a dispute arise about consequential damages resulting from delayed delivery, this phrase will be of value to the buyer.

The second matter relates to late delivery. The buyer should retain the right to cancel the Purchase Order in the event that the designated delivery date cannot be met. This right will be a valuable bargaining tool in expediting late delivery. It may also be desirable to state that the seller is obligated to ship by an expedited method, if late, but without any additional charge to the buyer.

Third is the opposite problem: early delivery. Particularly with respect to a large dollar-volume order or a blanket Purchase Order with scheduled releases, early delivery by the seller can aggravate cash flow problems of the buyer. The seller will invariably invoice on shipment and will expect payment on its specified terms as measured from the shipping date (or invoice date), disregarding the fact that shipment was improperly early. The buyer should reserve the right to return such goods delivered early at the seller's expense or to make payment based on the scheduled delivery rather than the actual delivery.

Fourth, the buyer should anticipate that the seller's Acknowledgment will include a paragraph that excuses late delivery for acts beyond the control of the parties. The buyer's paragraph should assent to excused late delivery but only on the condition that the seller promptly notify the buyer that some event has resulted in a necessary delay.

The delivery paragraph should read as follows:

6.2 *Delivery.* Time is of the essence in the performance of this order by Seller. If Seller fails to make delivery within the time specified, Buyer shall have the right to cancel this order and return any partial shipment previously made at Seller's expense. In the event that Seller makes early delivery, Buyer may, at its option, either retain the goods received or return them to the Seller at Seller's expense; if retained, time for payment and discount shall be based on the scheduled delivery date. In the event that Seller cannot meet the scheduled delivery date, or has failed to deliver on schedule, Seller shall ship by expedited means at Seller's expense. Seller shall not be liable for delay in delivery as a result of causes beyond Seller's control, provided that Seller promptly notifies Buyer of the events which result in the delay.

Shipping

Three matters should be covered here: packing, instructions, and insurance.

The buyer should specify that the goods should be suitably packed to obtain the lowest freight rate. To permit efficient receipt of goods in the shipping and receiving department, the buyer may want to specify that all containers must be marked with the buyer's Purchase Order and that any Bill of Lading must also bear the Purchase Order number. The buyer should also specify that it will not pay for any packing charges unless specifically agreed to in writing. This may be particularly important in purchasing heavy or large equipment.

It is standard commercial practice for the seller to provide that the risk of loss is transferred to the buyer on delivery of the goods to the carrier when sale is made FOB the seller's factory. It is inadvisable to attempt to preclude this shift of responsibility for loss or damage to the goods in the Purchase Order. Normally, the buyer's comprehensive insurance package policy will include All Risk Transportation Insurance that will cover such loss. Assuming that the buyer has such insurance, the seller should be advised that it should not procure insurance on the shipment on the buyer's behalf and charge the buyer for such double coverage. Since it would be unusual for the seller to procure such insurance for the buyer, this provision could be omitted.

Finally, the buyer may want to control the routing, method, and even the freight company for the shipment. If the buyer requires the goods immediately, it may be willing to pay for expedited shipping and will provide instructions to use the more expensive shipping method. Or the buyer may find that a particular carrier (in its geographic area) may be undesirable for lack of reliability or care in the handling of goods. The buyer may want to specify a specific carrier and have its instructions complied with.

The following paragraph incorporates several of these points:

6.3   *Shipping.* Goods must be packed and prepared for shipment to secure lowest transportation rates and comply with carrier regulations. Buyer will not pay for packing or crating unless stated in this order. Each container must be identified with Buyer's Purchase Order number that must also be indicated on Bills of Lading. Seller shall comply with Buyer's shipping and routing instructions and shall not use premium cost transportation unless authorized by Buyer.

Changes

The buyer would like to maintain the right to make changes in the Purchase Order at any time up to delivery. To what extent is this permissible, and what is the effect of a change order? These questions go to the heart of the purchase contract. If the buyer retains full right of cancellation of the entire order then the contract is illusory; that is, there simply is no promise to purchase. But if there is no promise to purchase, does the seller have the obligation to deliver? A contract is formed when the mutual promises of the parties serve as the consideration to create a binding obligation. If one party's promise may be withdrawn at will, is there a contract at all?

However, minor unilateral modifications of the contract should certainly be permissible, since they do not go to the substance of the agreement. For example, a change in the date on which delivery is required, a change of where the delivery is to be made, or a change in the specification of the goods (that does not materially alter the original goods) would clearly be minor variations of the purchase contract.

If, however, the buyer wants to change the quantity of goods ordered, it is more difficult to classify the variation as minor or substantial. The solution is to provide for an adjustment to the contract based on the change. For example, if the Purchase Order specified a quantity that qualified for a quantity discount, and the quantity is reduced, the price may be increased. Similarly, a change to a specification may increase the price. Or the change may have an effect on the promised delivery date that must be modified accordingly.

The following paragraph provides for maximum flexibility in order changes:

6.4 *Changes.* At any time prior to shipment, Buyer may make changes to this order with respect to the following: specification, method of shipment or packing, time and place of delivery, and quantity of goods. If any such change causes an increase or decrease in the cost of goods, or the time required for performance, an equitable adjustment shall be made accordingly. Seller must make any claim for adjustment under this clause within thirty (30) days from the date of receipt by Seller of the change to this order.

Inspection and Acceptance

This paragraph provides the purchaser with the right to reject goods and specifies the remedies to which the purchaser is entitled on such rejection. It is important to recognize the distinction between those rights of the purchaser based on the seller's warranty, or any implied warranty, and the broader right to reject goods. A rejection may be based on a breach of warranty, but it is not limited to that single type of breach. It is preferable to express the right to reject goods on the failure of the seller to comply with *any* of the terms of the Purchase Order.

It is common to first provide that acceptance of the goods is subject to final inspection at the premises of the buyer. The reason for this provision is to prevent a premature acceptance by the buyer should the buyer specify a performance test to be conducted by the seller or should the buyer visit the seller's premises before shipment of the goods. Occasionally, the buyer may visit the seller while the goods are being processed or tested, and the seller may contend that this constituted an acceptance by the buyer precluding any further inspection.

Under the UCC, it is clear that payment for the goods does not in itself constitute an acceptance and preclude any rejection based on final inspection. Nevertheless, some draftsmen prefer to point out that the right to final inspection survives such payment.

The clause should also provide the basis or criterion on which the buyer will reject goods. Normally, this is done through use of the term "nonconforming" goods. *Nonconforming goods* are those in which there is a defect in material or workmanship or those that otherwise fail to meet the specification the seller has established in its description of the goods and on which the purchase contract is based. Some draftsmen prefer to detail the method of inspection and the basis on which the buyer will reject goods in greater detail. For example, the Purchase Order may recite that inspection will be based on statistical sampling in accordance with Military Standard 105. The clause may then further provide that if defects within the sample exceed an amount acceptable to the buyer, the entire lot will be rejected. Whether this detail is advisable will depend on the specific method of incoming inspection used by the buyer and the cost of 100% screening in the event that sampling is used.

Having established the criterion for rejecting the goods, the clause should provide for the remedies the buyer may pursue. There are essentially six remedies a buyer may seek normally. There are two remedies involving return. First, the buyer may return the goods, at the risk and expense of the seller, for credit, without permitting the seller to replace the goods. Second, the goods may be returned to the seller, requiring prompt correction or replacement of the goods.

As opposed to returning the goods, the buyer may elect to retain the goods. The third remedy allows the buyer to offset any defect in the goods against the established purchase price, thus in effect constituting an acceptance of slightly defective goods at a correspondingly reduced price. Fourth, the seller may elect to retain the goods but to fix the defects or replace some component to render the goods acceptable and then charge the seller for material and labor used.

In addition to the options to return or retain the goods, the fifth remedy allows the buyer to cancel the Purchase Order. This may be particularly important for the blanket Purchase Order transaction with scheduled deliveries. The clause should provide that such cancellation is effective, except for those goods which are conforming and accepted, and that the right to cancel may be exercised whether only some or all of the goods are nonconforming. The sixth remedy gives the buyer the right to recover consequential and incidental damages suffered by the buyer because of the breach. Finally, the paragraph should point out that these six remedies are not exclusive but that the buyer retains all other remedies provided by law.

A recommended paragraph is as follows:

6.5 *Inspection and Acceptance.* All goods will be subject to final inspection and acceptance at the premises of Buyer. In the event of Seller's breach of any warranty or agreement of Seller, Buyer may (*a*) return nonconforming goods to Seller, at Seller's risk and expense, for full credit and without replacement; (*b*) return nonconforming goods, at Seller's risk and expense, and require prompt correction or replacement without additional cost to Buyer; (*c*) retain nonconforming goods and correct or replace such goods and charge Seller with the expense; or (*d*) retain nonconforming goods and set off losses against any amounts due seller. In the event of breach of any agreement of Seller, in addition to the remedies set forth above, Buyer may cancel any part or all of this order without liability, except in regard to conforming goods delivered and accepted by Buyer, regardless of whether the breach goes to part or all of the goods, and Buyer may recover consequential and incidental damages from Seller incurred by Buyer as a result of such breach. In addition to the rights and remedies provided in this clause, Buyer shall have all the rights and remedies provided by law, and such rights and remedies shall be cumulative and may be exercised from time to time.

Warranty

The Purchase Order may require certain warranties to be applicable to the goods. First, since the buyer will have chosen the goods based on information submitted by the seller, conformance to this information should be expressly warranted by the seller. The warranty may include specifications contained in technical literature of the seller, drawings provided by the seller, and performance data the seller has used to describe the goods. All these documents are simply incorporated by reference into the Purchase Order to constitute the basis of an express warranty by the seller.

Second, the buyer should state that the goods are expressly warranted by the seller to be "merchantable," a term used in the common law that is applicable to sales transactions and codified in the UCC. The term posits a standard against which the goods may be measured: the goods must be fit for the ordinary purposes for which such goods are used and generally acceptable in that line of trade under the description used in the Purchase Order. To paraphrase UCC Section 2-314, the goods must be of a quality that they will (a) pass without objection in the trade under the Purchase Order description; (b) if "fungible" (a mass of units of equivalent kind and quality which are for practical purposes indistinguishable and interchangeable), be of fair average quality; (c) be fit for the ordinary purposes for which such goods are used; (d) be generally of even kind, quality, and quantity within each unit and among units; (e) be adequately contained, packaged, and labeled; and (f) conform to the promises of fact made on the label or accompanying description. In a sale by a manufacturer or supplier of goods this warranty is implied unless it is specifically disclaimed by the seller. However, if the seller is not engaged in the business of supplying such goods the warranty of merchantability is not applicable. For example, if goods are purchased from a private individual not engaged in any business this warranty would not arise.

Third, there should be a warranty that the goods contain good material and workmanship and are free from any defects in material, labor, or fabrication. The object of this warranty is apparent.

Fourth, the seller should be made to expressly warrant that the goods are fit for the particular purposes of the buyer. This is another implied warranty that the common law created and which was incorporated into the UCC. The expression "fit for the particular purposes" of the buyer is also a term of art. As noted earlier, the warranty of merchantability establishes only that the goods are fit for "ordinary purposes" for which the goods are used. However, if the seller knows the *particular* purpose that the buyer intends to make of the goods and the buyer relies on the seller's skill or judgment in furnishing suitable goods, an additional warranty is created. Since it may be difficult for the buyer to prove in a later dispute what the seller knew, or should have known, and that the buyer relied on the seller's judgment in furnishing suitable goods, it is highly advantageous to the buyer to make this warranty express. An express warranty will obviate the proof necessary to establish an implied warranty. Without this express language, a valuable warranty may be lost.

To what extent can the buyer successfully fasten these warranties on the seller? Normally, a seller will warrant that the goods conform to the data or specification submitted, that the goods are of good material and workmanship, and that the goods are free from defects. But the warranties of merchantability and fitness for a particular purpose are commonly disclaimed by the seller. When properly done, this disclaimer is perfectly legal and enforceable. It is therefore highly likely that the buyer's terms for these warranties will be in direct conflict with the terms in the seller's Acknowledgment or Acceptance. Control of the warranty provisions is an excellent example of the importance of including an Acceptance clause by which the buyer's terms prevail in the battle of the forms. The buyer is in an advantageous position with respect to warranty provision conflicts. If the buyer's terms fail to control, the conflicting provisions are excised from the documents, but the conduct of the parties creates a contract, and the implied warranty sections of the UCC will be applicable. In other words, with respect to merchantability, the buyer is in as good a position as if its express warranty on merchantability controlled. With respect to fitness for a particular purpose, the buyer will have the added proofs, discussed previously, but it may still be able to establish the warranty.

The warranty clause should also state that the warranties will survive the acceptance of the goods by the buyer. It is commonly stated that such warranties survive inspection, acceptance, and payment. The reason for this provision is to forestall an argument by the seller that the warranties were extinguished when the buyer inspected and accepted the goods and then made payment. This argument may be advanced strenuously by the seller if there are defects in the goods that inspection should have disclosed but were not found.

The warranty clause should further identify what parties are to be protected by the warranty. This would of course include the buyer, but reference should also be made to the buyers' employees and customers and any users of the goods. The term "users" is a catch-all word that will include persons other than the buyer and its customers.

These are the standard provisions to be included in the warranty clause. It should be understood, however, that other promises extracted from the seller could also be included in warranty form. For example, it may be necessary in the buyer's business to assure that the seller has good title to the goods. If the buyer purchases used goods or equipment from dealers engaged in that business, it may be desirable to include a warranty of title. A warranty of title will further protect against liens or encumbrances a third party may have levied on the goods.

A form paragraph for the common warranties is as follows:

6.6   *Warranty.* All specifications, drawings, and other data submitted to Buyer are incorporated by reference into this order and the Seller expressly warrants that the goods or services shall conform to this data. Goods delivered are expressly warranted by Seller to be merchantable, of good material and workmanship, free from any defect in material, labor, or fabrication, and fit for the particular purpose of Buyer. All warranties shall survive inspection, tests, acceptance, and payment for goods and shall run to Buyer and its employees, customers, and other users.

Patent Indemnity

The sole purpose of this clause is to prevent the buyer from becoming embroiled in litigation between the seller and a patent owner. This clause obligates the seller to save the buyer harmless from liabilities for infringement and to fix on the seller the obligation to defend any lawsuit for infringement. The clause should protect not only buyer but also others in the chain of sale. It must include claims not only for patent infringement but also for other types of statutory and common law rights that may be asserted by a third party. It normally includes an exception if the goods are made to the buyer's specification. It occasionally includes specific provisions to protect the buyer against an injunction issued by a court against the buyer's use or sale of the goods.

The save harmless portion of the clause is relatively straightforward. It should include not merely liabilities and damages that may be assessed against the buyer in a suit brought by a third party but also against claims made by such third party as well as the lawsuit itself. Why is it necessary to have any protection at all? The reason stems from the nature of patent rights. The patent owner has the right to prevent not only the making of the infringing goods but also the use and sale. Therefore, the patent owner has the perfect right to press its claim against the buyer rather than the seller. Is it not likely that the third party would rather pursue the seller and stop the infringement at its source? It may be likely, but it is not necessarily so. The patent owner may prefer to sue the buyer in a local court, if they are both in the same geographic territory, rather than to institute a lawsuit in some remote court where the seller is located. The third party may pursue the buyer expecting an easy capitulation, particularly if the buyer is small. Conversely, if the buyer is large, the third party may see a more financially viable defendant. Or the buyer may be a competitor of the third party rather than the seller, and the suit may be used to harass and intimidate the buyer, causing disruption of the buyer's business for the competitive advantage the third party may obtain. Because patent infringement suits may result in large damage awards, the necessity of a save harmless is clear.

The clause should provide further that the seller will defend the buyer in any suit brought by a third party. Patent litigation is notoriously expensive. Even the cost of a nominal defense can be substantial. Thus the buyer should be relieved not only of the potential damage award under the save harmless provision but also should be relieved of the burden of defense.

Similar to the warranty clause, it is also desirable to set forth the identity of the persons who will be protected under the patent indemnity clause. Again, this should include the buyer and its customers and any users.

Although the clause is normally denominated an indemnification against a patent violation, other claims should also be included. In addition to patent infringement, a third party may press a claim for trademark infringement, copyright infringement, or unfair competition. The latter would include suits brought for breach of a confidential relationship, such as a trade secret claim. Like patent infringement suits, trade secret cases are prevalent in high-technology industries and can arise in diverse ways. They are also notoriously expensive.

The buyer should be protected against claims for goods designed and manufactured by the seller, but it cannot expect such protection if it has induced the infringement. The situation arises when the transaction does not involve standard, off-the-shelf goods of the seller. The buyer may approach the seller with a specific design and ask the seller to manufacture goods in accordance with such design. If it is the buyer's design that infringes the proprietary rights of a third party, then the buyer should be made to bear the consequences. Accordingly, it is common to set forth an exception in the patent indemnity clause stating that if the goods are manufactured in accordance with the buyer's design, the seller is not required to indemnify against a third-party claim. This exception will often be imposed by the seller in the absence of a provision in the buyer's Purchase Order. But the buyer can state the exception in a form most advantageous to itself. Occasionally, the buyer may provide a general specification or design, thus permitting the seller some latitude in the specific design of the manufactured goods. One design may infringe and another may not. The mere fact of the buyer's having provided a general specification should not cause it to lose its indemnification. To protect against this ambiguous case, it should be recited that the exception applies only when the seller used a design "required" to comply with the instructions, specification, or general design submitted by the buyer.

Although not mandatory, one additional provision may be included in the patent indemnity clause. In a patent infringement suit, the patent owner is entitled not only to damages but also to an injunction issued by a court that prevents the defendant from making, using, or selling the infringing product. If the subject matter of the transaction is a large, complex production machine, for example, and the patent owner is successful against the seller in an infringement suit, the injunction could prevent further use of the machine. This could greatly disrupt the buyer's business. If this prospect is likely, then the clause can provide that in the event of such injunction, the seller must (a) replace the infringing device, (b) procure a license from the patent owner permitting the buyer to continue use of the infringing device, or (c) remove the equipment and refund the purchase price. For the small business owner, the necessity of this additional provision in the Purchase Order form is optional. Consideration, however, may be given to this type of clause as a special term to be included in the purchase of a critical piece of equipment that is not easily obtainable from another source.

The recommended clause is as follows:

6.7 *Patent Indemnity.* The Seller agrees to defend at its own expense Buyer and its customers and users of the products of Buyer and to hold them harmless with respect to any and all claims that the products or materials furnished by the Seller under this order infringe any patent, trademark, copyright, or other proprietary rights of third parties with respect to all suits, demands, and liabilities arising out of any such claims. This provision shall not apply to any claim based on the Seller's use of a design required to comply with the written instructions of Buyer if such design is not normally utilized by Seller.

Indemnification

To indemnify a person is simply to promise to compensate or reimburse the person for a loss after it is established. As noted in the patent clause just discussed, such loss could be due to patent infringement. But indemnification is a broad concept encompassing any damages sustained by the buyer; it could be based on a personal injury claim brought by a third party against the buyer on a warranty claim. Occasionally, the indemnification clause in a Purchase Order is used in this broad sense and applies to losses sustained by the buyer arising from or in consequence of any performance based on the Purchase Order. However, it is more commonly used in a much narrower sense.

The indemnification is usually limited to losses that arise from actions taken by the seller's employees on the premises of the buyer. This is common when the goods must be installed on the buyer's premises. In the usual contract of insurance covering personal injury or property damage, the buyer is insured against any claims brought by persons on the buyer's premises because of acts of the buyer's own employees or agents. Such insurance does not cover claims arising from conduct on the buyer's premises, however, when it is the seller's employees or agents whose conduct causes the damage or injury. It is therefore desirable to specifically provide in the Purchase Order that the seller will indemnify the buyer against claims based on the conduct of the seller's employees.

This clause may read as follows:

6.8 *Indemnification.* If Seller's work under this order involves operations by Seller on the premises of Buyer or a customer of Buyer, Seller shall take all necessary precautions to prevent the occurrence of any injury to person or property during such work and, except to the extent that any such injury or damage is due solely and directly to Buyer's negligence, shall indemnify Buyer against all loss from any act or omission of Seller, and its agents, employees, or subcontractors. Seller shall maintain such Public Liability, Property Damage, and Employer's Liability and Compensation Insurance as will protect Buyer from such claims under any applicable Workman's Compensation laws.

Buyer's Property

The object of this clause is to clearly define the rights of the buyer to tooling, equipment, or material furnished or paid for by the buyer. It is a common occurrence for the buyer to furnish materials on which the seller will perform some services. These materials may be procured by the buyer from one source and sent to the seller for some secondary operation such as painting, machining, heat treating, or the like. Or the goods may have been created by the buyer and sent to the seller for similar purposes. A second type of occurrence is when materials or equipment are paid for by the buyer and maintained on the seller's premises. This could include tooling built by the seller, and for which the buyer has expressly agreed to pay, that is then maintained on the seller's premises for subsequent orders. Or it could be bulk materials purchased by the buyer and stored on the seller's premises and used to fill subsequent orders. In either event, it is necessary to clearly establish the buyer's right to such property and to also describe the obligations of the seller with respect to the property.

Defining the seller's obligations will greatly depend on the nature of the business and the goods involved. There are six duties of the seller that may be stated succinctly and are of general applicability. First, the seller should be obliged to use the material or tooling only for filling orders of the buyer. This serves the dual purpose of preventing use for a competitor of the buyer and controlling the wear and tear on the tooling. Second, the seller should be prohibited from disclosing, particularly tooling or equipment, to third parties. Special jigs, dies, or tooling can often disclose proprietary designs that have been created by the buyer and which are embodied in the equipment.

The other four terms relate specifically to maintenance and protection of the material or tooling itself. The seller's third obligation should be to safely store the material or tooling at its risk and to be responsible for any loss or damage of the buyer's property. Fourth, the tooling or material should be marked by the seller so that it remains readily identifiable as the property of buyer. For material, this may be done by marking the goods or by providing a bin or other storage area where the buyer's goods are apportioned from material of others. Fifth, the seller should be obligated to maintain the material or equipment in good condition, wear and tear excepted. Sixth, it should be made clear that the buyer has the right to remove the material or equipment from the seller's premises, and the seller should agree to follow the buyer's directions and to ship as instructed.

This list is not exhaustive. Again, the draftsman is reminded that the particular nature of the business may call for additional provisions and further definition of the seller's duties. A typical clause embodying the foregoing ideas is as follows:

6.9 *Buyer's Property.* All materials, tools, plates, artwork, film, drawings, specifications, and similar items furnished or paid for by Buyer shall be clearly identified as Buyer's property. Seller agrees that it will use such property only for filling orders of Buyer and will treat such property confidentially and not disclose it to any third party. Seller shall safely store such property, shall be responsible for loss or damage to such property, and shall return such property to Buyer in good condition, normal wear and tear excepted. Such property shall be subject to removal at Buyer's written request in which event Seller shall prepare such property for shipment and shall redeliver it to Buyer at no expense except for transportation.

Proprietary Information of Seller

This clause, and the one following, relates to the proprietary rights of the parties and their respective obligations with respect to information obtained from one another. In this clause, protection is provided for the buyer against a claim by the seller for theft of trade secrets or breach of a confidential relationship. Since information generally distributed by the seller enters the public domain, this clause is directed to information that the seller has prepared specifically for the buyer (and perhaps a few other selected customers). The information from the seller may not be contained in the goods alone. The seller may manufacture the goods using a proprietary process or some proprietary composition of material. In the course of negotiating the purchase, the seller may disclose such information to the buyer when explaining the quality or construction of the goods. The buyer must take care that it is not ensnared into a confidential status which could subsequently prevent it from disclosing such information to a competitor of the seller which is a second source of the goods.

This clause is short and explicit:

6.10 *Seller's Information.* Unless expressly agreed to in writing by Buyer, no information or knowledge disclosed to Buyer in the performance of or in connection with this order shall be claimed by Seller as confidential or proprietary, and any such information or knowledge shall be free from any restrictions on Buyer and is submitted to Buyer as part of the consideration for this order.

Buyer's Information

The converse of the above clause is to define the rights of the parties regarding any confidential information disclosed by the buyer to the seller. Such confidential information may be contained in drawings, specifications, or prototypes delivered by the buyer to the seller in the course of negotiating or performing the sale. The seller is simply obligated not to disclose such information and to hold it confidential. Similar to the above clause with respect to buyer's tangible property, the seller should be obligated to return the confidential information to buyer at buyer's request.

A typical clause reads:

6.11 *Buyer's Information.* Unless otherwise specifically agreed on in writing, all specifications, documents, and prototype articles delivered by Buyer to Seller are the property of Buyer. Such property is delivered solely for the purpose of Seller's performance of this order and on the express condition that the information contained therein shall not be disclosed to others or used for any purposes other than in connection with this order. Such property is to be returned to Buyer promptly on its written request during or after completion of Seller's performance. This obligation shall survive the cancellation, termination, or completion of this order.

Nonassignment

This clause is essentially boilerplate but tailored slightly for a purchase transaction. The purpose is to prevent the Purchase Order from being transferred to a supplier that the buyer would find less agreeable. Such an attempt by a seller would not be a common event, but the inclusion of the clause is justified because of the potential harm that may result when a large Purchase Order is involved.

The nonassignment clause further would prevent a transfer of money payable from the buyer to the seller. The problem arises when the seller assigns not the order but the resulting accounts receivable. If the goods are subsequently rejected, or the buyer must assert a claim for breach of warranty, such assignment may prevent the buyer from asserting a setoff or complete nonpayment. Since it is not unlikely that a seller will assign the accounts receivable, the clause provides for consent and reserves the right of setoff for any present or future claims of the buyer.

The matter may be carried one step further by precluding the seller from subconstracting to others a substantial portion of the order. The necessity for this additional protection is not believed to be sufficiently justifiable but is left as a matter of preference for the draftsman.

A typical paragraph would state:

6.12 *Nonassignment.* This Purchase Order or money payable as a result of this order shall not be assigned in whole or in part by operation of law or otherwise without Buyer's written consent. In the event of such consent, any assignee's rights shall be subject to set-off or recoupment for any present or future claims Buyer may have against Seller.

Termination

The right to terminate the Purchase Order may be made dependent on the occurrence of some specific act or may be permitted without cause.

In the event of bankruptcy or insolvency, the buyer should have the right to terminate the Purchase Order. As noted in other parts of this book, bankruptcy or insolvency by one contractual partner raises numerous difficulties for the other. Regardless of the relationship between the parties, it is almost always advisable to terminate the relationship rather than to attempt to deal with the bankrupt party's trustee, receiver, or creditors. This holds true for even a simple sales transaction. Delay and frustration are the common result when dealing with a bankrupt. A termination clause for bankruptcy is recommended.

The other event that should be made a ground for cancellation is a breach of any of the terms of the agreement by the seller. While the buyer may want to pursue other remedies, depending on the nature of the default, the buyer is also advised to have the right to terminate for a breach.

The matter of termination without cause is not so easily resolved. If the buyer can terminate at will, then the agreement itself may be illusory. If the buyer can terminate at any time before the goods are delivered, the promise to purchase is lacking, yet this is precisely the consideration that supports the legal enforceability of the agreement. Yet it is not uncommon to find a provision for termination without cause in many Purchase Orders. The right is generally accompanied by a specific remedy that is given to the seller. In short, the buyer generally agrees to make compensation to the seller based on the work performed prior to the date of termination. This affects the buyer's promise to purchase, providing some substance to the promise. The buyer effectively states: "I promise to purchase the goods on the terms and conditions as stated in this Purchase Order; but if I do not, I will compensate you for your incomplete performance." This is certainly not illusory.

If the right to terminate without cause is included, an adjustment provision may be set forth in considerable detail or in general terms. For purpose of brevity, it is suggested that only a general statement be made about the manner in which the buyer will compensate the seller for the partial performance. In exercising this right, care must be taken by the buyer to evaluate the possible repercussions of compensation. If the goods are off-the-shelf items, it is not likely that the seller will have incurred any cost allocable to the buyer's order and subsequent termination. On the other hand, if the goods are made to order, the seller may have incurred substantial costs in preparing to deliver the goods.

A form encompassing these three matters is as follows:

6.13   *Termination.* If Seller ceases to conduct its operations in the normal course of business or if any proceeding under the bankruptcy or insolvency laws is brought by or against Seller, Buyer may cancel this order without liability, except for deliveries previously made or for goods then completed and subsequently delivered in accordance with all terms of this order. If Seller fails to perform or comply with any of the provisions of this order, Buyer may terminate the order in whole or in part and Buyer reserves all rights and remedies provided by law in case of such failure of performance in addition to the right of termination. Buyer may terminate all or any part of this order, without cause, at any time on written notice to Seller; Buyer will thereafter pay Seller's costs, properly allocable to the termination, together with reasonable profit on the part of the work performed prior to termination.

Compliance with Laws

If a seller manufactures goods in violation of the law, government action may be taken against goods delivered to the buyer to prevent further sale or even seizure. There are myriad laws established by federal, state, and local governments. It is nearly impossible to intelligently foresee the ramifications for the buyer if goods are made illegally (labor laws) or are themselves illegal (hazardous or toxic). The buyer should attempt to protect itself from being drawn into a legal proceeding that may be expensive and time consuming. By placing an obligation on a seller to comply with all laws, a failure of the buyer to comply with the law would constitute a breach that would permit the buyer to terminate the agreement and to pursue other remedies.

This clause also offers protection for the buyer that has previously obligated itself to its customer to comply with federal, state, and local laws and regulations. Since the buyer has promised compliance to its customer, the chain must extend rearward to the supplies purchased by buyer.

In a general way, there are two categories of laws and regulations that must be complied with. First are those related to the seller's employment practices. This includes such laws and regulations as the Fair Labor Standards Act, Equal Employment Opportunity Order, Rehabilitation Act,

Veterans Act, and Minority Business Enterprises Executive Order. In the other category are laws that relate to the product, including Hazardous Materials Regulations, Occupational Safety and Health Act, Toxic Substance Control Act, Consumer Product Safety Act, and similar laws.

Rather than attempt to deal with all these matters in detail, it is recommended that a very broad omnibus paragraph be used to define the seller's obligation. A suitable clause would read:

6.14   *Compliance with Laws.*   Seller shall comply with all applicable federal, state, and local laws, rules, and regulations.

General

Several of the boilerplate paragraphs should be incorporated into the Purchase Order. Definitely to be included are the paragraphs on Governing Law (Form 3.3) and Entire Agreement (Form 3.2). It may also be desirable to include the paragraph entitled Headings Not Controlling (Form 3.4). Since space on the Purchase Order is definitely limited, a briefer form of these three paragraphs is suggested:

6.15   *General.*   This contract is subject to and shall be interpreted in accordance with the laws of the state of California. This order embodies the entire agreement of the parties, and no other agreements, verbal or otherwise, in relation thereto exist between the parties. No waiver by Buyer of any provision hereof shall be construed as a waiver by Buyer of its right to insist on compliance in the future. The paragraph headings in this order are for the convenience of the parties and shall not affect the construction of the provisions contained in this order.

Miscellaneous

There are numerous other provisions that could be added to any Purchase Order. The draftsman must weigh the desirability for conciseness and the space permitted against the desire to provide for as many contingencies as possible. Particular businesses may find that the nature of their purchasing relationships require additional clauses. Some are suggested here.

A clause may be included to cover implications of selling to the government. The clause may provide that to the extent that the buyer has a prime contract with the government all the terms and conditions of such prime contract are incorporated by reference into the Purchase Order. Rather than this all-inclusive provision, a qualifying phrase may be added stating that "if the order indicates" then the terms and conditions of the prime contract are included. Another way of attacking the problem is to state that the detailed provisions of the Defense Acquisition Regulations (DAR) are incorporated by reference.

Several matters not covered in the foregoing forms could be added that relate to the terms of payment. The buyer may set forth details about the method of rendering invoices, the place to which invoices should be sent, information that must be contained on the invoice, whether invoicing may precede a delivery, and whether freight charges must be prepaid. Since sellers commonly now provide for the payment of interest for late payment, the buyer may countermand this term by stating that it will not be obligated for any late charges, finance charges, or interest if the buyer fails to make payment when due. The buyer may also specify the applicable date for measuring discounts for prompt payment. The buyer may state that the time for prompt payment starts with the date of delivery or the date of receipt of the invoice rather than the date of the invoice itself. The buyer may provide that it will pay for partial shipments when delivered but that seller shall not invoice for the full shipment on only partial delivery. Certain sellers insist that they be permitted to ship slightly over or under quantities ordered for bulk goods. This may not be suitable to the buyer, and a term may be added forbidding the seller to utilize such practice.

Other matters that may be considered include publicity, proof of shipment, the right to setoff, access to the seller's plant to permit tests or review progress, and sales tax exemption information.

The draftsman should review current purchasing practices of the company that may contain unique circumstances requiring unique Purchase Order clauses.

Chapter Seven
Sales Contract

This chapter proposes terms and conditions for a sales contract from the seller's viewpoint. These terms and conditions may be used in various documents issued by the seller.

As earlier mentioned, the most common document containing seller's terms and conditions is the Acknowledgment, also referred to as an "Acceptance" or "Confirmation." An Acknowledgment is transmitted to a purchaser after the receipt of a purchase order. It provides the buyer with notice that its order has been accepted and a contract has been formed. It also provides delivery information to the buyer.

Sales terms and conditions may also be included in a Sales Order. This document is used in some industries by the seller's salesmen or representatives when calling on customers. The salesman and the buyer for the customer determine the goods, prices, and delivery schedules desired by the customer; these requirements are set down in writing on the Sales Order form. The seller's terms and conditions are generally set forth on the reverse side of the form. The Sales Order may also be used to confirm a verbal order from the customer. In either event, the buyer will execute the form at a place provided on it after filling in the order. The completed and executed form is a written agreement between the parties.

Sales terms and conditions that are favorable to the seller may also be included in a Quotation. In many industries, the buyer may solicit an offer from the seller by requesting that the seller prepare a Quotation in response to a general description of goods that the buyer desires to purchase. This Quotation comprises an offer to sell, and if a clean Purchase Order is forwarded by the buyer, a contract on the seller's terms contained in the Quotation is effected.

Another type of document in which favorable sales terms and conditions are included is the Sales Contract. This is generally a negotiated agreement for the sale of goods typically between a large customer and a seller. The parties contemplate that over a period of time the buyer will submit numerous orders for individual products to be delivered at specified locations at different dates. Since they recognize that the standard forms that each normally use may contain conflicting provisions, the parties may want to resolve any potential difficulties by negotiating all the terms at once. These terms will control the sale of goods between the parties during the contract. It normally does not constitute an order for specific goods and is sometimes referred to as a "Master Agreement." The contract will specifically state that its terms and conditions will control all sales transactions during the contract period without regard to printed forms which may be used for specific transactions.

The terms and conditions in all these different types of documents will be substantially the same, except for reference within the terms and conditions to the type of document employed. An Acknowledgment is a separate printed from that may be one of a multicopy form used by the seller to create an invoice, packing slip, factory work order, and so on. As noted in Chapter 6, it may also be a form submitted by the buyer requesting execution by the seller. This Acknowledgment, however, establishes the buyer's terms and conditions as prevailing and is not the type of Acknowledgment referred to in this chapter. The following form is prepared for use as an Acknowledgment and will be printed on the reverse side preceded by the title "TERMS AND CONDITIONS OF SALE." On the face side, the statement should appear: "This Acknowledgment is Subject to the Terms and Conditions Set Forth on This and the Reverse Side Hereof."

ACKNOWLEDGMENT

Acceptance

The Acceptance paragraph is the counterpart of the identically titled clause in the Purchase Order. The purpose of the paragraph is to establish the seller's terms and conditions as controlling for the sales transaction. As noted in the discussion of the Purchase Order, the best results for the seller may be obtained by stating that the acceptance is "expressly conditional on assent" to the terms and conditions of the Acknowledgment. The Acknowledgment may contain a blank for execution by the buyer that, if signed, will immediately form a contract between the buyer and seller on the terms and conditions set forth in the Acknowledgment. If the buyer does not sign the Acknowledgment and the Purchase Order contains conflicting terms and conditions, then the expressly-conditional-on-assent phrase will prevent an agreement from being formed by the exchange of documents. If the seller proceeds to deliver the goods that are accepted by the buyer a contract is formed by the conduct of the parties; the non-conflicting terms and conditions in the two documents and the terms of the UCC will control the transaction. The seller may aid this result by including a provision stating that delivery is only for the buyer's convenience and does not constitute an acceptance of the buyer's terms and conditions. Furthermore, the seller may attempt to have the last word with a provision stating that the acceptance of the delivery of the goods by buyer constitutes an acceptance of the terms and conditions of the Acknowledgment. The legal effect of this provision is uncertain.

These two provisions may prevail, provided that they are not in conflict with the buyer's terms on the same point. In other words, if the buyer's Purchase Order failed to state that delivery by the seller constitutes an acceptance of the buyer's terms, the seller's statement should prevail that delivery is only for the buyer's convenience and not an acceptance of the buyer's terms. The result would be that delivery had no effect on whose terms control. Moreover, if the Purchase Order failed to state that the buyer's acceptance of the goods did not constitute an acceptance of the seller's terms and conditions, the seller's statement, unopposed, may control. The net result thus depends on the completeness of the buyer's provisions in the Purchase Order regarding delivery and acceptance of the goods. The last word of the seller may obtain the desired result. At the very least, it is the most that the seller can do.

Finally, a brief explanation of the reason for setting forth the seller's position on acceptance, although not legally necessary, may be commercially desirable. The form paragraph follows:

7.1 *Controlling Terms and Conditions.* To provide prompt and efficient service, Seller cannot individually negotiate the terms and conditions of each sales contract. Accordingly, goods furnished and services rendered by Seller are sold only on the terms and conditions as stated herein. Seller's offer to sell is conditioned on Buyer's acceptance expressly limited to Seller's terms and conditions of sale. Seller's acceptance of any order from Buyer is expressly made conditional on Buyer's assent to these terms and conditions of sale unless otherwise specifically agreed to in writing by Seller. In the absence of such assent, the beginning of performance or delivery shall be for Buyer's convenience only and shall not be construed to be acceptance of Buyer's terms and conditions. If a contract is not earlier formed by mutual agreement in writing, acceptance of any goods or services by Buyer shall be deemed acceptance of the terms and conditions of this Acknowledgment.

Price and Payment

This clause establishes the price that will be effective for the sales trans-action. Preceding the statement establishing the price, the seller may want to provide that it reserves the right to change prices without prior notice. The seller must determine the event that will determine the price. Nor-mally, the price in effect on the date of receipt of order becomes the firm price for the sales transaction. However, in a highly inflationary economy, some sellers may want to specify that the price will be determined on the date of shipment. Alternatively, the seller may reserve the right to in-crease the price, after receipt of order but prior to shipment, in the event the seller's cost is increased either generally or for a specific increase in a commodity cost. For example, if a product has a substantial gold content, the seller may quote a price that will be increased by the cost differential between the date of receipt of order and shipment. The rapidly fluctuat-ing cost of this precious metal may therefore be reflected in the final price. Such term is often referred to as a "precious metal adder." Before implementing this right to increase the price, the seller should carefully consider the complexity and the potential dissatisfaction of the buyer with this type of arrangement.

In a Quotation, as opposed to an Acknowledgment, the seller should set forth that the price quoted will remain firm for a fixed period of time mea-sured from the date of the Quotation.

One of the complexities in setting forth the terms and conditions relat-ing to price in an Acknowledgment stems from the blanket Purchase Order with scheduled releases. The seller may hold a firm price only for a predetermined period of time, for example, 90 days. This will prevent a buyer from submitting a Purchase Order for a single delivery at some ex-tended future time, for example, 12 months after the order is placed. If a Purchase Order requests scheduled deliveries beyond the 90 days, the seller can set a maximum period for the last delivery. For example, the seller may state that prices shall remain firm for the term of the order or for 90 days from the order receipt date, whichever occurs first, but the order may not provide for scheduled deliveries beyond a six-month pe-riod. If the seller permits the buyer to schedule some deliveries and to notify the seller of the remaining delivery dates, the seller may demand that all release notices must be received within three months from the order receipt date. If any of the order is not released within the three-month period, the order will be deemed canceled and a new order must be placed with the price effective on the date of the later order. Whether this type of complex provision is required depends on the nature of the seller's business. If scheduled releases over a prolonged period are common, the seller should attempt to retain control over price unless the items can be immediately placed into production. Even so, the cost of carrying such items will increase the seller's price. During an economic period in which costs are relatively stable, the seller may be content to hold prices firm for a much longer period than 90 days.

The seller will want to establish that the prices quoted are for either the point of origin or the point of destination. Commonly, prices are quoted FOB the seller's place of manufacture. The term "Free on Board" means that the seller will not charge for the costs incurred in loading the goods onto common carrier vehicles but that the freight must be paid by the buyer.

The clause should also establish that the prices quoted are exclusive of taxes. This should include federal, state, and local taxes and excise, sales, and similar taxes. The seller may state that taxes will be billed separately unless the customer provides a tax exemption certificate (commonly called a "Resale Permit").

Terms of payment must also be specified. Any early payment discount offered should be explicitly set forth. If the seller offers some customers early payment discounts but not others, the standard terms and conditions may recite that the terms of payment are, for example, net 30 days, unless otherwise specified. If the seller charges interest on an unpaid balance, the amount of the interest and the date on which such interest will begin to accrue should be expressly stated. The seller must consider state usury laws when demanding interest on an unpaid balance.

It may also be desirable to state that payment shall not constitute acceptance of the goods. In the event the buyer claims that the seller has delivered nonconforming goods and withholds payment for this reason, this statement will assure the buyer that prompt payment will not jeopardize its rights to finally reject the goods. In other words, it is desirable to be paid during the dispute period, and the seller may remove the buyer's fears that payment will constitute acceptance. As a practical matter, it is common for a buyer to withhold payment when goods are nonconforming regardless of the legal obligation to pay.

Finally, the UCC provides additional rights to the seller in the event of nonpayment. The UCC provides that the seller may retain a security interest in the goods until payment is made. The complexity of a security interest is beyond the scope of this discussion, but it is a valuable right, particularly when the seller sells expensive equipment such as large machines. To protect a security interest it is necessary to file a "financing statement" with state authorities; the clause should provide that the buyer will cooperate in effecting this filing.

The form paragraph reads as follows:

7.2 *Price and Payment.* Seller reserves the right to change prices for the goods offered for sale without prior notice, subject to the following terms and conditions. Prices in effect on the date of receipt of order shall remain firm for the term of the order or for ninety (90) days from the order receipt date, whichever occurs first. If Buyer requests scheduled releases of the quantity on which the billing price is based on the order receipt date, Buyer must notify Seller of all scheduled release dates, within ninety (90) days from order receipt date, for shipment within six (6) months from the order receipt date. Failure to notify Seller within the 90-day period will result in cancellation of the order and a new order must be placed by Buyer. Releases shall not be scheduled beyond six (6) months from the order receipt date.

All prices are quoted FOB _____ unless otherwise specifically agreed to in writing by Seller. All prices are quoted and billed exclusive of federal, state, and local taxes and excise, sales, and similar taxes unless otherwise specified. Taxes applicable will be billed as separate items on Seller's invoices unless Buyer provides Seller with a properly executed tax exemption certificate.

Terms of payment are Net 30 Days from date of invoice unless otherwise specified by Seller in writing. In the event payment is not received within the 30-day period, any unpaid balance shall commence to bear interest at the rate of _____ percent (_____%) per year from the thirty-first (31st) day after delivery. Payment shall not constitute acceptance of the goods.

Seller retains and Buyer grants a security interest in the goods, including all additions to and replacements of such goods until Buyer has made payment in full in accordance with these terms and Buyer shall cooperate with Seller in executing documents, such as a Uniform Commercial Code (UCC) Financing Statement, and performing any filings and recordings as Seller may consider necessary for the protection of the security interest.

The seller may also want to consider specifying a minimum billing per order or release to a single destination. If so, the clause should contain a statement about whether different items may be mixed to meet the minimum order. It should also state that if the billing amount fails to reach the minimum, an amount will be added to bring the billing value up to the minimum, and this will be set forth on the invoice.

Termination or Modification

As noted in the discussion regarding the Purchase Order form, the buyer may attempt to retain the right to make changes in the Purchase Order after acceptance. The seller should countermand this attempt by stating its policy with respect to permitting such change. In its most simple form, the seller may state simply that there may be no modification or termination of the sales contract without the express written consent of the seller.

It is not uncommon, however, to permit a purchaser to change an order after written consent. This may be used by the seller to adjust the quantity discount when the buyer wants to decrease the quantity of goods ordered. If the seller retains the right to consent to change, approval may be given conditioned on a price adjustment.

If it permits complete termination or cancellation of the order, the seller will want to make provisions for the costs incurred. The seller may provide that the buyer must make payment of termination charges based on the expenses and costs incurred in the production of the goods prior to the date the termination is accepted by the seller. The termination charge may include an adjustment for price to reflect the reduction in quantities sold, as suggested earlier with respect to a "change order." It may also include expenses of disposing of materials on hand or on orders from suppliers and any losses resulting from the disposition, including a reasonable profit. It should also provide that termination charges do not affect goods previously delivered to the buyer for which full payment is expected.

It is left to the discretion of the draftsman whether to include detailed provisions regarding termination. A flat prohibition without the consent of the seller may be perfectly adequate. The concept that details should be provided regarding the effect of termination stems largely from defense contracts. In defense contracts, applicable regulations detail the effects of a termination and the obligation of the buyer (government) to the seller to make compensation for the production costs incurred in beginning work on the order. Whether this is necessary in the common commercial transaction may largely depend on the nature of the seller's business. If the seller builds goods that are unique for each customer, the desirability of detailed termination charges should be apparent. However, the necessity of this provision is vitiated if all the goods sold are catalog items, part of the standard product line of the seller.

A form paragraph with detailed termination provisions follows:

7.3   *Termination or Modification.* The sales contract may be modified or terminated by Buyer only on Seller's written consent. If all or part of the sales contract is terminated with Seller's written consent, Buyer shall pay termination charges based on expenses and costs incurred in the production of the goods prior to acceptance by Seller of the termination. The expenses and costs shall include, but not be limited to, adjustment in price to reflect a reduction in quantity ordered, expenses of disposing of materials on hand or on order and any losses resulting from such disposition, and a reasonable profit. Any goods delivered prior to Seller's consent to termination shall be paid for in full by Buyer.

Delivery

Five aspects of delivery should be covered, or at least considered, for the Acknowledgment form. First, the seller should unequivocally state that delivery dates are estimated and are not guaranteed. The seller should not be liable to the buyer for any damages that may result from the failure of the seller to meet the estimated delivery date. Furthermore, it should be stated that the estimated delivery date is conditional on receipt of information, if any is required, from the buyer. The seller should counter any attempt by the buyer, as discussed in reference to the Purchase Order, to obligate the seller to use premium transportation in the event that the delivery date is not met. Finally, the boilerplate provision relating to the effect of delays due to Acts of God that normally is set forth in a separate clause may be integrated into the delivery clause.

Second, the seller should retain the right to make delivery in installments. If goods are shipped in installments payment should be demanded for each installment separately.

Third, the seller should reserve the right to allocate its production or inventory. In the event the seller's production cannot keep pace with orders, the seller may want to service customers on other than a first-come–first-serve basis. A seller may want to ship only partially against a large order so that it has enough goods remaining to satisfy smaller, later orders. Disputes with customers may be avoided by advanced warning that it is the seller's policy to allocate goods when supply is short.

Fourth, the seller should make clear that in the event the buyer fails to make payments on prior orders, or prior delivery releases, it reserves the right to demand payment before shipping any further orders. Again, this will clarify the seller's policy, establish the seller's right, and help to avoid disputes with customers.

Fifth, a provision may be added when the seller deals in small, inexpensive items that are ordered in large volume. Sometimes referred to as the "Allowable Over and Under Shipment Policy," it allows the seller to ship slightly more or less of the items ordered within a prescribed range. This may be particularly advantageous to a seller that makes custom products (slightly tailored for each customer) which are not otherwise disposed of easily. The nature of many manufacturing processes provides less than a 100% yield. This means that to manufacture 500 units the production department may schedule 510 or 525 units, based on its experience that some units will be finally rejected by quality control tests. The manufacturer may then be left with slightly more than the customer has ordered and may want to dispose of these items from inventory. If the cost is small, the buyer may readily accede to this policy, recognizing that in its own production, inventory, and handling a few items may be lost or scrapped. If this is the nature of the seller's business, then the seller's policy with respect to shipments that are over and under the specified amount should be expressly set forth. It should be added that the customer will accept billing for the quantity delivered within the prescribed range of more or less than the quantity ordered.

The form paragraph should read as follows:

7.4   ***Delivery.***   All delivery indications are estimated and are dependent in part on prompt receipt from Buyer of all necessary information to service an order. Seller shall not be liable for any premium transportation or other costs or losses incurred by Buyer as a result of Seller's inability to deliver product in accordance with Buyer's requested delivery dates. Seller shall not be liable for delays in delivery or for failure to perform as a result of causes beyond the reasonable control of Seller, including, without limitation, Acts of God, acts or omissions of Buyer or civil or military authorities, fire, strikes, epidemics, quarantine, flood, earthquakes, riot, war, delays in transportation, or the inability to obtain necessary labor, materials, or supplies.

Seller reserves the right to make deliveries in installments. Partial shipments shall be billed as made and payments therefor are subject to the terms of payment noted in the foregoing. Seller may require full or partial payment or payment guarantee in advance of shipment whenever, in its sole discretion, it considers itself insecure with respect to Buyer's performance of the sales contract.

Seller reserves the right to allocate inventory and production if such allocation becomes necessary in the judgment of Seller.

Seller reserves the right to ship and bill for five percent (5%)

more or less than the exact quantity of items ordered. Buyer agrees to accept billing for the quantity delivered.

Risk of Loss

Prior to the adoption of the UCC, many of the rights and duties of the parties to a sales transaction were determined by which party had title to the goods. "Title" is not a single concept but rather is a group of rights that can be segregated so that each component can be individually handled. One of these is the risk of loss. It is common to provide that risk of loss will pass to the buyer at the point of shipment. It is recommended that the seller follow this policy.

If it carries All Risk Transportation Insurance, the seller may provide a service to its buyer by accepting the obligation to file claims for products lost or damaged in shipment. This policy is followed by some larger manufacturers, and the seller should ascertain from its insurance agent the cost of this insurance and whether this is a desirable policy for it to follow. If so, this may be expressly set forth in the clause relating to risk of loss.

The clause may also contain the seller's policy with respect to shipping instructions. Normally, the seller will agree to follow whatever shipping instructions are provided by the buyer. This allows the buyer to control the method of shipment, including the carrier that the buyer will normally demand. It is desirable to state that the instructions will be followed "where practicable." It should also be stated that if no shipping instructions are provided the seller will use its discretion in selecting the shipping method.

These items may be briefly stated in a clause as follows:

7.5   *Risk of Loss.* Sales are made FOB point of shipment; transportation is at Buyer's expense; risk of loss passes to Buyer at the point of shipment. When practicable, Seller will follow the shipping instructions of Buyer, but if no instructions are provided, Seller will use its discretion in selecting an appropriate transportation method.

Inspection, Return, and Remedies

The purchaser has the right to inspect goods on delivery to determine if they conform to the goods ordered. The seller should attempt to place a time limitation on the buyer's right to perform the inspection; otherwise, the law will only require the buyer to act within a "reasonable" period.

Commonly, a 30-day period is set by the seller from the date of receipt of the goods. During this period the buyer must submit any claim for nonconforming goods, providing that the defect is capable of discovery with reasonable inspection. It should be established that if the buyer fails to make a claim within the prescribed time period, this omission will constitute a waiver and an irrevocable acceptance of the goods.

The clause should further provide for the procedure to be used by the buyer in returning goods and the remedy to which the buyer is entitled. Goods may be returned because they are nonconforming; for example, they are not the goods ordered because of a mistake by the buyer in describing the goods or because the goods fail to meet the provisions of the warranty extended by the seller. In either event, the matter of return and the risk of loss or damage to the products during return should be expressly set forth.

To control and provide for an orderly return policy, the seller should specify that the buyer must seek written authorization before returning any goods. The seller may then condition its authorization on inspection of the goods at the buyer's premises. If the matter can be settled expeditiously and with minimum cost by inspection at the buyer's premises, this may save both parties considerable inconvenience. If it elects not to inspect the goods on the buyer's premises, the seller may instruct the buyer to ship the goods to the seller with transportation costs prepaid. If the goods are found to be nonconforming, it should be provided that the transportation charges will be reimbursed and the repaired or replacement goods reshipped to the buyer at the seller's expense. It may be desirable, although not necessary, to specify that any costs incurred for inspection or packing by the buyer are not the responsibility of the seller.

The seller may also set forth the remedies to which the buyer is entitled in the event that the goods are nonconforming. For example, the seller may specify that at its option it may repair any defective goods, replace the goods, or credit the buyer with the purchase price. The seller should make absolutely clear that this is the sole remedy of the buyer and that under no circumstances will the seller be liable for special, indirect, incidental, or consequential damages. Furthermore, the seller should disclaim any such damages whether they arise out of a claim in contract or in tort. The necessity of this limitation on liability cannot be overstressed. Often, it is not the cost of the goods themselves that can give rise to a substantial claim but damages which result from use. As a simple example, consider that if the goods fail after being installed in a complex system the resulting damages to other parts of the system or the costs of reinstalling replacement goods may far exceed the cost of the goods themselves. Although the effect of this clause, particularly with respect to personal injuries, may be less than successful in view of the continuing expansion of the liability of manufacturers under the doctrine of strict liability, the inclusion of the clause in the sales contract is at least a first measure of protection. The seller may also want to follow its disclaimer for consequential damages with the statement that in no event shall the seller's liability be greater than the purchase price of the goods.

The following clauses cover these matters:

7.6 *Inspection, Return, and Remedies.* Buyer shall inspect goods immediately on receipt. Claims for any alleged defect in Seller's performance under this sales contract that may be discovered on reasonable inspection must be set forth in writing and received by Seller within thirty (30) days of Buyer's receipt of the goods. Failure to make any claim within the 30-day period shall constitute a waiver of all claims and an irrevocable acceptance of the goods by Buyer.

If Buyer rejects the goods or claims that Seller has breached any of its obligations under this sales contract, whether of warranty or otherwise, Seller at its option may first inspect such goods at the premises of Buyer or may give written authorization to Buyer to return the goods to Seller, transportation charges prepaid, for examination by Seller. If the product is found to be defective, the transportation charges shall be reimbursed. Buyer shall bear the risk of loss until any goods, authorized to be returned, are redelivered to Seller. Seller shall not be liable for any inspection, packing, or labor costs in connection with return of the goods.

In the event Seller breaches any of its obligations under the sales contract, whether of warranty or otherwise, the sole and exclusive remedy of Buyer is limited to replacement, repair, or credit of the purchase price at Seller's option. In no event shall Seller be liable for special, indirect, incidental, or consequential damages, whether in contract or tort, nor shall any damages arising out of or connected with this sales contract or the manufacture, sale, delivery, or use of the goods exceed the purchase price of the goods.

Warranty

It is doubtful if there is a single small business operator in the United States who is not now aware of the crisis in product liability claims. The increasing concern of courts for persons injured while using products has created disastrous consequences for more than one small manufacturer. The doctrine of "strict liability" has encouraged the filing of an incredible number of product liability suits. Even if it has not been subject to such suit, the manufacturer may find itself faced with product liability insurance premiums that are equally disastrous. Because not all these claims are based on a breach of warranty, there is no panacea in a properly drafted warranty clause in a sales order. Nevertheless, a correctly drafted warranty clause will provide the manufacturer with at least some limitation of potential liability for claims that are based on warranty. This is especially the case when the buyer's claim is for the repair or replacement of goods rather than some personal injury that resulted from use of the goods.

A rudimentary understanding of warranty law is the first defense in providing protection. Warranties may be either express or implied. An *express warranty* is a statement or representation of the seller about the goods. For example, if the seller states that the goods "will be free from defects in material and workmanship" for a specified period of time, the seller has expressly bound itself to provide goods that are not defective. It is also possible for the seller to make an express warranty by sample. Obviously, these warranties are totally within the control of the seller; that is, if no statement is made or sample is shown, no express warranty arises.

Implied warranties are those created by courts or legislature to reverse the ancient maxim of caveat emptor. In the 49 states that have adopted the UCC (Louisiana excepted), there are two implied warranties that are of prime significance. As mentioned in Chapter 6, the first is the warranty of merchantability, and the second is the implied warranty of fitness for a particular purpose. Still, the manufacturer has control over these warranties, to a certain extent, because the UCC permits the manufacturer to expressly limit the application of these warranties. The conditions for such exclusion or modification of warranties is that the disclaimer (*a*) must be in writing, (*b*) must be conspicuous, and (*c*) must specifically mention merchantability and fitness for a particular purpose. The UCC permits other means for excluding warranties, with these being the most commonly used.

The above aspects of warranty law apply to all commercial transactions. But if the goods are intended for a consumer, a second body of law is engrafted onto these principles. Consumer warranties are controlled by the Magnuson-Moss Act enacted by the federal government and administered by the FTC. The provisions of this law are detailed and fairly complex. Essentially, they provide that written warranties for products above a rather nominal price must be designated as either "Limited" or "Full." The object is to force the manufacturer to make a full disclosure of the warranty, including the persons entitled to the warranty, the parts of a product that are warranted, the nature of the warranty for each part or the whole, and other details. Like the UCC provisions, the act permits the manufacturer, in a Limited warranty, to place certain limitations on the implied warranties of merchantability and fitness for a particular purpose. The manufacturer may also specify limitations on time or remedy—for example, limitations on consequential or incidental damages.

Although written purchase orders and sales contracts are not entirely confined to nonconsumer transactions, the sales contract here discussed focuses on transactions between commercial businesses. It therefore does not attempt to deal with the Magnuson-Moss consumer warranty law.

Most sellers expressly warrant that the goods sold will meet certain defined criteria. These criteria are generally set forth by incorporating into the warranty the manufacturer's data sheets, product descriptions, or other commercial or sales literature. It may also incorporate technical drawings that are distributed to potential customers. A manufacturer and a buyer may also discuss certain performance or physical characteristics of the goods and arrive at an agreed-on specification incorporated into the sales contract. These documents become the standard against which the express warranty obligation of the seller will be measured. It should be apparent that in preparing such documents the seller must be conscious that the claims made will become the basis of its warranty. Of course, it is not necessary, legally, to make any express warranty.

Sellers also commonly warrant that the goods will be free from defects in material and workmanship at the time of delivery. This means that fabrics will not have dyes that run, plastics will not crumble, and metals will not have hairline cracks that foretell immediate failure. It further means that metal housings will not have dents, finished furniture surfaces will not have scratches, and painted articles will not have unintended blotches of varying color.

Normally, the warranty is specifically limited to a fixed period of time. This differs greatly from industry to industry. Often, it is for a period of one year. A survey of what other manufacturers offer in the industry is a good guide to the extent of time during which a product should be warranted. However, a manufacturer may choose to use an extended warranty period as a sales incentive.

The warranty should also be limited to proper use of the goods. A sensitive test instrument designed for laboratory use should not be protected by warranty if dropped or left outdoors to rust. Nor should a product that has been improperly installed or maintained be covered by warranty. And if the buyer alters the product or performs an inept repair, the manufacturer should be relieved of its warranty responsibility. In short, the warranty should apply only when the buyer takes good care of the product and uses it in the manner that the manufacturer intended.

Finally, as noted previously, the seller should set forth in "conspicuous" language that it disclaims the implied warranty of merchantability and fitness. The condition of conspicuousness is generally satisfied by setting forth the disclaimer in bold or at least all capitalized words and preferably in a separate paragraph. In other words, the disclaimer should stand out clearly and be readily identifiable in the middle of the fine print.

There are various ways of providing for the determination by the seller of whether the claimed breach of warranty is in fact applicable and the remedies available to the buyer. These may be set forth in the warranty clause. Form 7.6 has been drafted so that the procedure for return of goods and the buyer's remedy is equally applicable to any breach of performance by the seller, whether of warranty or some other failure by the seller to comply with the order of the buyer. Whether goods are nonconforming or fail to meet the express warranty claim, the procedure for inspecting the defect and returning the goods and the remedies available to the buyer may be expressly made the same. This simplifies the interpretation and construction of the document as a whole.

The following warranty is drafted for a manufacturer selling goods to other manufacturers or industrial or commercial users. It does not purport to cover the special provisions applicable to consumer transactions. The clause reads as follows:

7.7 *Warranty.* Seller warrants to Buyer that all goods sold to Buyer will perform in accordance with the applicable data sheet, drawing, or agreed-on specification and at the time of sale will be free from defects in material and workmanship. This warranty shall apply for a period of one (1) year from the date of shipment unless the goods have been subjected to misuse, accident, damage, improper installation or maintenance, or alteration or repair by any one other than Seller or its authorized representative. Buyer shall notify Seller promptly in writing of any claim based on this warranty and the provisions of Paragraph _____ shall thereafter apply with respect to inspection and return. Remedies for breach of warranty are solely and exclusively limited to those set forth in Paragraph _____.

SELLER MAKES NO OTHER OR FURTHER WARRANTY, EXPRESS OR IMPLIED, INCLUDING ANY WARRANTY OF FITNESS FOR A PARTICULAR PURPOSE OR WARRANTY OF MERCHANTABILITY.

Patents

Nearly all sellers extend a warranty that the goods delivered are free of any claim for patent infringement. One reason for this self-imposed obligation is that in the absence of an express disclaimer the UCC fastens such warranty on the seller in any event. Another pragmatic reason is that if the buyer is sued for patent infringement, the buyer's defense will either be simple capitulation or at best a dispirited defense. To place the matter conversely, the seller is delivering the goods to many buyers and wants to protect its right to continue to manufacture and sell the goods. Accordingly, the seller's first concern is to state that it has the right to defend or settle any claim brought against the buyer for infringement of any patent. The seller then agrees to provide such defense and also to pay any final judgment entered against the buyer if the suit is allowed to be defended by the seller. Further protection by the seller is obtained by obligating the buyer to notify the seller promptly of any claim made by a third party for patent infringement. The seller may also obligate the buyer to provide the seller with information and assistance as required to defend or settle the claim.

The patent indemnity clause should, however, limit the seller's obligations. In the first place, as noted in Chapter 6, the goods sold by the seller may have been designed by the buyer. For example, the seller may be a contract manufacturer engaged in making products that are not of its proprietary design. The buyer comes to the manufacturer and specifies the product to be manufactured, providing drawings, data, and other technical information that essentially binds the seller to make the goods in a specific configuration or composition; thus the seller should not be obligated to defend against the infringement that has been caused by the buyer. The matter can be complicated if the buyer comes to the seller with a vague description of performance or construction that can be carried out with various designs. The best protection for the seller is to state that the buyer will hold it harmless if it "complies" with the buyer's instructions.

There are other limitations the seller should state. These involve some of the nuances of patent law and the desirability they have is more difficult to explain. Briefly, the seller should limit its liability to its product alone. It is possible for the seller to provide a product that is not covered by a third-party patent but if combined with a second product, perhaps made by the buyer, will produce a combination which infringes a third-party patent. The seller has no responsibility for this use under the patent law. Similarly, a seller may provide a product that with further fabrication or processing can be made into an infringing product. Again, the law fixes no responsibility on the seller. However, the patent laws do hold a seller liable for what is called "contributory infringement." If a seller provides a component of a patented machine, article of manufacture, combination or composition, or a material or apparatus for use in practicing a patent process, then the seller may be held liable if (*a*) the seller knows that the component is especially made for use in an infringement and (*b*) the product is not a staple article of commerce suitable for non-infringing use. The seller is, of course, protected if its product is suitable for other uses—for example, a product it manufactures and sells for a variety of uses by many customers. But if the buyer approaches the seller to manufacture a product that is special (although not in itself an infringement), the seller may be required to prove that it did not know that its product was made for use in an infringement. The seller may protect itself against such possibility by specifically disclaiming any patent warranty for such sale.

A party can also be held guilty of patent infringement if it "actively induces" infringement by another. If a seller provides a product that is capable of infringement (although not in itself an infringement) and provides instructions or other information to the buyer which informs or encourages the buyer to use the product in an infringing manner, the seller may be guilty of patent infringement. The seller should specifically disclaim any liability for infringement as a result of information furnished to the buyer.

The seller may also want to protect itself by limiting its damages in any patent infringement suit to the amount of money paid by the buyer to the seller for the goods. In effect, this constitutes a liquidated damage limitation in which the buyer and the seller agree that the maximum measure of liability will not exceed the purchase price. Limitation of damages by this type of clause is permitted under the UCC but only if the liquidated amount is reasonable in light of the anticipated or actual harm caused by the breach and there are difficulties of proof of loss that will prevent the injured party from obtaining an adequate remedy. Whether a limitation of the seller's liability to the price of the goods will meet this test is not altogether clear. In any event, it may provide some protection.

Finally, some manufacturers want to specify that the sale of the goods does not carry any implied license to use other patents of the seller such as a process or combination patent. For the small manufacturer, it is not likely that its patent portfolio is so extensive that a problem will exist. If the seller has several patents that relate to a family of products or processes, the seller may find it advisable to discuss the matter with a patent attorney to determine whether a disclaimer against an implied license is required.

The form paragraph is as follows:

7.8   *Patents.*   Seller shall have the right to defend or settle, and agrees to defend or settle, any claim brought against Buyer for the infringement of any U.S. patent by goods supplied by Seller. Subject to the limitations that follow, Seller agrees to pay any final judgment entered against Buyer in any suit defended by Seller. Buyer shall notify Seller promptly in writing of any claim for patent infringement and provide Seller with information and assistance as reasonably requested by Seller to defend or settle the claim.

Buyer shall hold Seller harmless against any expenses, damages, or loss for infringement of any U.S. patent or trademark that results from Seller's compliance with Buyer's designs, specifications, or instructions. Seller shall have no liability for any infringement arising from the combination of goods sold by Seller with any goods furnished by Buyer, any modification of the goods, the use of the goods in practicing any process, or any information furnished to Buyer for assistance.

In no event shall Seller's liability to Buyer under the provisions of this clause exceed the aggregate sum paid to Seller by Buyer for the goods.

General

In addition to the standard boilerplate paragraphs, there are some miscellaneous clauses a seller may include in the sales contract. One paragraph is a corollary to the Tooling paragraph used in the Purchase Order. If it creates or modifies equipment to produce goods for the buyer, the seller may want to specify that it owns such equipment. It also may want to explain when the buyer has title to equipment either paid for or provided by the buyer. The clause may state the obligations with respect to maintenance, repair, and storage of the equipment and which party shall bear any expenses incurred on returning or relocating buyer-owned equipment.

Another paragraph may cover indemnification by the buyer for injuries occurring to employees of the seller or the property of the seller, when on the buyer's premises. If the seller's product is normally installed on the buyer's premises by employees of the seller this protection may be well advised. This indemnification may be buttressed by obligating the buyer to procure liability insurance against claims arising from the performance by the seller on the premises of the buyer.

A seller who as a subcontractor manufactures products principally for other manufacturers engaged in the defense industry may find it necessary to comply with certain terms in its buyer's prime contract. It is not suggested that the seller incorporate the specific terms that the government will impose on the subcontractor into the Acknowledgment. Instead it is suggested that when the prime contract number is specifically set forth in the order the seller should add a paragraph stating in essence that for any order placed pursuant to a government prime contract the terms and conditions of the prime contract are incorporated into the Acknowledgment by reference. These government terms and conditions may conflict with the printed general terms and conditions recommended in this chapter. The seller should preface any such incorporation by reference with the statement that the general terms and conditions will have precedence unless absolutely in conflict with the terms and conditions of the prime contract.

A seller may also want to protect itself against a later claim for breach of a confidential disclosure agreement. The seller may state that any information relating to the order submitted by the buyer is accepted only on a nonconfidential basis.

From Chapter 3, the following paragraphs should be included: Entire Agreement (Form 3.2), Governing Law (Form 3.3), Severability (Form 3.9), and Nonassignment (Form 3.5). The seller may also want to include an arbitration provision.

Chapter Eight
Employment

A company enters into a contract of employment with each employee it hires. The employee agrees to perform certain duties in exchange for a stated compensation. Almost universally, these are oral contracts that the employer may terminate at will. Obviously, a written employment contract would be inappropriate for most employees. The question then is where the line should be drawn between the "ordinary" employee and the "special" employee for whom the employment contract should be reduced to writing. Although there are no hard and fast rules some general guidelines are available.

If an employee is paid special compensation, such as a bonus or perquisites that are reasonably complex, a written agreement is advisable. Bonuses paid for sales or profit performance will usually involve a written statement of the arrangement. If an employee is offered special benefits such as country club dues, relocation reimbursement, or special insurance policies, a written arrangement may be preferable.

A second area involves the highly qualified technical employee. The principal objective of an employment contract with this employee is to clarify obligations respecting the assignment of inventions and duties regarding trade secrets or confidential material that is created or used by the employee.

Viewed from the perspective of the employer, there are certain advantages that may be obtained from a written employment contract. The length of service can be established so that there is a measure of security in the employer's investment in the training and familiarization of the employee with the duties of the job. The duties of the employee, in advance of employment, can be defined explicitly so that there is no later misunderstanding with regard to the nature of the performance expected. The employee who may incur large expenses, such as an international marketing manager who is expected to engage in considerable foreign travel, may find that the expense policy of the company is inadequate. An employment contract would permit a careful definition of allowable expenses tailored to the specific job requirements. Highly compensated employees who have worked for large corporations are accustomed to relocation and are usually generously reimbursed for expenses due to the inconvenience of moving. A relocation policy can be expressly defined for the special employee.

Several of these advantages to the employer will also be advantageous to the employee. The certainty of a fixed term of employment may induce an employee living at a remote location prior to employment to relocate. A prospective employee may be uneasy about moving a family to a new location, particularly to a small town, if there is not some advance assurance that the employment will be for a lengthy period. An employee joining a small firm may also be concerned about the continuity of employment in the event the small firm sells out. Worse, the employee of a small business that is not in good financial condition may be concerned about termination of employment on bankruptcy or insolvency of the company. The effects of these difficulties on the employee can be defined in advance in a written contract. For the highly technical employee, there is the opposite side of the invention assignment issue—exclusion of incomplete inventions. The employee may wish that an invention be excluded from the normal requirement for the assignment of inventions. Furthermore, he or she may attempt to obligate the company to make royalty payments on the completed invention. Another example arises when a business is purchased and an owner-employee, in addition to the consideration for the business itself, intends and is expected to remain as a manager in charge of the newly acquired operation. An employee contract would be appropriate as part of the transaction.

In addition to these advantages, there is a legal issue that must not be overlooked. As explained in Chapter 1, the Statute of Frauds applies to any oral agreement between parties in which the performance cannot be completed in less than one year. Therefore, if a term of employment longer than one year is intended, it is mandatory that the agreement be reduced to writing to be valid.

The usual employment contract is not complex. It comprises five basic elements: employment, duties, compensation and benefits, duration, and usually proprietary rights. However, these basic elements have diverse expression because of the considerable latitude in the types of duties performed and the nature of employment.

EMPLOYMENT CONTRACT

Either the formal or letter format is acceptable for an employment contract. When the negotiation is conducted between the parties through written communications the letter format is usual. Format is left to the discretion of the draftsman.

Employment

The first clause in the agreement sets forth the relationship that is established. This clause may contain the term of the agreement, or as in the sample agreement of this chapter, it may constitute a separate paragraph.

8.1 *Employment.* Company hires Employee, and Employee accepts employment, on the following terms and conditions.

Duties

Description. The second clause of the agreement will usually set forth the duties to be performed by the employee. The highly qualified employee for whom a written employment contract is recommended will normally be hired to perform a specialized function for the employer. The employee may be hired as an officer, such as president, vice-president, secretary, or treasurer. In the technical area, the employee may be hired as director of engineering or as a research and development engineer. In the sales area, the employee may be the marketing manager, national sales manager, or even regional sales manager. In the accounting area, the employee may be the manager of finance or controller. Other positions would include general manager, director of manufacturing, computer programmer, material control manager, or plant manager.

It is left to the draftsman to prepare the job description for the particular employment situation. The form in this chapter describes duties for a vice-president of research and development who reports to the president of the company. If the company policy manual contains job descriptions these may be used verbatim. Even without formal job descriptions, the description of duties prepared for the employment ad is a good starting point for drafting.

In addition to the specific duties described the matter of change of duties should be covered. The agreement may provide that either the duties will be changed only on mutual consent of the parties or that the employer retains the right to assign the employee new duties. This is a matter of negotiation between the parties. In any event, the employee should remain subject to the employer's direction with respect to the manner in which these duties are to be carried out.

If the employee is an officer of the corporation, the description of the duties may be obtained directly from the bylaws of the corporation. It should be stated that the president remains subject to directions from the board of directors. Furthermore, the bylaws should be reviewed, since there may be restrictions on the scope of the activities that may be performed by the president. For example, the president may be limited with respect to the amount of borrowing or the size of capital equipment purchases. Even if such restrictions do not appear in the bylaws it may be desirable to place such restrictions in the employment contract. For corporation officers other than the president, it should be remembered that these officers are appointed by the board of directors and a board meeting should be conducted to obtain approval. It is good practice to prepare the employment contract for the officer prior to the meeting of the board so that it may be reviewed and specifically approved in regard to the terms and conditions.

Title.   Related to the matter of duties, and change of duties, is the title given to the employee. Because of the authority vested in a position bearing a particular title, and the prestige both within and without the corporation, the employee may be highly sensitive to a change of title. Titles should be as carefully chosen as the description of the duties of the job, and the right to change title should be negotiated.

Relocation.   The matter of relocation of the employee should also be included in this clause. If relocation is to be entirely at the employer's discretion this should be expressly set forth. If mutual consent is required the agreement should provide for the possibility that the parties cannot agree. If an employment contract is used for a salesman or regional sales manager and includes a specific territory assignment, the matter of relocation is particularly important. For these positions, it is highly likely that over a prolonged period the territory of the salesman or manager will be changed.

The clause should also expressly set forth the parties' intentions with respect to the amount of time the employee is expected to spend on the job. If the employee is to devote his or her full time to the job this should be set forth. This is usually followed by a statement that the employee will not render any services for any other organization without the prior written consent of the employer. A forthright statement of the employer's expectations in regard to the time the employee is expected to expend can prevent serious disagreements at a later time. Occasionally, the employer may permit the employee to work part-time in a noncompeting business. In such case, it should be made clear that such outside work may not be performed during normal working hours or at the employer's place of business.

Physical Examination. One final matter that may be included in the clause is the obligation of the employee to submit to a physical examination before employment and annually thereafter. Since such examination is usually paid for by the employer, the matter may be considered a benefit rather than a duty. However, expressing it as a duty may be advantageous if the employee runs into ill health that jeopardizes quality and continuity of performance. The employer may be able to aid an employee who is reluctant to seek medical advice for problems of emotional distress, problem drinking, or similar psychological illnesses. Getting the employee to submit to an examination may be a fruitful first step in the employee's rehabilitation.

A clause for the vice-president of research and development describing the duties and other obligations of the employee is as follows:

8.2 *Duties*

(a) Employee shall serve as the Vice-President of Research and Development of Company. Employee shall direct all the research and development activities of Company, particularly relating but not limited to [solid state memory devices]. Employee will perform all services, acts, and things necessary or desirable to advance the technological position of Company.

(b) Employee will utilize the best of the Employee's abilities and experience to conscientiously perform the required duties. Employee will devote the entire productive time and attention of Employee to the business of Company and shall not render any services of a business or professional nature to any other organization, whether with or without compensation, without the prior written consent of the President.

(c) Company may change the duties or title of Employee at any time during the term of this agreement; if such change is unacceptable to Employee, Employee may at its option terminate this agreement, and such termination shall constitute the sole remedy of Employee for such change.

(d) Employee will submit to a physical examination at any time requested by Company, and Employee will be entitled to such examination at least annually. Company will bear the entire cost of such examination, and Employee agrees that the results will be available to Company for review and evaluation.

Compensation and Benefits

As always, price constitutes one of the critical elements of an agreement. The compensation paragraph, in addition to providing for the base salary, may also include provisions for bonus payments, expenses, automobiles, vacations, medical and life insurance, relocation expenses, and perhaps some special compensation arrangement. Each of these matters may be placed in a separate paragraph, with the appropriate heading, or combined in a single paragraph.

Base Salary. The base salary is usually expressed as an annual amount payable in installments during the period of employment.

During a period of high inflation, consideration should be given to adjusting the annual salary for the declining value of the dollar. It is not necessary that the agreement specify a formula for such adjustment. The parties may simply negotiate additional compensation on an annual basis and amend the employment contract to define the new salary level. However, since such adjustment is entirely discretionary with the employer, the employee may want the assurance of an adjustment based on a specific formula. Typically, the Consumer Price Index is chosen as an expression of the rate of inflation. It may be advisable during periods of rampant inflation to mitigate the full effect of a cost-of-living adjustment by placing a ceiling on the increase. The extent of such ceiling is a matter of negotiation between the parties.

Bonus. The compensation may also include a bonus. As a general matter, bonus payments are usually made either in cash or stock. No attempt is made here to discuss a stock bonus arrangement, since the matter has become extremely complex in view of the tax laws, particularly Section 83 of the Internal Revenue Act of 1969. It is strongly advised that if stock bonus compensation is to be paid the services of a tax specialist should be retained.

The cash bonus may be a fixed amount, sales based or profit based. It is, of course, the object of a bonus to attempt to relate the employee's performance as directly as possible to the activity that the employee controls. In other words, an employee engaged in sales activities should be remunerated by a bonus that is based on sales increases as measured against prior results or a quota. The salesperson who has responsibility for only a limited geographic territory should have the sales from that territory used as the base. One type of sales formula would establish a fixed salary and a bonus that is determined monthly, quarterly, or annually and paid in addition to the fixed compensation.

Alternatively, compensation may be expressed as a percentage of total sales, with the employee permitted a draw against the commissions earned. Care should be taken to adequately define what constitutes "sales" and when the commissions are earned (booking, shipment, or collection). Suitable language can be taken from the Commission Payments paragraph in the Sales Representative agreement (Form 5.5).

A profit-based bonus should be used only when the employee has total responsibility for a profit center. It is typically used for a president, general manager, or division manager. The base against which performance is measured may be fixed dollars of net profit or return on capital or assets. Great care must be taken in defining what are "profits." Various terms are used by accountants and in different industries for the same concept. Certainly, a distinction exists between "net operating income" (profit before interest expenses and extraordinary income or loss), "pretax income" (net profit before federal and state income taxes), and "net income" (after-tax profit). If the business is operated as a proprietorship or partnership, should the salaries of the partners or sole proprietor be deducted before determining profit? Should the employee's bonus itself be deducted from profit, with the bonus then reiteratively calculated? There are many potential traps and misunderstandings that may arise by too glib a definition of "profit." One way of avoiding these problems is to have the independent accounting firm for the company prepare a skeletal form of the entity's income statement that may then be included in the agreement as an exhibit. In any profit-based bonus formula it should be set forth that the computation of profits as determined by the firm's independent certified public accountants is final and binding on the parties.

The bonus paragraph must also provide for when the bonus is to be paid and what will be the effect of termination by the employee prior to payment of the bonus. This latter problem may be handled in the Term clause or in the Compensation clause; in this chapter the Compensation form states that the bonus is payable only if the employee is employed at the end of the year.

Expenses. Expenses may also be covered in this clause; however, a separate heading is commonly used. There are two ways of treating expenses. First, the company may establish a fixed amount payable to the employee to cover all expenses incurred in connection with employment. This may be a monthly, quarterly, or annual amount. The employee's actual expenses may be less than or greater than the established amount, but no reimbursement to the company or additional amounts are allowed. Because of the difficulty in establishing a fixed amount and the inflexibility of this approach, it is rarely used except for one or two top-management employees.

The second and more pervasive method of handling expenses is to pay for actual, out-of-pocket expenses. The definition of "reimbursable expenses" may be general, referring simply to entertainment, travel, and possibly gifts. Alternatively, the agreement may provide that reimbursable business expenses are limited to those set forth in the policy manual of the employer which are incorporated by reference into the agreement. The former alternative is widely used. A related matter is to obligate the employee to provide the company with enough information so that the expenses will be properly deductible from state and federal income taxes. This may be done in detail by specifying that a record must be kept for each entertainment or travel occurrence and that documentary evidence be supplied as necessary to establish such expenses as deductible. An alternative approach is to generally state that all such expenses must be properly deductible on state and federal income tax returns of the company, including whatever documentary evidence is required by the tax authorities. This latter approach is preferable, since during the course of employment tax regulations may change resulting in the detailed statement of requirements becoming obsolete.

In the event expenses of the employee are found nondeductible during a tax audit, the company may provide a remedy for the breach of the employee's duty to properly report and document expenses. The agreement may state that in the event of a disallowance the employee will be required to reimburse the company. Some employees may balk at this provision. If the company has a poor audit record on expenses there is a likelihood that the tax auditor will rather stringently examine expense records and supporting documents. The employee may thus be prejudiced by the company's past liberal expense policies, particularly if an owner-employee has treated tax regulations with disdain.

Automobile. For the highly compensated employee for whom an employment contract is usually drawn the company will ordinarily provide an automobile. If the automobile is used only for business the employee will not be taxed for this perquisite. A proportionate part of the use of the automobile will be taxed as compensation to the employee if a tax auditor determines that it was used at least in part for personal reasons. Of course, the company is entitled to a deduction in either event. For this reason the agreement need not provide that the automobile be confined to business use.

The agreement may provide that the automobile will be of a certain make or may establish a maximum price for an automobile that the employee may select. The clause may further provide that a like automobile will be purchased for the employee annually, or more usually, biennially. The clause should state that the employer will pay all operating expenses for the automobile and that the employer will obtain insurance coverage, usually stating a minimum amount for bodily injury and property damage. The insurance coverage is of importance not only to the employee but also to the company.

Vacation. The amount and details of vacation permitted the employee is another benefit that may also be covered in this clause or a separate clause. Sick leave may also be specified. Including these provisions is by no means mandatory. The company may have an established vacation and sick leave policy that will be controlling in the absence of any specific reference to these matters in the agreement.

Insurance. Medical and dental insurance benefits are usual perquisites permitted the key employee. If it does not differ from coverage for all employees, this benefit need not be included in the contract, since the employee will qualify for coverage without specific mention. Special medical benefits were previously permitted for officers under a specific section of the Internal Revenue Code, but this benefit is no longer deductible by the company. In many companies, however, there is special extended coverage for key employees.

Life insurance may also be covered, if this benefit is different from the insurance normally provided under a group life insurance policy for all employees of the company. It is permissible under the present tax laws and regulations to provide group life insurance coverage for key employees up to $50,000, although this amount is greater than the amount purchased for the ordinary employee. If this maximum is exceeded, the premiums will constitute compensation to the employee and will be taxable. A qualified insurance agent should be consulted who will be familiar with current tax rules in setting any specific amount of insurance that the company obligates itself to provide.

Payments for disability may also be considered as an additional perquisite. This is usually given only to top-management employees. It normally provides that in the event of permanent disability the employee will continue to be compensated at a reduced rate for the remainder of the term of the agreement.

Relocation. There are several benefits relating to relocation of the employee that may be specified in the agreement. This matter may be left to company policy unless unusual in some sense. Naturally, if the company has no established policy the employee may want to have the matter spelled out in full. The most common provision is for moving expenses that would include travel, moving the employee's household goods, and expenses during the move. The latter may be spelled out as including a trip for house hunting by the employee and family where travel, lodging, and meals are covered, as well as lodging and meals while occupying temporary quarters for a limited period of time. Large corporations now provide many relocated employees with benefits relating to home purchase. If the company has no policy in this regard, it would be well to establish in the employment agreement the extent of such benefit, if any. The benefit may include repurchase of the employee's prior residence, at the option of the employee, with the value established by a qualified appraiser. The widespread adoption of employee relocation benefits has spawned several relocation service firms that may be helpful for ascertaining the extent of benefits other companies are offering.

The foregoing list of benefits and methods of compensation covers the "garden variety" situations. Special compensation packages are unlimited in variety and are greatly dependent on prevailing tax laws. There also appears to be a fad in compensation packages. Deferred compensation, for example, was at one time highly popular but is now seldom used. "Cafeteria" plans (selection by the employee among a variety of benefits) are now in vogue. The technical employee may want to negotiate compensation that includes royalties or other remuneration for inventions that are assigned to the employer. An employee who is being trained for a position may be compensated specially, at a reduced rate during the training period and at the full rate thereafter. Certain employees, even if "exempt" under the Fair Labor Standards Act, may be compensated for overtime.

The following form paragraph is skeletal. Rather than attempt to cover special compensatory arrangements, or a glut of benefits, this form includes provisions for basic salary, bonus, expenses, and automobile. The format and language of additional provisions should be suggested by these exemplary paragraphs:

8.3   *Compensation and Benefits*

(a)   As compensation for services, Employee will receive during the term of this agreement a salary of _____ dollars ($) per annum, payable in equal bimonthly installments on the sixth (6th) and twenty-first (21st) day of each month during the employment term.

(b)   In addition to salary, Employee will be paid an annual bonus in the amount of _____ dollars ($), payable at the end of each year of employment but only if Employee is employed under this agreement at the end of that year; employee is not entitled to any pro-rata bonus payment.

(c)   Company will promptly reimburse Employee for all reasonable business expenses incurred by Employee in connection with the business of Company, including entertainment and travel. Employee will maintain records and written receipts for such expenditures as required by federal and state tax authorities to substantiate such expenditures as an income tax deduction for Company.

(d) Employee will be furnished the use of a new automobile, at the selection of Employee, but not to exceed the price of _____ dollars ($), on beginning employment and shall be entitled to a new automobile of comparable make, model, and option after two years of employment and thereafter biennially during the term of this agreement. Company will procure and maintain in force an automobile liability policy covering the automobile with coverage, including Employee, in the minimum amounts of _____ dollars ($) for bodily injury in one accident and _____ dollars ($) for property damage in one accident. Company will pay all operating expenses for business related use.

Duration

As noted previously, it is one of the objectives of the employment contract to provide the employee and employer with the security of a fixed, relatively long arrangement. What constitutes a long term is left to negotiation between the parties. One cautionary note for long-term agreements is the possibility that a state law may limit the maximum term. For example, in California, the maximum term is seven years. Normally, this will not be a matter of great concern, since three- and five-year terms are more normally used.

Renewal. The agreement may provide for the manner in which employment may be continued after expiration, although this is not mandatory. If the term is specified, and no more is stated, the agreement will expire and continued employment will be at the will of the employer. Alternatively, the term may be automatically renewed unless one party gives notice to the other within a specified period prior to the end of the term. Renewals may be for a like or different period of time and may thereafter be automatically renewed. Or renewal may be at the option of one or the other of the parties. Finally, if the contract has been prepared solely to set forth the rights and duties of the parties and a definite term is not desired, the agreement may be made terminable, without cause, by either or both of the parties on giving a stated notice.

Performance. If it has a fixed term—is cancelable only for cause—the agreement must provide for termination on the occurrence of specified events. The first of these to be considered is termination by the employer for failure of the employee to perform the duties as stated in the second paragraph of the agreement. The manner in which this is usually couched is the "willful breach or habitual neglect" of the employee's duties. The effect of this language is to limit the employer's rights for nonperformance to intentional or grossly careless performance by the employee. If a dispute should arise after termination of employment, the employer would be put to the burden of establishing something more than mere failure of the employee to competently perform the duties recited. An employer may find that the whiz kid hired at a high salary performs at a level below expectations, but this is not grounds for termination. However, an employee with long or repeated unexplained absences or one who becomes a serious problem drinker could be established as habitually neglectful. Although the matter can never be free from doubt, and courts and jury will frequently err on the side of the employee, this language should adequately protect the employee and employer.

Death or Disability. Death of the employee should also be stated as an event that terminates the agreement. The obvious should not be overlooked. Permanent disability of the employee may also be recited as grounds for termination. Such provision should be consistent with any disability payment benefits as discussed previously. This matter may be more difficult to draft than at first perceived. Normally, the term "permanent disability" is used, although this term is certainly not unambiguous. Medical authorities will easily disagree on whether a disability is permanent, temporary, or unascertainable. A disability may be either complete or limited. The definition could be extended for pages, as sometimes appears in disability insurance policies. The matter may be given definiteness by simply stating that any opinion given by a licensed medical practitioner retained by the employer is final. If the company maintains a disability insurance policy on management employees, the definition in such policy may be incorporated by reference.

Business Failure. For a small business that is not well established the possibility of financial failure always exists. Both parties will be protected if the agreement is terminated automatically if the company ceases further operations. The employee may also want to be relieved from the contract if the company goes into bankruptcy, makes an assignment for the benefits of creditors, or is otherwise financially insolvent. This would also protect the employer from the burden of the contract if financial rehabilitation is possible but requires a severe pruning of employment.

Death of Owner. If the company is a sole proprietorship or a partnership, the death of one of the owners may severely disable the financial viability of the organization. The employee may want to negotiate for a termination of the contract in the event of such occurrence.

Sale of Business. An employee with any small company will also be concerned with the effects of the sale of the business. The draftsman should reflect on what is the most desirable result. An acquiring corporation will not be anxious to purchase a business burdened with long-term employment contracts for numerous key employees that include lucrative compensation provisions. Conversely, key employees may be one of the most valuable assets of a small business. If the contract is a true arm's length transaction, it is preferable to have the contract nonterminable in the event of a merger, an acquisition, or a sale of assets. The employee may view the matter differently. Some key employees join small organizations specifically to avoid the cumbersome organization of large corporations. On sale, the employee may prefer to be discharged. Not all key employees, however, will be so inclined. Clearly, this is a matter for negotiation. The form provided subsequently takes the point of view of the employer and follows the recommendation that the agreement remain binding and assure the employee that the acquiring corporation will remain bound by the provisions of the agreement.

Effect on Compensation. Finally, provision may be made for the effect of termination on compensation. As for regular salary, the Compensation paragraph provides that the employee will receive compensation during the term of the agreement; if the agreement is terminated, compensation ends. The effect on special compensation arrangements should be carefully considered. It is not uncommon to provide that a bonus payment is paid only if the employee remains employed on the date of payment, regardless of the measure used to determine the bonus. However, this could depend on the reason for which the agreement is terminated. Certainly, for breach of the agreement by the employee no bonus should be paid. But if the agreement is terminated on the death of one of the partners in a partnership business as suggested earlier, it may be equitable to provide for a pro-rata bonus. It may even be desired to provide for severance pay in the event of such occurrence. These matters are left for resolution by the draftsman in accordance with the situation.

The sample paragraph is as follows:

8.4   *Term and Termination*

  (a)   This agreement will begin on _____, 19_____, and termi-
        nate on _____, 19_____, except as provided in the fol-
        lowing.

  (b)   This agreement may be terminated by Company by giving ten
        (10) days notice to Employee if Employee willfully breaches
        or habitually neglects the duties required to be performed
        under Paragraph _____

  (c)   This agreement will automatically terminate on the death or
        permanent disability of Employee; *permanent disability* for the
        purpose of this agreement means the mental or physical in-
        ability of Employee to perform Employee's normal job with
        Company as evidenced by a certificate of a medical examiner
        satisfactory to Company, certifying such inability and further
        certifying that such condition is likely to be permanent.

  (d)   In the event Company ceases operation of all its business or
        becomes insolvent, makes an assignment for the benefit of
        creditors, is adjudged bankrupt, or has a receiver appointed,
        this agreement may be terminated without notice by either
        party.

  (e)   In the event Company is acquired, is the nonsurviving party
        in a merger, or transfers substantially all its assets, this agree-
        ment shall not be terminated and Company agrees to take all
        actions necessary to insure that the transferee is bound by the
        provisions of this agreement.

Competition and Proprietary Matters

Under this section three aspects of the employee's relationship are considered: inventions, unfair competition, and noncompetition. It is important to distinguish between the latter two matters. *Unfair competition*
is a vague legal doctrine that provides one party with a right which is
enforceable against another for various business improprieties. In the
context of the employee relationship, it arises because the employer en-
trusts the employee with certain proprietary information that the employee is obligated not to disclose to others or to use for the employee's
gain. By contrast, *noncompetition* refers to a duty or obligation the
employee assumes in consideration for payments, such as compensation,
made by the employer. Such competition may be perfectly fair, except as
it has been proscribed by agreement of the parties. Noncompetition obligations may be subdivided into those applying during employment and
those that take effect after termination. Noncompetition in the postem-

ployment period is most familiar when one party sells a business to another and agrees not to compete with the purchaser for a period of time and in a defined geographical area. It may also arise from a simple employment relationship, although the freedom of the parties to contract is circumscribed by certain state laws.

Each of these three categories of competition and proprietary rights should be considered in every employment contract.

Noncompetition during Employment.   Noncompetition during employment should be a broad and all-encompassing prohibition against competition from the employee. The proscription is related to the employee's obligation to devote the entire time and effort of the employee to the business of the company as set forth in Form 8.2. It is more specific in the sense that although an employee may be permitted to devote time to other commercial or financial endeavors outside working hours in Form 8.2 the employer may not be willing to permit such activity if it is competitive. For example, the employee may make after-hours investments in real estate or publicly traded stock. This would be permissible conduct under the "time and effort" duty of Form 8.2. But if the employee invests in a private business that is directly competitive to the business of the company, the employer should be entitled to prohibit the employee from such conduct. Prohibiting such conduct is part of the bargained-for consideration that the employee agrees to give in return for compensation. Courts are not reluctant to enforce a broad proscription against competition during employment.

Noncompetition after Employment.   After employment, the scope of the noncompetition prohibition must be phrased more carefully. The reason is that there are two competing policies that the law must accommodate. First, the employer should be entitled to its bargained-for consideration. But there is a reluctance to preclude an ex-employee from engaging in commercial activities even if in direct competition with the past employer. A person should be allowed to "earn a living." The touchstone used to distinguish between lawful and unlawful obligations is whether the agreement is a "reasonable restraint" against competition. In short, the law requires that the proscription be closely related to the protection that the employer requires. This is measured by the time period over which the prohibition applies as well as the geographical territory encompassed. For example, consider a local business such as a retail plumbing business. If an ex-employee is precluded from engaging in the retail plumbing business for 30 years throughout the United States, all courts would hold that the noncompetition restraint is too broad. If the agreement calls for noncompetition for a period of only a year or two, and only in the immediate geographical territory in which the business drew its customers, a court may be more receptive to enforcing such restraint. In fact, if the proscription is drawn too broadly, the court may blue-pencil the restriction to narrow both the time and territory involved and then uphold the restraint.

In drafting a postemployment clause, therefore, the draftsman should attempt to foresee the reasonable bounds of the restraint required to protect the employer's business. The point of a noncompetition clause is the attempt to prevent an ex-employee, who may have personal contacts with the customers of the employer, from taking advantage of such personal relationships built at the expense of the employer. It does not rest on the idea that the ex-employee is using confidential or proprietary information gained during employment to compete with the employer. This is a matter for unfair competition, and the basis of the prohibition is an implied contract rather than an express promise. In many instances it is nevertheless true that an ex-employee competing with a prior employer may be in breach of a noncompetition clause and simultaneously guilty of unfair competition.

Superimposed on the "reasonable restraint" concept, as developed by the courts in expressing the common law, are state laws that restrict the rights of the parties to arrive at their own bargain. It is necessary to consult the law in the particular state in which the company is doing business to determine if there is some superseding state law that goes beyond the reasonable restraint rule. In California, there is a flat prohibition against any agreement between an employee and employer that prevents the employee from competing with the employer after the term of employment ends. Any noncompetition clause in an employment agreement will be struck down and declared unlawful in California. Other states are much less restrictive and follow the common law doctrine of reasonable restraint.

If a noncompetition clause is permissible under state law, provision should be made for obtaining injunctive relief. Chapter 3 contains a discussion of the nature of injunctive relief and suggests a clause for this remedy. The importance of injunctive relief in a noncompetition dispute is the immediacy necessary for an effective remedy. Typically, a case may take one or more years before it comes to trial by which time the ex-employee's competing business may be in full flower. Attempting to establish a measure of damages resulting from the breach of this provision would be extremely difficult. Furthermore, from the employer's viewpoint, a money award will not compensate the employer for the continuing and future damage that will result from the ex-employee's competing business.

Enforcement of the noncompetition clause requires immediate action; remedies referred to as a temporary restraining order or preliminary injunction may be available within a short time after filing suit. If a strong case can be made, temporary relief may be granted terminating the competitive activity until trial. Form 3.10 will remove one defense to a request for injunctive relief—that the remedy of damages is adequate.

Unfair Competition. The second category to be considered is unfair competition. For a technical employee this is highly important and may be the primary reason for entering into a written contract. The agreement should provide a broad definition of proprietary matters (trade secrets) that the employer considers confidential and which the employee may be expected to learn. There are countless definitions of what constitutes a trade secret; the term is not defined in any state or federal laws. Two elements which appear to be fundamental are that (*a*) the information is maintained by the employer in a manner such that it is not generally disclosed to the public and (*b*) the information is valuable in a commercial sense. Some courts have held that a trade secret must be unique, but it is generally agreed that a trade secret need not be an invention. Protecting proprietary information by keeping it secret has become relatively common in business today. Some businessmen and attorneys reason that even if an idea is patentable, the monopoly granted by the federal government has a limited life of 17 years. Competitors are then free to use the idea. By contrast, if an idea can be maintained in secrecy the monopoly extends indefinitely. Manufacturing methods and processes are particularly amenable to trade secret protection, since by disclosing the intricate details of the process to only a limited number of employees, the idea can in fact be kept secret. However, if the idea is embodied in a product sold in commerce and the secret can be extracted from the product by reverse engineering, any competitor is free to do so. Thus whether an idea should be protected by trade secret rather than some statutory means of protection greatly depends on the nature of the idea itself.

Technical trade secrets are not the only class of information that may be protected under the law of unfair competition. One type of information that an ex-employee may be prevented from using relates to customers. A common example that has appeared in many litigated cases involves a route salesman, such as a milkman, who calls on a list of customers. The ex-employee who had access to a compilation of names and requirements of customers and who solicits these customers after termination is guilty of unfair competition that a court will enjoin. A proper employment agreement for an employee who has access to such information should preclude the employee from soliciting persons or firms on the list after termination.

Defensive Protection.   In addition to protecting against improper use or disclosure of the employer's proprietary information, the agreement should also protect against the improper receipt of proprietary information from a new employee. This is the defensive nature of the proprietary information question discussed in Chapter 4 with reference to a consultant. In fact, the provisions for both offensive and defensive proprietary protection are nearly identical to those set forth in Form 4.8. They may be incorporated directly into the employee agreement with simply a change in the identification of parties. The last sentence of the first paragraph in Form 4.8 could also be omitted.

Inventions.   Finally, there is the matter of inventions made by the employee during the term of employment. As noted in the foregoing, the matter is identical to the question that arises in the consulting relationship, and the same clause may be used in the employment agreement. There is, however, a difference between the relationship of a company with a consultant and an employee. If an invention assignment clause is included in the agreement, this difference is unimportant, but it is one that a small business manager should be aware of. There is a doctrine in the common law referred to as "shop rights" that confers on an employer the right to use any invention conceived by an employee during regular working hours while using the tools and materials of the employer. Because shop rights are rather strictly construed by the courts and the proof required to establish the right is time consuming and expensive, the doctrine is no substitute for a properly drawn invention assignment clause. However, if an employee without a written agreement develops an invention on the job, the employer should recognize that it has an implied license to continue to use the idea even if the employee leaves.

The draftsman should also be aware of state interest in the matter of invention rights between an employer and employee. Several states, including California, have enacted laws that define the rights of an employee-inventor to the fruits of the employee's creativity. In California, a recent bill prohibits an assignment clause from covering inventions made by an employee on his or her own time and with noncompany materials and tools so long as it does not relate to the employer's business or is a result of the employee's work for the employer. It should be possible to obtain information regarding such laws from local professional or technical societies. Prudence dictates that at the very least the obligation of the employee should be preceded by the following: "Subject to the laws and regulations of this state . . ."

Since the clause for inventions is available in Form 4.9 and the clause for protecting trade secrets is available in Form 4.8, the following form covers the matter of competition during employment, a noncompete clause (to be used when state law allows), and a clause for use when the employee (e.g., a salesman) had access to customer lists.

8.5 *Confidential and Proprietary Matters*

(a) Employee shall not, during the term of this agreement, directly or indirectly, either as an employee, employer, consultant, principal, corporate officer, director, or in any other capacity, engage in any business that is in competition with the present or prospective business of Company.

(b) For a period of two (2) years after termination of employment, Employee shall not, directly or indirectly, either as an employee, employer, principal, corporate officer, director, or in any other capacity engage in any business throughout the State of _____ that is in competition with the business of Company.

(c) All lists or other records relating to the customers of Company, whether prepared by Employee or given to Employee during the term of this agreement, are the exclusive property of Company and shall be returned immediately to Company on termination of employment. Employee shall not for a period of two (2) years after termination of employment use the information contained in such list or other records to disclose the names or other information pertaining to customers of Company, nor shall Employee solicit, either alone or with any other person or firm, any of the customers of Company with whom Employee had a relationship during the term of this employment.

General

The agreement must include clauses for Notices (Form 3.1), Governing Law (Form 3.3), and Entire Agreement (Form 3.2). An Arbitration clause (Form 3.11) may also be considered.

As suggested previously, there are dangers in the possibility that the provisions of the employment contract covering invention assignment or noncompetition after employment may violate state law. It is therefore recommended that a Severability clause (Form 3.9) be included in the agreement.

There is at least one more clause that may be considered in an employment contract. There are continuing developments in the law relating to wrongful discharge of an employee. Suits are based not only on breach of contract but also on tort (e.g., mental distress, humiliation, and damage to reputation). These suits, even if frivolously brought, can disrupt the company's business. Such suits may be speculative in the sense that success may depend on establishing a new class of rights for employees. The draftsman may therefore want to consider a clause that fixes a duty on the unsuccessful litigant to pay the attorneys' fees of the prevailing party. A suggested form is as follows:

8.6   *Attorney's Fees and Costs.*   If any legal action or other proceeding is brought for the enforcement of this agreement, the successful or prevailing party shall be entitled to recover reasonable attorneys' fees and other costs incurred in that action or proceeding, in addition to any other relief to which it may be entitled.

Closing

The standard form of closing as suggested in Chapter 2 should be used. The agreement may be executed prior to the actual start of employment, although care should be exercised that an appropriate date is used from which the term of the agreement is measured.

Chapter Nine
Licensing

PATENTS AND OTHER PROPRIETARY RIGHTS

Before proceeding to discuss contracts relating to intellectual property, a brief description of the types of properties involved will aid in understanding the transactions. First, and perhaps of greatest industrial importance, are patents. Patents may be obtained in the United States or in foreign countries; only U.S. patents are discussed in this chapter. Second is an amorphous type of property, variously referred to as "know-how," "trade secrets," "technical data," or "confidential information." A third type of property comprises copyrights. A fourth type is common law or statutory trademarks.

Patents

A patent is granted by the U.S. government and provides an inventor with the right to exclude others from making, using, or selling the invention. These rights are created by statute based on a specific clause in the U.S. Constitution. By one method of classification, there are utility, design, and plant patents. The utility patent is the most common and may be obtained on any new and useful process, machine, manufacture, or composition of matter. A utility patent has a life of 17 years.

There are several misconceptions about patents. First, a patent does not provide the owner with the right to make, use, or sell an invention but provides the right to exclude others from doing so. A patent that broadly defines an invention is generally referred to as being "dominant"; a patent of less importance may be referred to as an "improvement" or "subservient" patent. It follows that one inventor may obtain broad rights to a particular invention, and another inventor may make an improvement on the broad concept. The latter may be precluded from making, using, or selling the improved invention unless a license is obtained from the owner of the broad patent. Thus the improvement patent owner does not have an exclusive right to manufacture, use, or sell.

Second, there is the misconception involving the improvement patent. It is not a special class of patent; it differs from a basic invention only in a matter of degree. When a patent is issued, there is no determination by the U.S. Patent Office that the patent is either an improvement or a dominant patent. This conclusion can be drawn only by comparing the scope of the claimed invention to the state of the art.

Third, patents are not renewable. When the patent expires at the end of 17 years the invention falls into the public domain and may be freely used by the general public. From one perspective a patent may be viewed as a contract between the government and the inventor. The inventor agrees to provide a full disclosure of his invention that may be used by the public after the patent expires. This disclosure is made in consideration of a limited-term exclusive right to prevent others from making, using, or selling the invention during the patent life.

The procedure for obtaining a patent involves filing a patent application with the U.S. Patent Office. This application includes an abstract, a description (commonly referred to as a "specification"), drawings (if required), claims (which define the scope of the patent), and an oath or declaration that the inventor in fact made the invention and believes himself to be the first inventor of the patented subject matter. It is filed in the U.S. Patent Office with a fee and requires, after filing, a disclosure or summary of all prior art known to the inventor at the time of filing. The Patent Office proceeds to examine the application to determine whether the device is new and useful and whether it would have been obvious to one having ordinary skill in the art.

Procedural aspects of the application are also examined. If the examiner finds relevant prior art the application may be rejected, at which time the applicant may amend the scope of the claimed invention or argue that the examiner is in error. After one or more of such rejections and responses the application may be finally rejected and abandoned. Alternatively, the Patent Office may agree that an invention which can be protected is claimed and a patent will issue. This procedure and the technique and knowledge required to successfully prosecute the application is complex and is ordinarily handled by an attorney specializing in this branch of the law.

The criteria for patentability is twofold. First, the process, machine, article, or composition of matter must be new and useful. Second, it must be unobvious to one having ordinary skill in the art. Meeting the former criterion can be established by relatively objective standards. The latter involves complex considerations of the state of the art at the time the invention is made and is never free from subjective determination.

After a patent is issued it is not indisputable. If the patent owner attempts to exercise its exclusive right by bringing a suit for patent infringement to prevent the alleged infringer from making, using, or selling the invention, the alleged infringer may defend by claiming that the patent is invalid. The same criteria used by the Patent Office in its determination that the invention merited patenting is applied again by the court as a final arbiter. The defendant (infringer) offers prior art to show that the idea was neither new nor nonobvious. If the patent is found valid after the defendant exhausts all appeals to higher courts, the defendant is conclusively prevented from attacking the validity of the patent at a later time.

In addition to proving patent validity, the patent owner must also prove that the alleged infringer is using the invention as defined by the patent. This requires a careful determination of the scope of the invention—a rigorous examination of how the patentee described the invention. If infringement is found, the case is established (after any appeals) and the patent owner is entitled to monetary damages and an injunction preventing the defendant from making, using, or selling the invention.

Closely involved with the enforcement of patents is a doctrine that is related to antitrust law termed "patent misuse." Because it may be viewed as a legal monopoly, a patent allows the patent owner to engage in certain practices that would otherwise violate the antitrust laws. For example, a patent owner may license a competitor to make, use, or sell the invention in one territory and reserve another territory for itself. Without benefit of the patent, this would be a horizontal territorial division of markets that would be illegal under the antitrust laws. Conduct that constitutes patent misuse is not tested by standards as rigorous as those used to establish an antitrust violation. Moreover, the penalty is unenforceability of the patent until the patent owner purges the improper conduct; it does not require the payment of damages as in the typical private antitrust lawsuit. Patent misuse is often raised as a defense by an alleged infringer in a patent infringement suit. The patent owner, in its licensing practices, must be careful to avoid violating the doctrine of patent misuse.

Trade Secrets

Trade secrets are protected not by statutes of federal or state governments but through the common law. Common law is a dynamic, developing body of law shaped by courts in response to specific cases. It may vary from jurisdiction to jurisdiction and from time to time. Drafting a proper trade secret agreement is more complex than a simple patent license agreement.

The most common definition of a *trade secret* is this: any formula, pattern, device, or compilation of information that is used in a business and which gives the business an opportunity to obtain an advantage over competitors who do not know or use the secret. It generally relates to the production of goods, marketing techniques, or management methods. It is generally in continuous use in the operation of the business as opposed to a single event that may also be kept secret—for example, a closed bid submitted for a contract. It consists of acquired knowledge, skill, or information relating to the operation of a business. It lasts indefinitely so long as it is not independently discovered by a third person. Typical documents that may incorporate a trade secret include drawings, designs, circuit diagrams, printed circuit board layouts, specifications, laboratory reports, technical data, test data, descriptions of manufacturing processes, designs or patterns of manufacturing equipment, cost information, sources of supply, market studies, customer lists, or financial or statistical data compilations.

A secret disclosed in a publication available to the general public or by transmission to a party that is not contractually bound to maintain the secret in confidence enters the public domain and may be used by anyone. A trade secret comes into existence as a result of the developer's intent and effective use of procedures to maintain the information in confidence.

The law has developed various theories to justify the right of a business to protect its proprietary information. At an early time, trade secrets were equated with property. Later, courts relied on a relationship of trust between the parties and a concept of fair commercial practices. More recently, there is a trend to find the legal basis for protecting trade secrets in contracts between the parties. Such contracts include license agreements, employment agreements, confidential disclosure agreements, agreements not to compete, or consulting agreements. These contracts expressly provide that certain information may not be used or publicly disclosed. If the contract is breached, the remedy may be monetary damages or an injunction. Underlying any of these theories, however, is a basic standard of commercial morality or fairness. Thus a contract between an employer and an employee that prevents the employee, after the employment is terminated, from using knowledge or skills obtained while working for the employer may be found unenforceable. The rationale for invalidating such agreement is the broader policy interest which demands that an ex-employee be permitted to earn a living by working for someone else or going into business for himself. Trade secret law will never be free of subjective judgments, fairness, conscience, equity, and broad policy interests.

Copyrights

A new copyright law was enacted by Congress and became effective in 1978. Copyrights, like patents, are granted by the federal government in accordance with statutes enacted pursuant to the U.S. Constitution. Copyrights protect artistic creations and are of immense value in the publishing industry; they are of less concern to most industrial businesses. However, certain documents and artistic creations such as advertising, manuals, and computer software programs can be protected by copyright and may be of considerable value.

A copyright lasts for the life of the author, plus 56 years. It prevents anyone from copying the artistic creation. If a third person independently creates an identical composition, the copyright, unlike a patent, provides no protection. Accordingly, to prove infringement of a copyright, the owner must show that the alleged infringer had access to the original work or a copy of it and that the similarity of the works is such that an act of copying is a fair conclusion to be drawn.

Trademarks

The line between copyrights and trademarks is not easily drawn by most businessmen. This apparently results from confusion caused by the use of the letter C in a circle to protect copyrights and the letter R in a circle to protect federally registered trademarks. Admittedly, a slogan or jingle could be covered by either copyright or trademark or both. Nevertheless, the concepts are entirely distinct as are the methods for obtaining the copyright and trademark, the manner of enforcing the rights, and the remedies that the law provides for infringement of the rights.

A brief explanation of the manner in which trademarks are created and protected is found in Chapter 5 in the discussion of distributor agreements. Any one of these four types of proprietary rights may be licensed. Furthermore, the licensed rights may include a combination of these types of properties. A frequently occurring combination is a patent and know-how (trade secrets).

LICENSED SUBJECT MATTER

During the course of invention, an idea or concept may be carried into commercial production. This is particularly true when the inventor is employed in industry. The details of the production methods and processes may be as valuable to a prospective licensee as the patent itself. The first consideration in preparing a license, therefore, is whether the company should license the patent alone or whether the trade secrets for carrying the idea into practical, commercial production should also be included for an appropriate fee.

Perhaps the primary determinant in this decision is the sophistication or expertise of the licensee. If the licensee is engaged in manufacturing in the field in which the invention has been made, the licensee may be entirely capable of transmuting the bare invention, as disclosed in the patent, into a commercial product. If not, technical assistance may be required. The second consideration for the developer may be the extent of documentation already prepared or the cost of preparing documentation that would be required in a manufacturing license.

When it is supplemented with additional technical information, the patent license may be referred to as "know-how" or by some similar term. Generally, the term "trade secret" is not used in licensing nonpatented subject matter to avoid any suggestion that the subject matter is of some special character, as opposed to garden-variety engineering. Although this would be unnecessary if the term "trade secret" is interpreted in the broad manner as initially set forth previously, it is still generally followed because of restrictive interpretations of the term by some courts. In addition to the documentary materials listed earlier, the licensed know-how may include physical objects such as prototypes, composition samples, test fixtures, photographs, or slides and films. Know-how may also include technical assistance from skilled personnel employed by the licensor who are familiar with the information being transferred. Normally, the oral transfer of information accompanies the documentation and is usually done by agreeing to supply a particular employee at a specified location to assist employees of the licensee. Technical assistance is usually paid for on a per-diem basis, plus expenses, much like a consulting arrangement, rather than the typical royalty payment.

If know-how is licensed the parties must be careful to specifically define the know-how from several points of view. First, the licensor should insert a time limit after which the licensor will not transfer any additional information it derives from its continuing engineering development without further compensation from the licensee. Conversely, the licensor may agree to continuously provide the licensee with all new developments relating to the product or process as they are made by the licensor. Second, the technical data must be identified with some particularity. On the one hand, the sheer volume of technical information will usually preclude it from being attached to the agreement. Furthermore, it may be undesirable to have such confidential information attached to the agreement because of the possible inadvertent disclosure to nonbound persons. The license agreement should therefore identify the documents and drawings by title, description, document number, or similar designation, preferably including the date. The licensee is as interested in specific designation of the licensed subject matter as the licensor. If the information licensed enters the public domain without fault of the licensee, the obligation of the licensee to make continued payments ceases. A careful definition will prevent future disputes.

There are certain advantages to licensing both the patent and know-how. First, a patent application pending in the U.S. Patent Office may be licensed, rather than an issued patent. In the absence of any know-how transfer in the agreement, no further royalties need be paid if the application does not issue. Thus the licensor's right to compensation may depend entirely on patent issuance. Second, the licensee will be relieved of any further license payment obligation if an issued patent is found invalid by a court. Or if the patent, in litigation against another person, is found to be noninfringed because the claims of the patent are narrowly construed, the licensee may be in a position to take advantage of such holding and refuse to make further payments. In these situations, loss of the patent results in the cessation of any further payments. However, if the licensor combines a patent license with a license to use technical information and this technical information has genuine substance, the entire situation may not be lost.

In licensing both patent and know-how subject matter in a single license, it is extremely important to segregate the grant of the patent license and the obligation to make patent royalty payments from the transfer of the know-how and the obligation to make payments for such transfer. Unless these matters are segregated, a court may find that a loss of either the patent or the know-how completely destroys the consideration to the licensee and relieves the licensee from any further payments. For example, in the situations mentioned previously in which the patent fails, the licensor may continue to receive payments for transfer of the know-how, providing that the agreement shows that separate payments were made for each. Conversely, it is possible that during the life of a patent the know-how will be disclosed to the public through no fault of the licensee; this will discharge any obligation of the licensee from further know-how payment. However, the licensor may still receive payment for the patent rights if the consideration for each is segregated, even if such payments for the know-how end.

The proportion of payments between patent and know-how rights to be made by the licensee must be negotiated and will presumably reflect the relative value. The term of the agreement must be no longer than the life of the patent. Typically, payments for the know-how end much earlier—for example, 10 years.

LICENSE AGREEMENT

A bare patent license agreement is described in this section. Normally, a license agreement is in a formal format. In addition to the standard opening clause, it may be desirable to include recital paragraphs in which certain definitions are set forth. Alternatively, one of the principal paragraphs in the body of the agreement may contain all the definitions of terms used in the agreement.

Grant

This paragraph provides the licensee with the right to make, use, and sell the invention. It is not necessary that all three of these rights be licensed. The licensor may grant only the right to make and use, with no right to sell the end product. Various combinations are possible, depending on the subject matter of the patent. A patent may include a method for manufacturing an intermediate chemical compound and also products made from such compound. The licensor may divide these rights between various processors and manufacturers.

The Grant clause must specifically set forth whether the grant is exclusive or nonexclusive. If an exclusive license is granted the license will exclude the licensor from the invention. Thus if the licensor intends to compete with the licensee it must reserve a license for itself. Obviously, the licensee is more likely to pay a larger sum for an exclusive right vis-à-vis a nonexclusive right. An exclusive license may be necessary to induce a licensee to invest the funds required for manufacturing facilities or market development. If an exclusive license is granted, however, the licensor must take care that the invention will be properly exploited. This is normally done by requiring minimum annual royalty payments. An alternative to the minimum royalty may be an extremely high nonrefundable down payment that may be used to force the licensee to exploit the invention to recoup its investment. In an exclusive license, a best-efforts clause is not sufficient; minimum annual royalty payments are advised.

The grant of the license should be for a specified territory. If only a U.S. patent is owned then the territory may be all or some portion of the

United States. Typically, the license is granted for the entire country. If foreign patents are involved, there are various possibilities for licensing particular territories on an exclusive basis, others nonexclusively, and still others in some combination of rights. A business manager would be well advised to seek legal assistance in granting foreign licenses.

If it is desirable to allow the licensee to grant sublicenses to others this must be made express in the agreement. In the absence of such statement, there is no right to sublicense. In most sublicensing arrangements, the licensor is attempting to use the licensee's stature or existing business organization to facilitate the licensing of a large number of potential users of the patent. For the assistance of the licensee, the licensor and licensee often split the royalties collected from sublicensees.

There are many other limitations on the grant that may be placed in this clause. It is possible, for example, to allow the licensee to manufacture only a fixed number of products. Or the licensee may be limited to a particular field of use; for example, the patent could cover an electronic circuit that could be used in various apparatus, but the license could limit use of the patent for circuits that are employed only in one type of apparatus, for example, radios. Other licenses could then be given in other fields in which the circuit could be used. Or the license may include some but not all of the claims of the patent. Some patents may cover both a component and various assemblies utilizing such components. These will be covered by different claims, and the claims may be licensed to some but not others.

A Grant clause for an exclusive license of a single patent may read as follows:

9.1 *Grant.* LICENSOR hereby grants to LICENSEE an exclusive license to manufacture, use, and sell devices covered by United States Letters Patent No. _____ for the life of the patent throughout the United States and its territories and possessions.

If the patent covers a method or process rather than an article of manufacture, apparatus, or machine, the license right may be described as "the exclusive license to practice and use the method." If both an article and a method are contained in the same patent, these two phrases are simply combined. If recital paragraphs or a definition paragraph has previously identified a group of patents with a definition such as "Letters Patent," this phrase can be substituted for the specific patent. If a patent has not yet issued but an application is pending, the subject matter licensed may be described as ". . . covered by United States Patent Application Serial

No. _____, entitled _____, filed
_____, and any
United States Letter Patent that may issue thereon . . ."

It is common to establish the term of the agreement in the Grant clause by stating that the license is for the life of the patent. The term must not extend beyond the life of the patent, since this would constitute patent misuse. The license, as previously noted, may also be restricted geographically. If only a portion of the United States is included in the license, the limited territory should be defined in the Grant clause directly or by using the term "Licensed Territory" and defining this term in another portion of the agreement. It must be remembered that in granting an exclusive license, the licensor itself will be precluded from practicing the invention. Therefore, if it intends to manufacture, use, or sell devices under the patent, the licensor should make the license "subject to a retained right in the licensor to make, use, and sell."

Payments

Although there are many variations of payment methods for a patent license, these can be broadly categorized into fixed or variable sums. A fixed sum license, as the name implies, involves a fixed number of dollars regardless of the extent of use of the patent. These dollars may be paid in a lump sum or by installment payments over a period of years. The variable sum method of payment, however, is more usual. Under the variable formula, the more use a licensee makes of the invention, the greater the sum paid to the licensor.

In the ordinary variable sum license, the payments, called "royalties," are made during the life of the patent. Typically, a down payment is made by the licensee that generally compensates the licensor, at least in part, for the development costs incurred in creating the invention. This down payment may be a fixed amount bearing no relationship to future royalties or may be an "advance royalty" that is credited against future earned royalties. In other words, it is a sum, usually nonrefundable, representing the royalties that the licensee must pay for the first units manufactured and sold.

The variable royalty rate is typically uniform and is based on units sold or net sales in dollars. A variation is a formula in which the royalties ascend or descend as volume increases. For example, a royalty formula may call for payments of 5% of the sales price for the first 10,000 units, 4% for the next 20,000 units, and so forth.

If the subject matter of the patent is a method rather than an article or composition, several royalty formulas may be used. The number of units processed using the patented method may be used to measure the utilization of the invention. This same measure may be used when licensing a machine. For example, a licensee may pay 2¢ for each unit processed by a patented machine. In a chemical-type process, the measure may also be the cost or the quantity of supplies introduced into the patented method. Still another variation would be the total sales volume of the resulting product from the method.

As suggested previously, the royalty base may comprise either units or dollars of the licensed product manufactured or sold. If the dollar volume of products sold is used as the base, this is generally referred to as "net sales" of the licensed product, and this term must be defined either in the payment paragraph or at some other place in the agreement.

For any variable sum license, there may be either a minimum or a maximum. As indicated earlier with respect to the exclusive license, some minimum annual payment is required in exchange for exclusivity. This may be stated in several ways with distinct results. It may be stated that the licensee shall pay a minimum royalty of a certain amount during each year in which the license is in effect. This would be a nonconditional obligation on the part of the licensee, and on failure to make such minimum payments, the licensor could sue and recover the sum. On the other hand, the license may state that minimum annual royalty payments must be made to maintain either an exclusive license or any license at all. In other words, the remedy of the licensor is not the recovery of the minimum annual royalty but the right to end the exclusive rights and turn the agreement into a nonexclusive license or to cancel the license in its entirety. At the other extreme, a maximum royalty sum may be stated in the agreement that, when reached, will constitute full payment for the license rights, with the licensee thereafter having a royalty-free license under the patent. This is sometimes referred to as a "knockout" provision. It provides the licensee with a reward, much like the descending royalty formula, for full exploitation of the licensed invention. The difficulty is that both parties will have a hard time arriving at a maximum sum.

The following clause is a relatively straightforward variable sum payment clause calling for an advance royalty payment, a flat percentage of the net sales of products sold during the term of the license, and minimum annual royalty payments. The date for payment is also specified.

9.2   *Payments.* LICENSEE shall make the following payments to LICENSOR:

    (a)   An advance royalty payment of _____ dollars ($_____), such sum to be paid within thirty (30) days after the date this agreement is executed; such sum shall be credited against and deducted from earned royalty payments becoming due under Subparagraph (b), but shall not be refundable in the event of termination of this agreement.

(b)   Earned royalty payments at the rate of ten percent (10%) of Net Selling Price of devices made and sold under this license. "Net Selling Price" shall mean the invoice price, minus transportation, insurance, sales or excise taxes, and credits allowed for returned goods. Devices shall be considered sold when invoiced, or, if not invoiced, when delivered, or, if payment is made before delivery, when paid for.

Royalty payments shall be paid by LICENSEE to LICENSOR on or before the last day of the month following the end of each calendar quarter during which this agreement is in effect for devices sold during such calendar quarter.

If payments made by LICENSEE to LICENSOR in any one year during the term of this agreement, other than the first year, do not exceed _____ dollars ($_____), LICENSOR at its option may terminate the exclusive right granted under this license, and LICENSEE shall thereafter have a nonexclusive license.

Reports and Records

In any variable sum license agreement, the licensor should reserve the right to audit the books and records of the licensee. The licensor may also require the licensee to provide a royalty report with each payment setting forth details of the royalty calculation.

A simple clause reads as follows:

9.3   *Reports and Records.* LICENSEE shall submit to LICENSOR a written royalty report with each royalty payment made in accordance with Paragraph _____. The report shall set forth in detail the amount of net sales of devices sold by LICENSEE during the applicable period and a calculation of the payment due. LICENSEE shall keep complete and accurate records for purposes of calculating payments and will permit an authorized agent or representative of LICENSOR to inspect and audit and make copies of such records, at any reasonable time during business hours, to vertify the records and amount due LICENSOR.

Term and Termination

In the Grant clause set forth previously, the term of the license was set forth as being coextensive with the life of the patent. The licensor may choose any shorter period, although this would be unusual, since the licensee would require the full term to justify the capital expenditures and product and market development costs. If more than one patent is licensed the licensor must be careful not to extract payment for an expired patent. Any such requirement is unlawful. This prohibition may be inadvertently violated if the agreement includes multiple patents and is made coextensive with the life of the "last patent to expire." If the royalty is not reduced on the expiration of one of the earlier-to-expire patents, it is assumed that a portion of the continuing royalty is in consideration of the expired patent and is thus improper. Accordingly, if a group of patents is licensed, the license royalty rate must be reduced incrementally on the expiration of each patent in the package until the final patent expires.

Termination for cause must also be covered in the license agreement. Neither party will generally be receptive to cancellation without cause. This will be particularly true for the licensee that has made an investment in exploiting the invention which it will not permit the licensor to appropriate. However, cancellation for cause must be carefully considered, since the agreement normally has a long life during which various difficulties may arise.

One of the obvious reasons for terminating the agreement is a breach by one of the parties to fulfill its obligations. A typical breach by the licensee would be failure to make royalty payments, to maintain books and records, or failure to mark patented items with a notice, as discussed subsequently. Although the sole obligation of the licensor in most licenses is only to grant the license, a breach by the licensor is also possible. If the license is exclusive and the patent is later held invalid, the licensor will have failed to perform its obligation of providing exclusivity. The termination-for-breach clause will provide the licensee with the right to terminate. Even if the license grants only a nonexclusive right, invalidity of the patent will constitute a breach. In a nonexclusive license, the licensee actually receives only immunity from the patentee's right to exclude others from practicing the invention. The price for this immunity is the payment of royalty. If the patent is held invalid, there is no longer any need for the immunity and there is a failure of consideration for continued payments. Thus each party should have the right to terminate the agreement in the event of a breach by the other.

Another matter is the possibility of financial difficulty by the licensee. Financial failure will either jeopardize the full exploitation of the invention or, in its worst case, may jeopardize payment of the royalties. The licensor should arm itself with the right to terminate in the event the licensee becomes financially impaired.

This clause should also provide that in the event of termination, the licensee is not relieved of the obligation to make payments for units made and sold prior to the termination. If the license includes know-how or confidential information, the post-termination subparagraph should clearly obligate the licensee to discontinue using any of such information, to continue the obligation to maintain such information in confidence, and to return all documents and other technical data that contain the confidential information.

The following clause does not include any statement of term but sets forth the basis for termination and defines the rights in the post-termination period.

9.4   *Termination.*   If either party fails to perform any one or more of its obligations required by this agreement and does not remedy the same within thirty (30) days after receipt of a written statement specifying the details thereof or if either party discontinues business, becomes insolvent, has a receiver appointed, goes into liquidation, or becomes a party to any action relating to bankruptcy or insolvency that is instituted and not dismissed within thirty (30) days, the nondefaulting party may terminate this agreement on giving thirty (30) days notice to the defaulting party of its intent to terminate, and this agreement shall terminate at the end of such notice period.

Termination of this agreement pursuant to any of its provisions shall not relieve LICENSEE of its obligations incurred prior to such termination and shall not impair any of LICENSOR's rights or remedies as set forth in this agreement or provided by law. On termination, there will be immediately due to LICENSOR by LICENSEE any unpaid royalty payments.

Patent Notice

The licensor should obligate the licensee to mark each of the patented items with the patent number. The marking of patented items affects damages that are recoverable from infringers. If devices are marked with the patent number, this act is considered to be constructive notice of the patent owner's exclusive right to all the world effective immediately upon the sale of the items with the notice. Because of such notice, an infringer is made to account for damages for all infringing articles made after the sale with a patent notice. If a notice is not used, a patentee may recover damages from an infringer only after giving express notice to the infringer. The difference in the damage period may be extensive. The licensor should therefore fix on the licensee the obligation to mark the products to maximize the patentee's potential damages in the event of suit against an infringer.

A short paragraph for the patent notice is as follows:

9.5 *Patent Notice.* All devices manufactured and sold by LICENSEE, unless otherwise approved by LICENSOR, shall bear notice of any patent that in LICENSOR's judgment covers the device.

Other Provisions

There are literally hundreds of other provisions that could be considered in a patent license agreement. Many of these are subtle and require the advice and counsel of a patent lawyer before being incorporated into a license. Some are unnecessary in a simple straightforward license, but as the transaction grows more complex, various provisions may be desirable. Only a few are suggested here.

The licensee may require that the licensor warrant its title to the patent license. Whereas a title search may be conducted in the U.S. Patent Office by a potential licensee to confirm the licensor's rights, a warranty may still be appropriate in some cases. The licensor may have failed to obtain the complete right, title, and interest to the patent by virtue of a faulty assignment from its employee-inventor or a prior patent owner. A history of financial difficulty, perhaps involving bankruptcy, may cast a shadow on the licensor's complete and full title to the patent. Other problems of ownership may make a warranty desirable.

Generally, nothing is said in a license agreement regarding enforcement of the patent. In the absence of any statement, there is no obligation on the part of the licensor to prosecute infringers. If the license is exclusive, the failure to prosecute infringers may be grounds for termination. But if the license is nonexclusive, the question is not entirely free of doubt. Only in rare instances will a licensee have sufficient leverage to force the licensor to assume the obligations of enforcing the patent rights. This may be a mandatory obligation or may give the licensee the right to terminate the license in the event that it notifies the licensor of an infringement and the licensor fails to act.

Another matter that should be considered is proper exploitation of the invention. As noted previously, there will normally be a minimum annual royalty if the license is exclusive. But if the license is nonexclusive, a licensee will normally object to any minimum annual payments. The licensor's only alternative is to attempt to saddle the licensee with the duty to exploit the invention through a "best-efforts" clause. It will be difficult even under the best of circumstances for a licensor to prove that a licensee failed to use its best efforts in exploiting an invention. Nevertheless, the use of a best-effort clause provides at least a minimum level of protection to the licensor.

When both parties to a license agreement are engaged in research, development, and design of products covered by the license, the parties' continuing efforts may give rise to additional rights. Either the licensor or licensee may make improvements that may be patentable. The parties may desire to settle at the time of entering into the license their respective rights relative to these future inventions. Inventions by the licensor may be added to the subject matter of the agreement automatically, or at the option of the licensee, and will bear the same royalty. When an improvement is made by the licensee, the licensor may want to obtain some rights thereto, either for its own purpose or, if the license is nonexclusive, to distribute to its other licensees. It may oblige the licensee to "grant back" rights under any improvement patents. This type of provision can easily run afoul of the antitrust law. Careful consideration and counsel are advised before implementing a grant-back clause. If used, it is advised that the licensor take back only a nonexclusive license together with the right to sublicense. This avoids the charge that the licensor is using the grant-back clause as a net to encompass the entire technology.

As mentioned earlier, the license may be entered into before a patent is issued. Before a patent issues, the applicant has no right to exclude others from making, using, or selling the invention prior to the date of issuance of the patent. Thus, if a license is signed prior to patent issuance, the licensee is actually making royalty payments for the advantage of early disclosure by the patentee as well as the "option" to have a license in the event the application matures into a patent. Since the latter may constitute the most valuable right received by the licensee, the licensee may have a justifiable interest in seeing that the licensor vigorously prosecutes the application to successful conclusion. Consequently, a license agreement covering a patent application may include an obligation on the licensor to prosecute the application.

General

The standard clauses for Notices (Form 3.1), Governing Law (Form 3.3), Entire Agreement (Form 3.2), Assignability (Form 3.6), and Headings Not Controlling (Form 3.4) are definitely required. Because of the potential possibility of a violation of antitrust laws or the application of the patent misuse doctrine, a Severability clause (Form 3.9) is highly advised. It is also advised on behalf of the licensee to obtain a Most Favorable Terms (Form 3.14) clause. The parties should consider an Arbitration clause (Form 3.11).

Chapter Ten
Conclusion

At the risk of being redundant, it must be stressed once more that the draftsman should analyze the facts concerning a transaction prior to negotiation and the drafting of an agreement. The objectives of the company must be clearly established through internal consultations with company managers involved in the activity covered by the agreement. If the agreement concerns one of the areas discussed in this text, the appropriate chapter should be reviewed and an outline of the points to be included prepared. Form paragraphs will require amplification to encompass the unique aspects of the transaction. Other matters raised in the discussion of company objectives may not be included at all in the form paragraphs; on the other hand, it may be necessary to create entirely new paragraphs.

If the subject matter is not covered in the text, it is still possible to draft a well-constructed, clear, and legally binding agreement. The beginning and end are available in Chapter 2; Chapter 3 provides the ordinary boilerplate. Drafting should start with a *detailed* outline. The outline can be prepared by asking a series of questions, of which the following are only exemplary.

What are the specific acts which each party is required to perform to achieve the main purpose of the agreement? What remedy should be available to the nondefaulting party if the act is not properly performed? Termination? Specific performance? Liquidated damages? What are the foreseeable events that may occur and what should be the effect on the arrangement? Insolvency? Death? How long will the agreement last and how will it be terminated? Indefinitely? Terminable only for breach or for some other good cause? Should there be automatic renewal? Will the arrangement involve the disclosure of confidential information that is of considerable value? What means should be used to prevent unauthorized disclosure?

In nearly every transaction, payment is the primary obligation of one of the parties. What is the specific amount of the payment? Will it be a lump sum, paid in installments, variable, or incentive based? If variable, what is the basis for measuring the amount? Sales? Profit? When will the consideration be due? When must it be paid? What events may change or modify the amount owed? Sale returns? Noncollectibility of a receivable? What should be the effect on payment, if any, if there is a premature termination? Should there be a right to acceleration if an installment payment is late? Are there terms that require specific definition? Sold? Net income? Will there be a maximum for payments? A minimum? Should there be a right to examine the books and records for verification?

If rights are granted or an appointment is made, what is the precise nature of the rights? Exclusive? Retention of rights in the grantor? Should there be a territory limitation? Time? Quantity? Customer? May the grantee appoint others or subdivide the rights in some manner?

Is a warranty required? What type of warranty? Performance? Title? Should there be save harmless protection? What will be the remedy for a breach of warranty? Should there be a disclaimer of warranty? Of consequential damages?

It is obvious that the above list of inquiries could be extended for pages—and still the necessary inquiry for the specific transaction for which the agreement is to be prepared would not be covered.

The point is that many arrangements are either unique or have some unusual aspects. Simply seizing one of the form paragraphs in this text, without reflecting on its applicability to the transaction under consideration, will lead to disaster. If the arrangement is too complex, the matter should be turned over to an attorney. Even then, a draft may be prepared and submitted to the attorney for review. At the very least it may be sufficient as an outline to be used by the attorney and may perhaps save legal expense.

If the agreement must be prepared "from scratch," write or dictate a draft from the prepared outline in simple, direct, business conversational English. Prepare the draft like a letter or report, concentrating on making a clear statement for each point, as if you were explaining the transaction to a third person. Then, after perhaps a second draft or some cleaning up, *give* it to a third person, such as the company accountant. Ask for a critical review. What isn't clear? What hasn't been covered? Ask what his or her understanding of the arrangement as a whole is. Invite him or her to add, delete, or modify. (Pride of authorship has no place in agreement drafting.) Then prepare a new draft. Put it into a drawer for a day or two. Read it again. Draft it again. When your secretary looks a little wan and pale when you request another typed draft—you're *almost* done.

If the process appears too arduous, consider the benefits. It is probably the first agreement you will ever enter into that you fully understand.

Moreover, the exercise has likely raised matters that could easily have escaped your notice if the agreement had been drafted by someone else. It is possible that the arrangement has lost some of its rosy color as a result of your assiduous analysis. The value of a realistic appraisal of the benefits and burdens of the arrangement *before* the agreement is executed may be priceless.

As a final word, review the two agreements contained in the Appendix. Both are for hypothetical situations. Each illustrates a more complex contract but is constructed from the basic elements discussed in the text.

The employment agreement is for a founder, major shareholder, and current president of a closely held corporation. The president is 55 years old and has occupied this position for 26 years. The agreement has been prepared in order to solidify the relationship between the president and the company. It sets forth the benefits the president is entitled to and defines his role in the company until retirement.

The company has stock purchase and stock option plans for upper management employees; the plans have resulted in the distribution of stock to a small number of key employees who are interested in the continued management of the company. The company has no plans to be acquired or to sell shares in a registered public offering.

The president has a ranch in Albuquerque, New Mexico where he is active in breeding and raising horses for profit and pleasure. Under a current diversification program the company is internally developing a new product line for a new division and the president is actively participating in this activity. The long-range plan of the company is to locate a plant in Albuquerque when the division has become operational and attains a predetermined sales level.

In the agreement in the Appendix, the first paragraph provides for employment until mandatory retirement of the employee unless, upon election of the employee with company approval, an earlier retirement is chosen. The agreement may be terminated earlier upon the occurrence of certain events, which are described later.

While the employee is hired as the president, the company has retained the right, in Paragraph 2, to relieve the employee of this position. The employee has bargained for the right to select early retirement in the event that he relinquishes this position, and the company has agreed to consent to such early retirement in these circumstances. The agreement makes clear that, other than early retirement, the employee will have no other claims against the company for the demotion. Paragraph 2 also requires the employee to work full-time for the company; however, the employee is given one month in each year to spend on his ranch to raise and breed horses. This time is in addition to normal vacation.

The compensation, in Paragraph 3, is divided into a base salary and an incentive salary. The base salary is adjusted for inflation through the provision of a cost-of-living escalator based on the Consumer Price Index. The incentive salary is based on pretax profit after subtracting a return on the net worth of the business. Both "net profit" and "net worth" are carefully defined. Since the incentive salary is based on the company fiscal year, and the agreement is executed in midyear, provision is made for the payment of incentive salary for partial years. The incentive salary payment date is specified and a maximum is placed on the amount.

Although the company has a qualified pension and profit-sharing plan which includes the president, it is desired to supplement the benefits of this plan with a nonqualified deferred compensation plan. In Paragraph 4, deferred compensation is based on the employee's salary preceding retirement and includes three types of payment. One payment is required regardless of the postretirement activities of the president. Another payment is for active advisory services to be performed by the ex-president after retirement; payment is contingent on actual services rendered. These advisory payments will reduce Social Security benefits. The third deferred compensation payment is in consideration of a promise not to compete with the company after retirement.

Since the president is 55 years old, physical or mental disability is a foreseeable event. The event must be carefully defined because the consequences are serious. The company does not wish to be burdened with an invalid chief executive officer; in Paragraph 5, therefore, termination after disability is at the discretion of the company. Furthermore, permanent disability is related to deferred compensation by making termination for disability equivalent to retirement. Because a portion of the deferred compensation is dependent upon active performance of advisory services, which would presumably be impossible if the president was permanently disabled, this requirement is excused.

Other than carrying a $250,000 group life insurance policy covering the president, the company does not provide any other death benefits while the president is employed. This benefit is specified in Paragraph 6. Under Internal Revenue Code Sec. 79(a), the premium payments on the excess of the policy benefit over $50,000 will be taxed to the employee according to an established formula. The occurrence of death after retirement, during the 10-year payout of deferred compensation, is covered in the deferred compensation provision in Paragraph 4.

When drafting an agreement where there are several foreseeable events that may affect certain obligations and benefits of the parties, care must be exercised in relating all of the events, rights, and duties. The same event may require mention in several different paragraphs. It is easy to lose track of the relationships, particularly in a complex agreement. After a first draft is prepared, the draftsman should pick an event and review the entire agreement noting all paragraphs where each duty and right are related to the event. For example, the sample employment agreement may be reviewed to determine the effect of death during employment on base salary compensation, incentive compensation, termination, and low-interest loans. Similarly, events such as retirement or voluntary termination can be traced to determine their effect on various benefits for the employee. Reviewing the agreement with a particular event in mind will aid in disclosing omissions or inconsistencies. A thorough "What if . . ." analysis is indispensable as a drafting tool.

The president has expressed the desire, prior to retirement, to manage the new division when it is moved to Albuquerque. In such event, the president has indicated that he would relocate his residence from the upper Midwest city where he now resides to Albuquerque. The employment contract, in Paragraph 7, provides relocation expenses for the president.

The agreement also provides for ordinary medical and group life insurance, a vacation, an automobile, and a standard expense reimbursement provision. To enable himself to pursue his interest in raising and breeding horses, the president has borrowed money from the company from time to time. Low-interest loans are an excellent executive compensation perquisite. Thus Paragraph 12 gives the president the right to borrow money up to a maximum aggregate amount.

Although the agreement will last until the employee retires, the company reserved the right, in Paragraph 13, to terminate the president for certain causes. The president also has the right to terminate without cause. The effect of different types of termination on various employee's rights and benefits are specified. The remaining terms of the agreement are boilerplate.

Considering the entire agreement, it is apparent that the president had substantial bargaining power in arriving at the final terms and conditions. The agreement is not atypical of what could be expected in a situation such as that described. Although there are a few unique benefits in the agreement in the Appendix, nearly every agreement requires *some* tailoring to specific circumstances.

The second agreement in the Appendix is a hybrid consulting and purchase agreement. It calls for custom computer software development. The hypothetical situation involves a firm, Structural Dynamics, Inc. (SDI), that provides structural design and engineering services to the construction industry. SDI has developed a new method for performing a structural steel analysis for buildings, such as gymnasiums, amphitheatres, and stadiums, that are built using a new construction technique. It believes that its method for structural analysis is unique and offers a significant competitive advantage for this type of service. It has previously developed other methods that have been programmed, but these methods were appreciably simpler than the new method. It does not have an in-house computer but employs a computer time-sharing service to run its older programs. The new method is performed using two of the older programs, several desk-top engineering computers, and manual calculations. Creating a program for the new method is beyond the technical expertise of SDI and, in any event, would require so much time that the company would be unable to carry out its present workload. The older programs were also developed under custom software programming contracts, so SDI is familiar with the many pitfalls in this type of contract.

Modern Systems, Inc. is a software development firm that specializes in programs for scientific and engineering applications. During initial discussions, Modern proposed doing the work on a time and materials basis. SDI was apprehensive about this type of payment because it is aware that creating a program involves many unforeseen difficulties which could lead to exhorbitant costs. Moreover, it has not previously used Modern's services. On the other hand, Modern has indicated that it cannot provide a fixed price until it has fully evaluated the extent of the work that would be required to complete the program.

To resolve the impasse, the parties agreed to enter into two agreements. The first will require preliminary design services; in this job, a functional specification and a preliminary design specification will be prepared. This will enable Modern to assess the amount of programming required. Also during the preliminary design job, a project plan will be prepared that will include a master schedule for the project as well as other details regarding personnel, rates, and so on. If SDI is satisfied with the preliminary design package, the main project will proceed. Since the preliminary design job is less extensive than the principal programming job, Modern will be able to quote a firm price in a proposal.

The second agreement will involve the principal design, programming, and testing services. All work during the principal job, called the "Project," will be in accordance with the documents developed during the preliminary job. The maximum payment for the project will be determined during the preliminary work and will be incorporated into the second contract.

After some reflection, the parties agreed that the two agreements could be integrated into a single contract providing that it was unequivocally clear that SDI could terminate the agreement after the preliminary job if it was not satisfied. This integration would make the job of drafting simpler.

The drafting problem for the agreement between Modern and SDI is complicated by the nature of the subject matter. Software is intangible and the process for creating it is, if not mysterious, at least abstruse. When a building contractor or special machinery manufacturer is engaged, the owner can visually monitor progress during construction. It is much more difficult, however, to see a computer program being built. From the point of view of the draftsman, the trick is to identify whatever *is* tangible during the development and to use the tangibles as a measure of progress. The tangibles are referred to as "deliverables." An additional technique for monitoring is to require progress reports throughout the development cycle. Unfortunately, proper monitoring involves considerable expenditure of time by the purchaser; progress reports must be carefully reviewed and evaluated. But there is no viable alternative.

To fully understand the agreement between SDI and Modern, a few words about the software development process are required. A software development project employs a number of professionals specializing in different facets of the job. These include system analysts, program designers, programmers, program test specialists, documentation support personnel, and, most importantly, a senior project manager. The senior project manager has complete control over and authority for the project and is the interface with the customer. Except for the project manager, none of the personnel are engaged full-time and continuously on the project.

The project can be divided into major parts, called phases. Depending on the project management employed, there may be five or six phases: definition, design, programming, testing, and installing. To complicate matters, most of these phases overlap. If the project is extensive, the phases are broken up into tasks. Some of the tasks must be completed prior to starting other tasks or phases. These tasks, and all of the phases, are critical to on-time completion of the project. They are therefore singled out for monitoring and are called "milestones." At the completion of the milestones, documentation is produced that records the work completed. This documentation constitutes the deliverables that are contractually required.

When the software program is completed, it must be demonstrated as having solved the problem. The final demonstration is called an "acceptance test." It is the crucial phase of the development process. In a complex program, there will always be "bugs," as they are called by programmers. Many bugs are innocuous and can be easily fixed; others may be due to a fundamental design deficiency. It is not always easy to separate the harmless from the lethal bugs. During the acceptance test, the program is measured against the functional specification to determine compliance. The appearance of harmless bugs, although preventing full compliance, may be ignored in judging the success of the program. The program, therefore, is required only to show "substantial compliance" to the functional specification during the acceptance test. Any minor bugs are later corrected during a warranty period.

Turning now to the agreement between Modern and SDI in the Appendix, the reader will see that only a few of the special problems are discussed. In Paragraph 2(c), although the preliminary design job is smaller than the project, it is still broken down into four parts. As each part is completed, evidenced by delivery of a report or documentation, a portion of the fixed price is paid. If performance is not on-time, SDI can terminate. Compare this with the payment provisions for the project in Paragraph 4(c). Also note the structure of the agreement; Paragraph 2 is for the preliminary job, Paragraph 4 is for the project, and each is subdivided into similar parts to provide a parallel that facilitates reading and locating of particular provisions.

In Paragraph 4(c), there is a fixed price stated (to be supplied after the preliminary job is completed), but the price is a maximum. Modern will be paid for time and materials, which may be less than the maximum and Modern must bill for time spent and produce time records to prove the actual time expenditures. Payment is made, as in the preliminary job, on completion of events (milestones), but SDI will hold back a portion of each payment to secure the final completion. Furthermore, if billed time is less than the maximum, the difference is credited against future milestones. Unlike the preliminary job, if the milestone is completed off schedule, SDI can either terminate or charge a late payment. As a practical matter, termination may be a poor remedy because the prior investment would be partially lost if SDI terminated and hired a new firm. The late payment provision is a better remedy to motivate Modern into committing further manpower to meet the schedule, particularly since all late payments are waived if completion is on time.

In Paragraphs 2(d) and 4(d), there is a provision for protecting SDI against loss of ownership of the work product in the event the agreement is terminated prematurely. The paragraphs lock in ownership, following each payment, to all written materials that are created prior to the payment. Consequently, with the passing of each milestone, SDI can terminate without cause and will still be assured that the benefit from the services will not be lost.

Another nonordinary provision is in Paragraph 5(b). Modern warrants that the development is original and was specifically for this project. Since various pieces of existing software are often used to develop a program, it is important to the ownership rights of SDI that none of the pieces belong to any third party. Although the warranty also covers patents and copyrights, most software is protected by trade secret; the warranty that trade secrets of others were not used is clearly more valuable.

Finally, in Paragraph 8, there is an explicit statement of the responsibility of SDI. In a transaction of this type, a certain amount of cooperation from the customer is required. However, a phrase such as "mutually co-operate" is too ambiguous and is an invitation to the vendor to use some minor incident as an excuse to performance. It is preferable to set forth the specific duties of the customer in detail.

Neither of the agreements in the Appendix is perfect. Despite serious and prolonged effort, I have rarely reviewed an agreement drafted months or years earlier with complete satisfaction. Like any other endeavor, each individual effort is a learning exercise. I hope this text will provide a shortcut to at least a minimum level of competence.

Appendix

EMPLOYMENT AGREEMENT

THIS AGREEMENT is made this _____ day of _____, 19__, by and between XYZ COMPANY ("Company"), a Minnesota corporation, having its principal place of business in Minneapolis, Minnesota and John Parker, an individual, residing at 1234 Dennison Avenue, Minneapolis, Minnesota ("Employee").

BACKGROUND

Employee is one of the founders of the Company and has been its president for 26 years, during which time the Company has received substantial benefits from the extraordinary services he has performed;

The Company desires to have Employee continue to serve as its president until his retirement and to compensate him for his services both prior and subsequent to his retirement.

THE PARTIES THEREFORE AGREE AS FOLLOWS:

1. *Appointment.* The Company hereby hires Employee as president of the Company for a period beginning on the date of this agreement and ending on mandatory retirement of Employee on _____, 19__, or, if Employee elects and the Company approves, at an early retirement date selected by Employee, unless earlier terminated in accordance with the terms hereinafter set forth.
2. *Duties and Authority*
    (a) Employee will occupy the position of President and Chief Executive Officer of the Company and may be elected to serve as a director of the Company. In the event Employee is relieved from the position of president, Employee may elect early retirement and Company agrees to consent to such early retirement.

This right to early retirement will be the sole remedy of Employee for having been relieved from the position of president.

(b)   As president, Employee will have the powers of a general manager, subject to the control of the Board of Directors, and have general supervision, direction, and control over the business and affairs of the corporation and its officers. Employee will be primarily responsible for carrying out all orders and resolutions of the Board of Directors and such duties as may from time to time be assigned to Employee by the Board of Directors.

(c)   In the absence of the Chairman of the Board at any Shareholders or Board of Directors meeting, Employee will preside over that Shareholders meeting, and, in the event Employee is then a director of the Company, will preside over that Board of Directors meeting.

(d)   Employee shall devote his entire productive time, ability, and attention to the business of the Company; however, Company acknowledges that Employee is engaged in the raising and breeding of quarter horses for profit and agrees that Employee may spend up to one month during each year of this agreement at Employee's ranch, in addition to the vacation set forth in Paragraph 9, and may devote such other time to such business as Employee's duties reasonably permit.

(e)   Employee will not, during the term of this agreement, directly or indirectly engage in any business, either as an employee, employer, consultant, principal, corporate officer, or in any other capacity, whether or not compensated, without the prior written consent of Company.

3. *Compensation.* Employee will receive compensation during the term of this agreement as follows:

(a)   A base salary of One Hundred Thousand Dollars ($100,000.00) per year, payable in equal weekly installments on the last day of each week. The base salary shall be adjusted at the end of each year of employment to reflect any change in the cost of living by multiplying the salary for the prior year by a fraction, the numerator of which is the National Consumer Price Index (NCPI) for the month most recently released by the Bureau of Labor Statistics of the United States Department of Labor and the denominator of which is the NCPI for the identical month in the preceding year. If this index is discontinued, changed, or unavailable, Company shall determine and utilize a similar criterion for reflecting any increase in the cost of living.

(b)   An incentive salary equal to ten percent (10%) of the difference between: (i) the adjusted net profits (hereinafter defined) of the Company and (ii) ten percent (10%) of the net worth (hereinafter defined) of the Company, during each fiscal year beginning or ending during the term of this agreement. "Adjusted net profit" shall be the net profit before federal and state income taxes, determined in accordance with accepted accounting practices by the independent accounting firm employed by the Company as auditors and adjusted to exclude: (i) any incentive salary payments paid pursuant to this agreement; (ii) any contributions to pension and/or profit-sharing plans; (iii) any extraordinary gains or losses (including, but not limited to, gains or losses on disposition of assets); (iv) any refund or deficiency of federal and state income taxes paid in a prior year; and (v) any provision for federal or state income taxes made in prior years which is subsequently determined as unnecessary. The determination of the adjusted net profits made by the independent accounting firm employed by the Company shall be final and binding upon Employee and the Company. "Net worth" for purpose of computing the incentive salary shall be the stockholder's equity at the beginning of the fiscal year. For the first and last fiscal years ending and beginning, respectively, during the term of this agreement, the incentive salary shall be computed for the proportion of the fiscal year coextensive with this agreement. The incentive salary shall be paid within ninety (90) days after the end of each fiscal year. The maximum incentive salary payable for any one year shall not exceed two hundred percent (200%) of the base salary of Employee.

4. *Deferred Compensation.* In the event that Employee retires after performing services for the Company until Employee reaches the age of 65, or retires at an earlier age with the approval of the Company, Employee will be entitled to deferred compensation payments after retirement upon the following terms and conditions:

(a) For a period of ten (10) years ("Retirement Period") Employee will receive some or all of the following: (i) Base Payments equal to thirty percent (30%) of the average total salary (base salary plus incentive salary) paid to Employee during the last three (3) full years of employment prior to the month of retirement ("Retirement Salary Base"). (ii) Advisor Payments equal to thirty percent (30%) of the Retirement Salary Base, provided that Employee serves as an advisor and consultant to the Company regarding its business. To earn the advisor payments, Employee will hold himself available to perform services at reasonable times at the request of the Board of Directors of the Company, consistent with any business activities Employee may be engaged in at such time. The Board of Directors of the Company shall have the right to require the presence of Employee at any Board of Directors meeting, not exceeding more than one per month, to act and serve in the advisory capacity. Attendance at these Board of Directors meetings shall not be required should Employee's health prevent attendance; however, Company shall have the right to demand a written statement from Employee prepared by a licensed medical examiner evidencing inability of Employee to attend the meeting or meetings. Employee will be reimbursed for all reasonable and necessary travel and incidental expenses incurred by Employee in connection with the performance of advisory services. (iii) Noncompetition Payments equal to forty percent (40%) of the Retirement Base Salary provided that Employee will not, directly or indirectly, perform any business, commercial, or consulting services to any person, firm, or organization or become associated as manager, employee, director, or owner of any business organization competing directly or indirectly with the Company, whether or not compensated, without the prior written consent of Company. In the event that Company and Employee are unable to agree on whether a particular business in which Employee attempts to engage is directly or indirectly in competition with the Company, the matter will be submitted to arbitration under the provisions of Paragraph 20.

(b) The deferred compensation payments shall be made in equal monthly installments starting in the month following the month of retirement.

(c) In the event of the death of Employee prior to the expiration of the "Retirement Period," the Company will pay all remaining Base Payments specified in subparagraph (a)(i), and no other deferred compensation payments, to any beneficiary of Employee designated by Employee in a written document filed with the Company, or in the absence of such designation, the estate of Employee. The Company may elect to pay these remaining Base Payments in a lump sum or in the equal monthly installments specified in subparagraph (b).

(d) Employee shall not sell, assign, transfer, or pledge, or in any other way dispose of or encumber, voluntarily or involuntarily, by gift, testamentary disposition, inheritance, transfer to an inter-vivos trust, seizure and sale by legal process, operation of law, bankruptcy, winding up of a corporation, or otherwise, the right to receive any deferred compensation pursuant to this agreement.

5. *Permanent Disability*

   (a) In the event Employee becomes permanently disabled (hereinafter defined) during employment with Company, Company may terminate this agreement by giving thirty (30) days notice to Employee of its intent to terminate, and, unless Employee resumes performance of the duties set forth in Paragraph 2 within five (5) days of the date of notice and continues performance for the remainder of the notice period, this agreement will terminate at the end of the thirty (30) day period. "Permanently disabled" for the purpose of this agreement will mean the inability, due to physical or mental ill health, or any reason beyond the control of Employee, to perform Employee's duties for thirty (30) consecutive days or for an aggregate of sixty (60) days during any one employment year irrespective of whether such days are consecutive.

   (b) Upon termination of employment under the provisions of subparagraph (a), Employee may have any deferred compensation to which the Employee may be entitled under the provisions of Paragraph 4 paid to him upon giving notice to the Company. For the purposes of Paragraph 4, termination under subparagraph (a) of this paragraph shall be considered "retirement"; Employee will be excused from performing advisory services as required under Paragraph 4(b)(ii) but shall nevertheless be entitled to Advisor Payments except to the extent limited by death of Employee as set forth in Paragraph 4 (c).

6. *Death.* In the event that Employee dies during the term of this agreement, this agreement shall immediately terminate.

7. *Relocation.* In the event Employee is transferred and assigned to a new principal place of work located more than fifty (50) miles from Employee's present residence, Company will pay for all reasonable relocation expenses including:

   (a) Transportation fares, meals, and lodging for Employee, his spouse, and family from Employee's present residence to any new residence located near the new principal place of work;

   (b) Moving of Employee's household goods and the personal effects of Employee and Employee's family from Employee's present residence to the new residence;

   (c) Lodging and meals for Employee and Employee's family for a period of no more than sixty (60) consecutive days while occupying temporary living quarters located near the new principal place of work;

(d) Round trip travel, meals, and lodging expenses for Employee and Employee's family for no more than two (2) househunting trips to locate a new residence, each trip not to exceed fourteen (14) days; and

(e) Expenses in connection with the sale of the residence of Employee including realtor fees, mortgage prepayment penalties, termite inspector fees, title insurance policy and revenue stamps, escrow fees, fees for drawing documents, state or local sales taxes, mortgage discount points (if in lieu of a prepayment penalty), and seller's attorneys fees (not to exceed one percent (1%) of the sales price). At the option of Employee and in lieu of reimbursement for these expenses, Employee may sell the residence of Employee to the Company at the fair market value of the residence determined by an appraiser chosen by the Company. The appraisal will be performed within ten (10) days after notice of transfer and notice of appraised value will be submitted by report to Employee. Employee will have the right to sell the residence to the Company at the appraised price by giving notice of intent to sell within thirty (30) days from the date of the appraisal report. The term "residence" shall mean the property occupied by Employee as the principal residence at the time of transfer and does not include summer homes, multiple-family dwellings, houseboats, boats, or airplanes but does include condominium or cooperative apartment units and duplexes (two family) occupied by Employee.

8. *Medical and Group Life Insurance.* Company agrees to include Employee in the group medical and hospital plan of Company and will provide group life insurance for Employee in the amount of Two Hundred and Fifty Thousand Dollars ($250,000.00) during the term of employment.

9. *Vacation.* Employee shall be entitled to four (4) weeks of paid vacation during each year of employment; the time for the vacation shall be mutually agreed upon by Employee and Company.

10. *Automobile.* Company will provide to Employee, during the term of this agreement, the use of a new automobile, of Employee's choice, at a price not to exceed Twenty Five Thousand Dollars ($25,000.00) and will replace the automobile with a new one every two (2) years. Company will pay all automobile operating expenses incurred by Employee in the performance of Employee's business

duties. The Company will procure and maintain in force an automobile liability policy for the automobile with coverage, including Employee, in the minimum amount of One Million Dollars ($1,000,000) combined single limit on bodily injury and property damage.

11. *Expense Reimbursement.* Employee shall be entitled to reimbursement for all reasonable expenses, including travel and entertainment, incurred by Employee in the performance of Employee's duties. Employee will maintain records and written receipts as required by federal and state tax authorities to substantiate expenses as an income tax deduction for Company and shall submit vouchers for expenses for which reimbursement is made.

12. *Low Interest Loan*

   (a) From time to time, Employee may borrow sums from Company up to a maximum aggregate of One Hundred Thousand Dollars ($100,000). Each loan shall be evidenced by a Promissory Note, payable in not more than sixty (60) monthly principal installment payments starting with the first day of the month following the month in which the loan is made, with interest at the rate of _____ percent (____%) per year (payable on the date on which the monthly principal installment payments are due) on the unpaid balance of the loan or loans outstanding.

   (b) In the event Employee severs employment with Company for reasons other than permanent disability, death, or retirement while a loan or loans are outstanding, the unpaid principal amount then outstanding shall be due and payable within thirty (30) days after the date of termination. In the event severance of employment is due to permanent disability, death, or retirement, Employee, or the legal representatives of Employee, shall repay any outstanding loan in accordance with the terms of the promissory note.

   (c) Should there be a default in the payment of any installment of principal or interest when due, then the entire sum of principal and interest, at the option of the Company, shall immediately become due and payable without demand or notice. In case this note shall not be paid when due according to its terms, Employee shall pay all costs of collection and reasonable attorney's fees whether or not suit is filed on the note.

13. *Termination*

   (a) This agreement may be terminated by Company by giving ten (10) days notice to Employee if Employee willfully breaches or habitually neglects the duties to be performed under Paragraph 2, or engages in any conduct which is dishonest or damages the reputation of Company.

(b) This agreement may be terminated by Employee, without cause, by giving ninety (90) days notice to Company.

(c) In the event employment is terminated pursuant to subparagraphs (a) or (b), Employee will be entitled to only base salary compensation earned prior to the date of termination as provided for in Paragraph 3 of this agreement computed prorata up to and including the date of termination. Employee shall not receive the incentive salary payments or the deferred compensation payments provided for in Paragraphs 3(b) and 4, respectively.

(d) In the event Company is acquired, is a nonsurviving party in a merger, or transfers substantially all of its assets, this agreement shall not be terminated and Company agrees to take all actions necessary to ensure that the transferee or surviving Company is bound by the provisions of this agreement.

14. *Notices.* Any notice provided for in this agreement shall be given in writing. Notices shall be effective from the date of service, if served personally on the party to whom notice is to be given, or on the second day after mailing, if mailed by first class mail, postage prepaid. Notices shall be properly addressed to the parties at their respective addresses or to such other address as either party may later specify by notice to the other.

15. *Entire Agreement.* This agreement constitutes the entire agreement between the parties relating to the subject matter contained in it and supersedes all prior and contemporaneous representations, agreements, or understandings between the parties. No amendment or supplement of this agreement shall be binding unless executed in writing by the parties. No waiver of any one provision of this agreement shall constitute a waiver of any other provision, nor shall any one waiver constitute a continuing waiver. No waiver shall be binding unless executed in writing by the parties against whom the waiver is asserted.

16. *Governing Law.* This agreement shall be construed and interpreted in accordance with, and be governed by, the laws of the State of Minnesota.

17. *Headings Not Controlling.* The subject headings of the paragraphs of this agreement are included for purposes of convenience only and shall not affect interpretation of the paragraph.

18. *Assignability.* This agreement may not be assigned by either party, except by Company to a corporation that assumes in writing all the

obligations of the Company and is the successor of all, or substantially all, the business of Company.

19. *Severability.* If any provision of this agreement is held by a court of competent jurisdiction to be invalid or unenforceable, the remainder of the agreement shall remain in full force and shall in no way be impaired.

20. *Arbitration.* Any controversy or claim arising out of or relating to this contract, or the breach thereof, shall be settled by arbitration in accordance with the Rules of the American Arbitration Association and judgment upon the award rendered by the arbitrators may be entered in any court having jurisdiction thereof.

THIS AGREEMENT has been executed by the parties on the _____ day of _____, 19__ by JOHN PARKER and by WILLIAM FRENCH on behalf of the Company, having been duly authorized by resolution of the Board of Directors, passed without the vote of Employee, to execute this agreement.

XYZ COMPANY

_____   By _____
                Secretary   WILLIAM FRENCH, Vice President

_____
                          JOHN PARKER

SOFTWARE SERVICES AGREEMENT

MODERN SYSTEMS, INC.
1111 World Road
Springfield, Massachusetts 01101
Gentlemen:

As we have discussed, Structural Dynamics, Inc. is engaged in providing structural engineering design and analysis services for architectural firms, contractors, and similar businesses and professions.

We have conceived and developed a method for performing these design and analysis services that is original and unique and represents a significant advance in the state of the art.

Modern Systems, Inc., according to your representation, is engaged in providing custom computer software development (programming) services and specializes in scientific and engineering applications programs.

We would like to engage you to create a computer program, utilizing our design and analysis methods and procedures, for use by us in our internal operations and business.

Based on these facts and our expressed intentions, the remainder of this letter will set forth the terms and conditions that will govern our relationship in the above described undertaking. If you signify your acceptance of these terms and conditions by executing this letter at the place indicated, this letter will constitute a legally enforceable agreement between us.

1. *Scope.* The services to be performed under this agreement are divided into two independent jobs: a preliminary design job and a principal design, programming, and testing job. At the conclusion of the preliminary job, we will have the right to decide whether to terminate this agreement or to proceed with the principal job. You will perform the preliminary design services and, upon our decision to proceed, the principal design, programming, and testing services in consideration of the payment and upon the terms and conditions that follow.

2. *Preliminary Design Job*

    (a) *Scope.* We have developed a Functional Description of our Method of Structural Design and Analysis, attached to this agreement as Exhibit A. You have reviewed this Functional Description and have provided a Proposal for preliminary design services, attached to this agreement as Exhibit B. You will design and develop in accordance with the Proposal the following: Functional (Requirements) Specification; Documentation and Programming Standards; and Preliminary Design Specification. Those specifications, documentation, and standards are hereinafter referred to as "Preliminary Design Materials." You will also develop a Project Plan that will include: a firm price quote, including time and materials for completion of the project; identification of the Senior Project Manager for the project; a summary of hourly rates for all job positions in your company; resumes of all employees having the title of "Programmer" or a higher job position title; and a master schedule for completion of the project. The master schedule of the Project Plan shall be divided into a series of Phases, each Phase including one or more Tasks, with the end of selected critical Tasks and the end of each Phase designated as Milestones. The goal of each Milestone will be specifically defined as required to complete the project. The master schedule shall set forth the date on which each Milestone shall be completed, the Deliverables that must be submitted, and the portion of the firm price quote allocated, as a maximum, for each Milestone Task.

    (b) *Performance.* You will begin the preliminary design services within five (5) days after execution of this agreement and will complete these services within one hundred and twenty (120) days from the date of execution. "Completion," for the purpose of the preliminary design, shall mean the delivery of the Preliminary Design Materials, Project Plan, and a Feasibility Report. The "Feasibility Report" shall set forth your candid and considered evaluation and judgment of the successful, on-time, and within-budget feasibility of the project based on the preliminary design services performed and your resources. You will provide written Preliminary Design Progress Reports, signed by the systems analyst or other person with responsibility for performing the preliminary design services, at the end of each thirty (30) day period during the preliminary design. Each Preliminary Design Progress Report shall include: a statement of the work completed since the last report; problems encountered that may affect the timely delivery of the Preliminary Materials, Project Plan, and Feasibility Report; and the number of man-hours expended to the date of the report.

(c) *Payment.* We agree to pay you the fixed price of _____ Dollars ($_____) as full payment for all preliminary design services, in installments, within ten (10) days after each event is completed as follows:

Performance Event	Percent of Fixed Price	Completion Required
Execution of contract	20	None
First Report	15	Preliminary design progress report
Second Report	15	Preliminary design progress report
Third Report	15	Preliminary design progress report
Completion	35	Deliver preliminary materials, project plan, and feasibility report

In the event we fail to make timely payment of each installment, or you fail to timely provide the item specified under Completion Required, the nondefaulting party may terminate this agreement immediately upon notice to the defaulting party.

(d) *Proprietary Rights.* After each installment payment, exclusive ownership of all written materials and documentation, including but not limited to draft functional and preliminary design specifications, draft documentation and programming standards, work sheets, flow charts, program narrative, data flow diagrams, decision tables, and related preliminary design work-product that have been created by you prior to the date of payment shall be vested in us and, should this agreement be terminated, you will deliver all copies of written materials and documentation to us. After the final installment payment, following Completion, exclusive ownership of all Preliminary Materials, the Project Plan, and the Feasibility Report shall be vested in us.

3. *Decision to Proceed.* After completion of the preliminary design job, as described above, we will have a period of thirty (30) days from the date of Completion to decide whether we wish to proceed with the principal design, programming, and testing job (Project). In the event that we decide to proceed, we will give you notice of acceptance in writing:

   (a) The notice shall specify that the Preliminary Design Materials and Project Plan are accepted as submitted, in which event the Preliminary Design Materials and Project Plan will be incorporated into this agreement as though set forth in full at this time; or

   (b) The notice shall specify all objections, requested changes, deletions, or other modifications of the Preliminary Design Material and Project Plan; we will promptly meet thereafter to resolve the proposed modifications and, if the modifications are agreed upon by written joint acceptance, the accepted Preliminary Design Materials and Project Plan will be incorporated into this agreement as though set forth in full at this time. Should we be unable to arrive at mutually agreeable Preliminary Design Materials and a Project Plan within ten (10) days from the date of the notice (unless extended by mutual agreement), this agreement will terminate and neither party shall thereafter have any obligation to the other except as set forth in Paragraph 6.

   (c) We will designate a Project Coordinator, familiar with the Functional Description, as our representative to cooperate with you on the project.

4. *Principal Design, Programming, and Testing Job (Project)*

   (a) *Scope.* The design, programming, and testing services you will perform shall be in accordance with the accepted Preliminary Design Materials and Project Plan resulting from the preliminary design job described above.

(b) *Performance.* You will begin the Project within fifteen (15) days from the date of notice of acceptance or the date of written joint acceptance (in the event modifications were proposed by notice) and will complete all required services in accordance with the master schedule of the Project Plan. You will commit employees and resources as required to complete the project in accordance with the master schedule.

You will provide a written Task Progress Report, signed by the Senior Project Manager, at the end of each Task completed during the Project. Completion of each Milestone specified in the master schedule of the Project Plan will require you: (i) to submit the "Deliverables," as required under the Project Plan; (ii) to contemporaneously provide an oral and written executive Milestone Project Report at a meeting attended by our Project Coordinator and your Senior Project Manager at a time to be agreed upon; and (iii) to obtain our written acceptance. Each written Task Progress Report shall include: a statement of work completed in the Task and the relationship of the work completed to other Tasks and the Phase; problems encountered which are beyond your control (e.g., strikes, riots, acts of God, power or computer hardware failure) and the effect on the Project Plan master schedule; problems encountered due to our cooperation and the effect on the Project Plan master schedule; and a proposed plan to remedy any problems encountered. Each Milestone Project Report shall include, in addition to the information required in each Task Progress Report, the status of the entire project, and a summary of all time and material expended since completion of the last Milestone Project Report.

"Deliverables" include source code listings, manuals, narratives, and other program documentation as specified in the master schedule in accordance with the Documentation and Programming Standards of the Preliminary Design Materials.

In the event you fail to complete any Milestone on the date specified in the master schedule of the Project Plan, we may terminate this agreement within five (5) days after the specified date by giving you notice of our intent to terminate within fifteen (15) days, unless within the fifteen (15) days you complete the Milestone Task (including submission of required Deliverables and the Milestone Project Report) which shall void the notice; otherwise, the agreement will terminate at the expiration of the fifteen (15) days.

During the Project, you will assign the Senior Project Manager to full-time effort on this Project and you will not replace the assigned Senior Project Manager except with our express written consent. You will use your best efforts to maintain continuity of other employees assigned to this Project. For good cause (including failure to meet the master schedule of the Project Plan, failure to cooperate, habitual neglect, or the like), you will remove the Senior Project Manager from this Project upon ten (10) days written notice from us. In the event the Senior Project Manager terminates employment with you, you will assign an alternate only with our express written consent.

You will maintain the hourly rates for all job positions set forth in the Project Plan during the term of this agreement. Upon starting this Project, you will identify (by job title and resume) by notice to us the personnel assigned to this Project; any personnel later assigned to this Project will be similarly identified.

(c)   *Payment.* We agree to pay you for time and materials spent on this Project up to the maximum of _____ Dollars ($_____) as set forth in the Project Plan, to be completed at the time of the decision to proceed, with a maximum for each Milestone as follows:

Milestone	Maximum Payment
	$_____
_____	_____
_____	_____
_____	_____
Final Acceptance Test Completion	_____

Upon completion of each Milestone, you will submit a statement of time spent on the Tasks comprising the Milestone, including the name of each employee, the number of hours spent by all employees on the Tasks comprising the Milestone, and the billing rate of those employees. You will keep full and accurate records showing time spent and will permit us to inspect such records from time to time, during normal business hours, to verify any statement. The statement shall include an itemized list of materials charged to the Tasks comprising the Milestone.

The maximum payment for each Milestone and the entire Project are based on the Preliminary Design Materials and the Project Plan. There will be no change or modification to the Preliminary Design Materials or Project Plan except by written agreement through a Change Order Form. To initiate a change, the party desiring the change will prepare the Change Order Form, specifying in detail the change proposed, the additional time and materials required, and the reason for the change and submit it to the other party, which must respond with an acceptance or rejection within ten (10) days from the date of submission. If rejected, the parties agree to meet and use their best efforts to agree upon the requirements for change and the amount of additional time and materials required. Upon acceptance, the maximum amount of payment for the applicable Milestone and the entire Project shall be adjusted accordingly.

Within ten (10) days after presentation of the statement, we will pay ninety percent (90%) of the amount billed, and we will hold back ten percent (10%) for security that all services under this agreement are performed. The holdback amount will be paid within ten (10) days after Completion. You will not submit a statement amount in excess of the maximum payment specified for each Milestone. In the event that the statement amount is less than the maximum for each Milestone, subsequent Milestone maximum payments will be increased by such amount.

In the event that any Milestone is not completed on the date specified in the master schedule of the Project Plan we may terminate this agreement or we may charge a late penalty of Five Hundred Dollars ($500.00) per day for each day of delay beyond the specified date. The penalty shall be charged to the holdback account. In the event that one or more Milestones are not completed on time, but the entire Project is completed on the date specified in the master schedule of the Project Plan, all late penalties will be waived by us. In the event this agreement is terminated by us on account of your default, prior to completion of the Project, we will be entitled to retain the late penalties as liquidated damages for your failure to complete any Milestone on time.

Upon the completion of each Milestone, we may elect not to proceed with the Project and may terminate this agreement, without cause, by giving you ten (10) days notice of termination; in such event, we will pay to you all billed amounts to date and will also pay for all services rendered on all Tasks not billed, including any holdback, and we will waive any late penalties.

In the event we fail to make timely payments of your billing statement, you may terminate this agreement immediately upon notice to us.

(d) *Proprietary Rights.* After each installment payment, exclusive ownership of all written materials and documentation, including, but not limited to, all source programs and modules and all supporting documentation such as flow charts, program or module narratives, listings, and other program design or implementation aids that have been created by you prior to the date of payment shall be vested in us and after Completion, or should this agreement be terminated, you will deliver all copies of all programs and documentation to us.

(e) *Acceptance.* To complete the Acceptance Test Milestone, you will install the program, ready for use, train our employees, and notify us that you are prepared to commence the Acceptance Test. The Acceptance Test, which shall be conducted in accordance with an Acceptance Test Plan prepared as one of the Milestone Tasks, will be completed within ten (10) days of the notice date. Successful completion of the Acceptance Test shall require: (i) that the program substantially complies with the Functional Specification and the Final Program Design Specification (prepared as one of the Milestone Tasks); (ii) that the program will run on a repetitive basis on a variety of data, without failure; and (iii) that the documentation meets the requirements of the Documentation and Programming Standards. If the Acceptance Test is successful, we will give notice of acceptance that the Milestone is completed. If we fail to accept or reject within five (5) days after the completion of the Acceptance Test, the program shall be considered accepted. If the program fails to pass the Acceptance Test, we will notify you of rejection within five (5) days after the completion of the Acceptance Test, and you will modify or correct the program, notify us, and we will conduct another Acceptance Test within ten (10) days of the notice. If the Acceptance Test is again rejected, the late penalty provisions, as defined above, will apply to any further testing.

(f) *Completion.* As the final Milestone, you will complete delivery of all documentation. At the completion of this Milestone this Project shall be complete and this agreement will terminate.

5. *Warranty*

(a) *Performance.* You expressly warrant that the program delivered and run during the Acceptance Test shall continue after Completion to operate so as to meet the requirements of the Functional Specification for a period of ninety (90) days. In the event that the program fails to so operate, you will, without charge to us, correct any defects and make any additions, modifications, or adjustments as may be necessary to keep the program operating in accordance with the requirements of the Functional Specification during such time period.

(b) *Title.* You warrant that the program, all Preliminary Design Materials, and Deliverables produced under this agreement will be of original development by you and will be specifically developed for the fulfillment of this agreement. You will not disclose or divulge to us, nor induce us to use, any confidential information, know-how or trade secrets which you now possess or which may be acquired by you from any third party during the term of this agreement. You also warrant that the program, Preliminary Design Materials, and Deliverables will not infringe upon any patent or copyright. You will indemnify and hold us harmless from and against any liabilities, expenses, or claims against us alleging infringement of any patent, copyright, or a breach of obligation to any third party for unauthorized use of any trade secret, know-how, or other confidential information.

6. *Confidential Relationship*

(a) During the course of your performance of services, you will become aware of and receive information concerning our Method of Structural Design and Analysis, including the Functional Description and other information required for the completion of the Project. You will receive and hold in confidence all information acquired from us or produced by you in the course of performing all services under this agreement, including any programs, reports, plans, manuals, or other work product. You will not disclose any such information or any part thereof to any other person, firm, or corporation and will not use or publish the same, in whole or in part, without previous authorization in writing by us.

(b) You agree to disclose such information only to your employees who have executed a written agreement obligating them to receive and hold in confidence all such information received either from you or directly from us.

7. *Termination of Business.* In the event you cease conducting business in normal course, become insolvent, make a general assignment for the benefit of creditors, or permit the appointment of a receiver for your business or assets, or shall avail yourself of, or become subject to, any proceeding under the Federal Bankruptcy Act or any other statute of any state relating to insolvency or the protection of creditor's rights, then this agreement, at our option, shall terminate. Upon such termination, we shall have the entire right, title, and interest in and to all Preliminary Materials, Project Plan, Feasibility Report, Preliminary Design Progress Reports, Deliverables, Task Progress Reports, Milestone Project Reports (including those materials originated since the last Preliminary Progress Report if during the preliminary design, and Task Progress Reports and Milestone Project Reports if during the principal job of the agreement), and all other work product, which shall immediately vest in us, and we shall have immediate access to and possession of all such written materials and documentation and you shall assist us in every possible manner in arranging for the orderly transfer of such written materials and documentation and the continuation of the preliminary design or Project services by us or a party selected by us. In the event that we exercise our rights to access and possession of the written materials and documentation, you may invoice us for the services rendered since the last billing statement.

8. *Responsibility of Structural Dynamics.* You will have the responsibility for completion of the Project except that we will: (*a*) review and, if completed in substantial compliance with the applicable specification and the master schedule, accept all Reports and Deliverables; (*b*) prepare test data; (*c*) conduct the Acceptance Test; (*d*) convert the data base; and (*e*) make available the Project Coordinator for discussion, assistance, and liaison and other employees for training in the use and operation of the program.

9. *Independent Contractor.* You are an independent contractor with respect to all services performed under this agreement and you assume sole responsibility for any agents or employees hired or engaged by you in connection with the performance of services by you.

All expenses, liabilities, or other financial obligations incurred by you, or your agents or employees, in connection with the performance of this agreement shall be borne by you, and you shall be solely responsible for the payment of the expenses, liabilities and other financial obligations.

10. *Noncompetition.* You acknowledge that there are a relatively small number of suppliers that provide structural design services of the type we offer and that, in the course of performing the programming services, you will be exposed to our unique solution to structural design problems. Therefore, in addition to your obligation not to disclose or use confidential information obtained from us or produced during the Project, you will not for a period of two (2) years from the date of the Completion Task perform programming services for any person, firm, corporation, or organization engaged in offering structural engineering design and analysis services.

11. *Time of the Essence.* For any performance required under this agreement, time is of the essence.

12. *Notices.* Any notice provided for in this agreement shall be given in writing. Notices shall be effective on the date of service if served personally on the party to whom notice is to be given, or on the second day after mailing if mailed by first class mail, postage prepaid. Notices shall be properly addressed to the parties at their respective addresses set forth above or to such other address as either party may later specify by notice to the other.

13. *Nonassignment.* This agreement may not be assigned nor the rights and obligations otherwise transferred to a third party by either of the parties hereto; any attempted assignment or transfer shall be void.

14. *Arbitration.* Any controversy or claim arising out of or relating to this contract, or the breach thereof, is subject to arbitration. A party desiring arbitration shall give notice (containing a general description of the controversy) to the other party and designating, by name and address, an arbitrator. The other party shall designate an arbitrator within five (5) days from the date of such notice by giving notice including the name and address of a second arbitrator. The selected arbitrators shall choose a third arbitrator from a list of arbitrators submitted by the American Arbitration Association (AAA). Other than this selection of arbitrators, such controversy or claim shall be settled in accordance with the Rules of the AAA. Judgment on the award rendered by the arbitrators may be entered in any court having jurisdiction thereof.

15. *Headings Not Controlling.* The subject headings of the paragraphs

of this agreement are included for purposes of convenience only and shall not affect interpretation of the paragraphs.

16. *Entire Agreement.* This agreement constitutes the entire agreement between the parties relating to the subject matter contained in it and supersedes all prior and contemporaneous representations, agreements, or understandings between the parties. No amendment or supplement of this agreement shall be binding unless executed in writing by the parties. No waiver of any one provision of this agreement shall constitute a waiver of any other provision, nor shall any one waiver constitute a continuing waiver. No waiver shall be binding unless executed in writing by the party against whom the waiver is asserted.

17. *Governing Law.* This agreement shall be construed and interpreted in accordance with, and governed by, the laws of the state of California.

If the above terms and conditions are satisfactory to you, please execute this agreement at the place indicated below.

Sincerely,

STRUCTURAL DYNAMICS, INC.

Accepted this _____ day of _____, 1981.

MODERN SYSTEMS, INC.

By _____

Bibliography

Anderson, O. J., *Business Law*. Totowa, NJ: Littlefield, Adams & Co. (1980).

Bobrow, E. E., *Marketing through Manufacturers' Agents*. New York: Sales & Marketing Management (1976).

Bunn, C., Snead, H., and Speidel, R., *An Introduction to the Uniform Commercial Code*. Charlottesville, VA: Michie Company (1964).

Coppola, A. J., *The Law of Business Contracts*. Totowa, NJ: Littlefield, Adams & Co. (1977).

Corley, R., and Robert, W., *Fundamentals of Business Law*, 2nd ed. Englewood Cliffs, NJ: Prentice-Hall (1978).

Hawkland, W. D., *A Transactional Guide to the Uniform Commercial Code*. New York: American Law Institute (1964).

Howard, L. B., *Business Law*. New York: Barron's Educational Series Inc. (1956).

Krause, W. H., *How to Hire and Motivate Manufacturers' Representatives*. New York: AMACOM (1976).

Lane, M. J., *Legal Handbook for Small Business*. New York: AMACOM (1977).

Mandel, L., *The Preparation of Commercial Agreements*. New York: Practicing Law Institute (1978).

Rice, J. S., and Libbey, K., *Making the Law Work for You: A Guide for Small Businesses*. Chicago: Contemporary Books (1980).

Index